TRAVELLERS'
TALES

little best wishes

Renée Heumann

Michael Aden.

A collection of tales by
members of the
Travellers Club, London

Travellers' Tales

edited by

FRANK HERRMANN

and

MICHAEL ALLEN

CASTLEREAGH PRESS
LONDON 1999

First published in Great Britain 1999
by Castlereagh Press
Unit 15, Airfield Way, Christchurch,BH23 1PZ

© The Travellers Club 1999
for this collected edition

© Each individual author 1999
for his own contribution or contributions

The individual contributors have asserted their right
to be identified as the authors respectively of the
individual contributions and the Travellers Club
asserts its own right to be identified as the author
of the collected edition of this work, in accordance
with the Copyright, Designs & Patents Act 1988

A catalogue record for this book is available
from the British Library

ISBN 1 901825 01 9

Typeset by Andrew Burrell

Printed in Finland

Distributed in the UK by Ditka Books Limited,
Arbons House, Lavenham, Sudbury, Suffolk CO10 9RN

Contents

CONTENTS

*The front endpapers show the Library and the back endpapers
show the Coffee Room (dining room) at the Travellers Club.
Both are from watercolours by* DAVID GENTLEMAN, RDI, *in the
possession of the Club.*

Foreword

The Travellers Club in Pall Mall was founded in the aftermath of the Napoleonic Wars at the suggestion of Lord Castlereagh, then Foreign Secretary. Today (1999) it has about 1,200 members, drawn from many professions, particularly diplomats, lawyers, people from international business, journalism and authors.

The Club moved to its Clubhouse in 1832. Sandwiched between the Athenaeum and the Reform Club, it was the first major commission for the architect Sir Charles Barry, later to be best known for the gothic Palace of Westminster. Its finest features include the magnificent Library and the Coffee Room, as the dining room is traditionally called: both rooms are shown on the endpapers of this book.

The genesis of the book was at the centre table of the Coffee Room, where members dine when they wish to be sociable. It is here that one often hears them recounting interesting stories of their experiences. As listeners to such tales over the years, we felt it would be of interest to get some of these onto paper and to collect them into a volume for a wider audience. This book is the result of that exercise, travellers' tales in both senses of the word – experiences by members of the Club and accounts of interesting journeys.

The styles in which they are recorded are as diverse as the characters of the authors, and we have kept the pieces much as they were written. Remarkably, among the eighty contributions, there was little repetition. The two recurring themes that we did notice were a love of exploring volcanoes and, among the diplomats, *early* experiences in their careers which had become particularly firmly imprinted on their minds. There are also a number of contributions that provide intriguing sidelights on major historical events.

Sadly, we were too late to receive a contribution from one of the Club's best-known members: Monsignor Gilbey, who died in the summer of 1998 at the age of ninety-six. For several decades he had been almost the only member to live on the premises – so the Clubhouse became his home. When he introduced himself to a new member he would always say, 'My name is Gilbey: the gin family, you know'.

Late in 1996, the Monsignor was involved in a charming encounter with the Queen Mother, who gives members of her household a festive dinner in the Club Library each Christmas. The dinner over, Her Majesty was being escorted by the Club Secretary from the lift to her waiting car, when Monsignor Gilbey came round the corner making for the lift. It should be mentioned that by this time Gilbey was walking with a very considerable stoop, which made it almost impossible for him to look up. Fearful of a collision, the Club Secretary deftly stopped Gilbey and – knowing him to be a great admirer of the Queen Mother – presented him to Her Majesty, mentioning his great age, then 95. The Queen Mother said she believed she was a year older, to which the Monsignor responded courteously that he did not know of any lady older than himself other than one *extremely distinguished lady* whom he doubted he would meet in his Club. They chatted for a few minutes and the Queen Mother then continued towards the entrance, smilingly unruffled that she had not been recognized. It was not until the following day, when Monsignor Gilbey was asked how he had enjoyed meeting Her Majesty, that he was mortified to discover he had actually been introduced to his 'extremely distinguished lady' but had failed to realize it. He was with difficulty dissuaded from writing a letter of apology to the Queen Mother at Clarence House.

The sequence we have chosen for our stories has been arranged with one principle in mind: to set each in such a way that it reads well. Mainly this is a matter of establishing a contrast between each item, whether of subject or of mood. Thus tales with a similar subject – such as Africa or volcanoes, are apart rather than together. Nor does the sequence imply or acknowledge any hierarchy amongst the contributors. Some of their names will be familiar to the general reader; each is identified by a brief biography at the end of the volume.

The book tells us something about the members of an institution that has often seemed mysterious to outsiders, particularly after various allusions to it in the novels of Graham Greene. It certainly proves that they are still great travellers, many with a fine sense of humour. But, above all we hope that readers will find this miscellany to be entertaining.

FRANK HERRMANN AND MICHAEL ALLEN

Acknowledgements

The Editors would like to thank all those members of the Club, who proved themselves such able and enticing tellers of tales and gave so much of their time towards creating this book.

They would also like to express their gratitude to Patricia Herrmann who undertook the onerous task of converting the individual contributions into a cohesive entity. Finally, they are most grateful to the publisher, Jeremy Gambrill; and to Andrew Burrell, whose typographical skills over the typesetting made a difficult job seem quite simple.

TRAVELLERS'
TALES

Archmobile

There was a time when it was my agreeable duty to accompany His Grace the Archbishop of Canterbury on his foreign travels. When I use the word 'agreeable' my tongue is inclined slightly towards my cheek. The company of His Grace was at all times congenial, given the natural limitations of mortal nature. The mode of travel was not always so pleasing.

In our years together we traversed the globe. I have memories of bowling along the Alaska Highway at midnight in a pickup truck en route to Haines Junction, where a comfortable billet awaited us at a hostelry quaintly named *Mothers Cosy Corner*. In China we were ushered into the luxury of the former emperor's railway carriage. Meals were prepared over a wood-burning stove at one end of the car while we received them in the comfort of the observation lounge at the other end. Our rooms, each boasting a bathroom complete with bath, gave truth to the dictum that equality is a matter of degree.

The Archbishop was a good traveller. He was modest in his eating and drinking habits and quite able to travel in the re-cycled atmosphere of a jumbo jet and emerge to greet a welcoming party on the other side of the world as though he had just completed a Mediterranean cruise. He once assured me that, in his humble opinion, the majority of long-distance travellers were not suffering from jet lag. Rather, he believed, they were the victims of alcoholic poisoning. As a lifelong air traveller I am inclined to believe him.

I said that it was the mode of travel that gave us certain problems. Let me be more explicit. Without fail, wherever we went our hosts were most anxious to please. On one occasion, sometime in the eighties, we visited Canada. We dined with the Prime Minister of the day; took tea with the Governor General and met Canadians from the forests, mountains and plains of that great country. The second week of the tour found us in some rural backwater, the name of which escapes me. It might have been Granpappy Canyon, Lonnigans Reach or whatever. No matter, the name is of no consequence.

3

The good citizens of this delightful retreat were overwhelmed by the visit as they had hardly seen a clergyman before, let alone the Archbishop of Canterbury. They were, however, keen watchers of television and they had followed His Holiness the Pope as he travelled in Pontifical style across the globe. No doubt they would have wished that His Holiness might have spent an hour or two in their company but heaven had given them a different blessing and they had His Grace. They were determined to show what they could do.

They had noticed that the Holy Father frequently travelled across terra firma in a Popemobile. This was a luxury car with a transparent bullet-proof dome beneath which the Pope might stand and bless the multitudes. Popemobiles were not in regular production in Canada and the importation of one would have decimated the municipal budget for generations to come. The loyal Anglicans of Canada were not to be outdone.

The Archbishop's programme for his visit to this devout corner of the Anglican communion was full. The curious of the town (of whom there were many) were anxious to catch sight of His Grace. The church was too small to admit everyone. The solution? Let the Archbishop and his chaplain travel through the streets in an Archmobile.

On the morning of the visit we drove to the vicarage. As the vicar briefed us on the programme for the day I glanced through the study window and noticed a curious-looking vehicle on the front drive. Closer inspection revealed that it was a pickup truck that belonged to a local garage. The latter fact was obvious as the name of the garage was blazoned across the side of the vehicle. In the front seat sat a stout gentleman wearing a ten-gallon hat and chewing a large cigar. On the back of the truck there was a structure that resembled a primitive greenhouse. Rough wooden posts had been lashed together over which transparent polythene had been secured. My feelings of anxiety increased as we left the study and walked towards the mobile monstrosity.

'We were uncertain about the weather,' said the vicar. 'So many people want to see you, Archbishop, that we decided to drive you to the church in style. We didn't want you to get wet if it rained.'

As the early morning sun was already beating down with extraordinary ferocity, there seemed little danger of a soaking.

The Archbishop glanced nervously at the greenhouse and severely at me. The vicar moved towards the pickup.

'If you and the chaplain would ride in the back, your Grace, Mr Waite can follow in one of the cars.'

It was now the turn of the chaplain to give me an agonized look.

Gingerly the Archbishop and his faithful chaplain stepped onto a little platform and into the polythene. The fat driver started the engine, inserted a tape of suitable hymns into the tapedeck and edged forwards. I clambered into the air-conditioned bliss of my automobile and followed at a suitable distance.

'I guess it's mighty hot in there,' muttered my driver as we proceeded down the main street.

I guessed it was also as I could see the chaplain mopping his brow with a large red handkerchief. Suddenly I noticed that the chaplain had hoisted his cassock and appeared to be rummaging through his trouser pockets. Having found what he was looking for he began to attack the polythene for all he was worth. A large hole appeared in the side of the greenhouse and, to the delight of the faithful, the chaplain's perspiring head appeared.

By now we were almost at the church. When we stopped I leapt out of the car, ran towards the pickup and lifted the heavy plastic flap.

'Quick,' said the chaplain as he supported his charge. 'The Archbishop is soaked. Get the robecase. He must have a change of clothes otherwise he will get the death of a cold.'

A limp but still genial Archbishop emerged from the tropical hell into the warm Canadian sun and was speedily ushered into the vestry. He did get a change of clothing and remained well. The chaplain caught a cold. I resolved to take a great deal more care about our mode of transport in the future.

When we were safely home I commended the chaplain on sticking to the first rule of travellers everywhere: never leave home without a Swiss army penknife!

TERRY WAITE

A Leisurely Crossing

In 1955 my wife had to return home to Sydney, Australia for family reasons. Her mother had died the previous year, a few weeks after our first child was born. She left the UK in September, taking our thirteen-month old daughter with her. The following March I was to meet up with her in New York and then the three of us would return to London. I had been overworking and had been ill with glandular fever. My doctor thought a trip right away was an excellent idea and as I am a very good sailor and can really relax at sea, it was suggested that I took a leisurely crossing aboard a merchant ship. At that time, travel to the USA or Canada was very difficult. Currency restrictions were severe. I was on the teaching staff at the London Hospital Dental School and the dean of the dental faculty decided that a trip to see some of the work done in the eastern Canadian and American schools would be a good idea: it also meant that I would qualify for a small allocation of Canadian and American dollars.

Through a friend of mine in the mercantile shipping business, I booked a berth aboard a small cargo ship, the SS *Cairnesk*. This old, well-built coal-burning vessel was registered in Newcastle, but was taking on cargo at Grangemouth in the River Forth. I joined the ship in about mid-March. There were twelve passengers, all except myself emigrants, and a very nice bunch they were. There was one small family of mother, father and a young boy and girl aged ten and twelve. Eventually I realized that the father, a Devonian and ex-policeman, was one of the world's worst sailors: he was seasick almost as soon as we weighed anchor. I shared a cabin with a Geordie who was very pleasant, and very apprehensive at the prospect of his 'new' life in Canada.

After some delay loading the cargo, we sailed down the Forth and turned north. Although it was March and the equinoctial gales were anticipated, we were routed through the Pentland Firth – in fact going north about being the shorter journey – making for St John, New Brunswick, on the Bay of Fundy.

As soon as we hit the open ocean, the bad weather started. We literally crawled. We had four force-10 gales one after another. Then the weather cleared and for the first and only time in my life I saw the northern lights – and what a sight! Because I had been in the Navy, the rest of the passengers seemed to think I was a sort of Captain Cook, in spite of my explaining that I was nothing of the sort: I was just a dentist who had done my war service in the Royal Navy. The captain of the Cairnesk was a charming man and an extraordinarily fine seaman. He and I became very friendly and when he was relaxing from the bridge we had a few (very few) drinks and played pontoon.

The night after seeing the aurora borealis he called me up to his cabin and told me he had had a radio signal that we were heading for a freak hurricane. He asked me to keep a responsible eye on the passengers. The cabin steward called us early next morning and told us that we were indeed in a hurricane. It had hit us about 1 a.m.

Although I had seen some very severe weather during my five years' naval service, I had never experienced anything like this. We were 'hove to' making practically no headway but with our bows nose-in to the weather. The noise of the wind was horrendous and as the sea made its own fog, visibility was down to some 30 or 40 yards, as I remember. We were permanently sounding the ship's siren as a warning to any vessel that might have been in the vicinity. To add to our problems, the weather became very much colder, which meant there was a very heavy frost and possibly snow all over the upper deck, including the ship's lifeboats and, more worryingly, their lowering tackle.

As the day wore on, the weather worsened. The cargo then became loose, particularly some very long (probably 30 to 35 feet) steel plates which had been lashed down to the forecastle deck. These caused unbelievable damage as they slid from side to side: two of the bollards, which were about 2½ feet across and of solid iron, were split vertically, the forward derrick became loose and two of the crew, lashed together and to a stanchion, braved the seas to secure it. Part of the actual ship's side on the upper deck was carried away. Added to all this was the sound of the cargo below deck sliding about, making a hideous row.

I had advised the passengers that as the saloon was on the main deck level we would be less thrown about, and at least all together, if we stayed there. However, about mid-morning the ship's wheel must have slipped (the captain had two sailors trying to keep us steady on course) and we were broached to, and caught an enormous sea on our beam. The water smashed through the quite small portholes and we were flooded. Crockery and glass and furniture were smashed. The galley fire (coal) was doused. As a body, we rushed up to the next deck on the bridge structure, just under the officers' sea cabins. That was where the passenger accommodation was. Some people had minor cuts and bruises, and I was busy doing very minimal first aid and trying to reassure people – of what I had no idea and still cannot imagine.

In spite of all this we did have light-hearted moments. When we had joined the ship, the passengers, especially the children, were delighted to find that the ship's cook had brought on board a playful little ginger kitten. I believe the ship had mouse trouble. Having rushed up to the accommodation deck, I suddenly heard a rather dour Scot who had served in one of the kilted regiments yelling at the top of his voice for me. When I reached his cabin he was standing astraddle. 'For Christ's sake get my trousers down!' More than nonplussed, I did, to find that in its fright the kitten had taken refuge in our Scot's groin. He thanked me and then said, 'If I'd been wearing a kilt that would never have happened.' Our other slight relief was that the Devonian ex-policeman was too frightened to be seasick.

We had further damage to the ship. Our little library/rest room was partly carried away; the radio was smashed and in that weather there was no possible hope of getting any repairs; the steel ladders were buckled and the ship's boats were wrecked.

The captain confided to me that we were likely to be going through the eye of the storm. If this were to happen, we would have to turn the ship 180 degrees in a very, very short time to keep our bows into the wind. Fortunately it did not happen, and after another 24 hours we found ourselves in calmer water. I shall always be very grateful to porpoises: as the fog and rain cleared, there they were 'playing' the rollers. I was thankful, too, that ours was an old riveted ship: I learned afterwards that had she been a more modern riveted ship, she would have broken her back.

We now found ourselves in glorious spring weather, albeit very cold. When I saw the captain, who had been on the bridge continuously for 36 hours, I congratulated him. He then told me that as soon as they had repaired the radio he had heard we were just in the paths of icebergs that had been broken up by the storm. Subsequently I learned that on one of the Queen liners, which had been 300 miles south of us, 90 people had been injured as a result of the storm.

We were far too damaged to get as far as New Brunswick. We had to make for the nearest port, which was St John's, Newfoundland. We made landfall at about 11 o'clock in brilliant sunshine. Soon after we berthed, the weather broke, and by the afternoon we heard that the harbour had been blocked by ice.

I left the ship and flew to Montreal, my initial destination.

After meeting up with my wife and daughter in New York, we had a lovely and welcome holiday. The three of us flew back to London – in beautiful weather and we could often see the Atlantic below looking wonderful. Little did the other passengers know!

PETER MACKENZIE-YOUNG

A Timbuktu Perspective

I visited Timbuktu briefly in 1973, travelling by air from Bamako. Routine internal flights by Air Mali offer easy if unromantic access to the fabled city whose location – indeed whose very existence – had been a matter of controversy in Europe until its 'discovery' by explorers in the 1820s. Even now, it seems a long way from anywhere, and as we overflew the vast emptiness of that arid region and suddenly glimpsed Timbuktu itself, I remembered the first impressions and mixed emotions of the intrepid René Caillié in 1828 when, after a long and hazardous journey, he at last reached his destination, on foot.

For Caillié, his safe arrival was the fulfilment of a long-cherished dream, and the solution of a geographical mystery. Timbuktu had for several centuries enjoyed a legendary reputation, stemming from its fortunate situation as a market where two ancient trade routes – north/south across the Sahara and east/west along the Niger – crossed. Moreover it had been a cultural as well as a commercial centre, boasting at one time two universities.

So Caillié travelled hopefully; and having arrived he tried not to let his joy and thankfulness be eroded by the disappointingly shabby appearance of the town, though in his written account he admitted the anticlimax. The place 'did not answer my expectations. I had formed a totally different idea of the grandeur and wealth of Timbuktu. The city presented, at first view, nothing but a mass of ill-looking houses, built of earth. Nothing was to be seen in all directions but immense plains of quicksand of a yellowish-white colour.'

His description remained valid in 1973, and the only building not mud-coloured was the little whitewashed hotel. However, Timbuktu was well worth a visit, both for its legendary historical associations and for the friendliness of the townspeople. In the comparative cool of the evening my wife and I took a stroll through the streets of the town, which were of bare sand. In the doorway of a house a little ancient man greeted us in French, and invited us to have tea with him. We went into his front room, and sat on low stools on the floor which, like the street outside, was of bare sand. Our host brewed tea over a spirit lamp and served it in tiny brass cups; and the following conversation, in French, ensued, to the edification of a crowd of friends and relatives who drifted in from nowhere.

'Are you tourists?' the old man enquired.

'We are tourists,' we replied.

'What is your nationality?'

'We are English.'

'I have heard of England. It is an island, is it not?'

'It is an island.'

'Is it extremely small?'

'It is quite small.'

'Is it in mid-stream, or close to one of the banks?'

This flummoxed me, till I remembered a phrase of Milton's, 'the steep

Atlantick stream', and guessed that my host saw the Atlantic Ocean as a body of water with land on either side, as in a map. Viewed thus, the British Isles were undeniably closer to the right side than to the left. But was *rive* masculine or feminine? Was it *rive droit* or *rive droite*? I am ashamed to say that I funked the issue, and plumped for the safety of *rive gauche*. The whole thought process occupied a mere second or two, much less than it takes to describe.

'Closer to the left bank.'

'Ah, I have always thought so.'

Soon it was time to move on, and when we did so we were accompanied for a short distance by two grandsons of the old man.

'Our grandfather is exceptionally well informed,' said one.

'And he already knew that England was an island in the Niger,' said the other. 'The Niger is over four thousand kilometres long, and gives a livelihood to people of many countries. Why not the English?'

'Why not indeed?' I replied.

GEORGE WEBB

Kharakhoto Revisited

Our Chinese friends in the Inner Mongolia museum in Hohhot (I thought it was called Hotpot, but no matter, for the main dish in the town was indeed Mongolian hotpot) told us that there was no way we could get to Kharakhoto, in the middle of Gobi desert, some thousand miles away. Even they needed permission to travel in that area, which was close to the northern frontier of China. But I had a hunch it was worth a try, and after four days travelling westwards by bus and train, we found ourselves at the end of the Great Wall at Jiayugian, on the edge of the desert, with the 12,000-foot, eternally snow-covered mountains of the Qilian Shan on its southern flank.

There was a vast medieval gateway open to the west, the beginning of the ancient silk route. And there was a sign in Chinese which I like to think read 'To Istanbul'. There was also a pretty travel agent called Helen (real name Fan Xin Zhi) in the local hotel who, when I asked her if she could get us to Kharakhoto, flashed a dazzling smile and said, 'No problem!' We then had to point out to her its whereabouts on the map, 140 miles directly into the centre of the Gobi desert, near the oasis of Etsin Gol.

That was at ten o'clock in the morning. By one o'clock she had produced a four-wheel drive Mitsubishi Pajero, a driver, a guide and the promise of another local guide later, and had squared the police with a deft call on her mobile. I simply could not believe we might get there. Kharakhoto (Heicheng, or Black City) was discovered by the Russian explorer Count Kozlov in 1906, visited and extensively looted by Sir Aurel Stein in 1912, by Langdon Warner from Harvard in 1923, and by a Swedish expedition led by Sven Hedin in 1934. And by no one from Europe since. It was the garrison city for Genghis Khan and a staging post for the Mongol conquest of China, finally abandoned and dissolving into the desert sands with the collapse of Yuan dynasty in 1368 and the exit of the Mongols. I knew from the earlier travellers that the city in the desert, like the sands of ancient Egypt, had preserved not only pottery but also organic materials such as paper, silks, textiles and paintings. My particular interest was in Yuan ceramics and especially fragments of early fourteenth-century blue-and-white porcelain, of which the Topkapı Sarayı collection in Istanbul has perhaps the world's greatest selection.

We drove north, first along a tarmac track through a lunar landscape of blackened rocky outcrops that petered out into a dirt road through sandy flats. We saw eagles, hawks, flocks of tiny desert quails and, satisfyingly, a herd of wild Bactrian camels, which are indigenous to the Gobi desert. We were following, somewhat to the west, the course of the Etsin Gol, which rises in the Qilian Shan, not far from the source of the Yellow River which flows in a different direction for thousands of miles eastwards to the Pacific. In winter, with a temperature of around 40°F below, the Etsin Gol is frozen solid, with the water rushing below the black ice. In summer the flow is continuously fed by the melting snows as the temperature rises to 130°F above. The only sensible times to visit this inhospitable land are in spring and autumn, and although we chose the spring, what we didn't know was that this was the season of sandstorms, which hit us with a vengeance just as we arrived at the site.

And what a site! Perhaps a quarter of a mile across, the mud-brick city walls were still standing to a height of thirty feet, against them piled enormous sand dunes. Inside was more drifted sand, but the remains of buildings were clear, including three Buddhist stupas at the north-east corner. There were wooden structures poking out of the sand, perfectly preserved. And there was the pottery – an archaeologist's dream: tens of thousands of sherds lying on the surface all burnished clean by the flying sand and looking brand new. We gathered all we could, blue-and-white, celadon, *tzu chou* incised ware, in fact the whole range of late Song and Yuan Chinese ceramics. These were later deposited in the museum in Hohhot, on our return journey.

It was now well into the afternoon and I offered to share the Chinese equivalent of a tin of our sardines with our crew. Their faces fell, and they asked if I would be prepared to pay for lunch? As we were hardly in gourmet territory, I wondered what they meant. It turned out that they knew the local leader of the Turgut Mongols, and that he had a *yurt* some miles to the west. We found it in the middle of a stockade made of prehistoric-looking tamarisk tree-trunks, and a corral of charming black and white goats with devilish pointed horns. We met Mr and Mrs Mongol (I think that was their name) and entered the *yurt*, where we sat on low, cushioned benches around the central stove. Pretty painted wooden cabinets lined the circular walls. We were served lumps of white rock (dried white cheese of limestone-like consistency) and something that could have been tea, or soup, or both. Then an aluminium washing-up bowl appeared, full of noodles in a mutton broth. It was simply delicious.

My wife, Peggy, took an interest in the quilted felts on the floor, and in no time Mrs Mongol had her sewing-kit out and they were both hard at it demonstrating their mutual skills. This went down so well that Mrs Mongol dived into a cupboard and produced a bottle of colourless liquid (koumiss?) that tasted a bit like slivoviç. Served in thimble-sized glasses, I had seven in a row, which my wife said was quite enough. They then started on her, and everyone else, and quite soon we were all exceedingly merry.

So much so that when we left, the driver took a short cut across what he thought was a dried-up river bed, and we were soon up to our axles in quicksand. But the good spirits prevailed, and an hour later we had dug out the vehicle and were on our way.

JOHN CARSWELL

Mr Khatib

I see from today's paper that the Egyptians have been tidying up the Sphinx – 'restoring' is the word used. The process has taken ten years and cost £1.8m. Neither figure seems excessive, after 4,500 years. There is a picture in colour, showing laser beams scourging the leonine back, and an orchestra playing at top speed under the human jaw. The work has been done in the interests of 'tourism'; and the Sphinx, who is known to be omniscient, will be aware of that.

I was there several years ago, in the company of a Mr Khatib. Returning home after some government business in southern Africa, I took the chance of paying a visit to Cairo. The plane landed me at 5 a.m. and I drove to Shepheards Hotel, the new Shepheards on the Nile. There were not many visitors to Cairo at that time, and I was given a fine room. From the windows I had a splendid view of the Pyramids, ghostly in the morning haze, pure geometry. After breakfast I went to the information desk, and said to the three men in black suits standing behind it that I had the day to spend in Cairo. They fell on me like famished ravens unexpectedly thrown an early worm. They pecked at me in turn. 'You will visit the palaces, the mosques, the museums, the bazaars,' said the first. 'You will ascend the new tower, and doubtless take lunch in the revolving restaurant,' said the next. 'You should go on the river in a felucca – of course you will visit the Pyramids,' said the third.

I held up my hand. 'I shall go to the museums this morning,' I said, 'and spend the afternoon seeing the mosques.'

The first took over the dialogue. 'There are many mosques,' he said.

'Some of them, then.'

'I shall find you a good guide for the day.'

I considered guides in general to be redundant, a nuisance. Besides, there was the expense.

'No,' I said. 'I shall take one of these.' I held up a booklet I took from a pile – YOUR GUIDE TO CAIRO.

At this all three came back into the discussion. That, they said, was only for the tourists. A cultivated traveller such as myself must know the value of using the services of an expert guide. I resisted, but compromised in the end, agreeing to one for the mosques in the afternoon; then took myself off to the Cairo Museum.

After lunch I found the guide waiting at the information desk. A well-built man, with the solid, oblong head characteristic of many Egyptians, he was not really dark, and his small moustache was almost fair.

'I understand, sir,' he began, 'that you would like to visit the mosques and the bazaars.'

'I said nothing about the bazaars. I want to see the mosques, and perhaps one or two other places of historical interest.'

'You will find the bazaars of much historical interest.'

'I shall not shut my eyes if we come to one. I wish to go to the mosques, please.'

We agreed upon a fee of two Egyptian pounds (the Egyptian pound would then, and probably always will, buy more than the pound sterling). He handed me his card: 'Mustapha Khatib B.A.(Politics)', and in the corner 'Authorised Guide'. Politics! Nasser! A trap! I must be on my guard.

My guide put me into a taxi, appearing to be the most dilapidated in sight, sat down beside me, and addressed the driver's back in Arabic. In league together, I thought, they would drive me round and round until the meter showed an astronomical figure.

'We will go first to the El Mu'ayyad mosque,' said the guide. 'I tell the driver to make a long detour, so you will see many places of historical interest.' I decided on acceptance.

He began to point out the sights: the concrete building housing the Arab League, the Hilton hotel, the 'brand new' tower with its restaurant. It became clear that Mr Khatib's idea of what was of historical interest differed from mine; he meant the future historic.

We talked a little, about changes in Cairo, prices. His manner was quiet and agreeable. We reached the old part of the town, and drove down narrow streets, and along the side of the ancient fortifications. At the mosque the attendant put canvas slippers over our shoes. I was about to place five piastres in the upturned palm when my guide stopped me, saying, 'I will take care of that.' It was pleasant to feel the absence of pecuniary responsibility.

We went through the great outer doors of limewood with their elaborately decorated bronze plates, and forward to the green garden lying beyond. The mosque itself is now reduced in size and splendour, but I much admired the beams and panels of the ceiling, and the lace-like tracery and multicoloured glass in the row of small windows. My guide signalled to the guardian. He came up with an immense key, and unlocked the door of an inner room, where I saw the tomb of the Sultan El Mu'ayyad, who had built the mosque to keep a vow. The door was locked again when we left the room, and a coin passed. Another when we stepped into the taxi, to the man who had been standing there gripping the door handle. The Egyptians are generous to one another, I thought.

The street was full of people. The driver squeaked continuously on his bulb horn as he nosed through the crowds. Boys in striped *galabiyeh* banged on the car windows, and grinned at us. The guide did not respond to the cries of *bakshish, bakshish*! directed at me. He began to talk about Egypt's ever-growing population, and the enormous problem of finding food and work for them. Nevertheless, the government had accomplished much, he said: health had improved, and schooling was now compulsory. Above all,the building of the High Dam at Aswan would result in the bringing under cultivation of huge areas of desert. About this there had been much trouble.

Mr Khatib looked at me challengingly. But I turned the conversation away, and asked whether he had always been a guide.

'No,' he answered. 'I studied at the university, as you have seen' – he patted his jacket pocket where his cards lay – 'and I continued my studies for some time afterwards. Then I became a writer, and wrote for the newspapers and magazines. Unfortunately my contributions were not welcomed.'

'What did you write about?'

'Politics.'

Again! But we had arrived at our next mosque, that of Sultan Hassan at the foot of the Citadel. The business of the overshoes was repeated, with accompanying gratuity, and I saw the glint of a second coin as it fell into the palm of the man whose function it was to stand by the open door. Then all at once, as we passed inside the magnificent building, a shaft of light illuminated my mind: while the hand making the out-payments was the hand of Mustapha Khatib, the treasury into which it was dipping was mine. I had surrendered control over my pocket. The thought disturbed me to such an extent that I couldn't give attention to the architecture of the mosque, or to Mr Khatib's description of it, masterpieces of Arab art though I believe both to have been. I am unable to recall any details of the mosque. But I remember that on our again entering the taxi my guide, having evidently run out of small change (and I was not surprised), handed the man supporting the tottering vehicle a currency note.

Inside, my guide said, 'Now, sir, we will tackle the bazaars.'

'No, Mr Khatib. I said I wanted to see mosques. I have seen nothing yet.'

'Very well, sir. As you will, of course. I take you to the Mahomet Ali mosque. It is up here, on the Citadel. We can walk.'

'That's a good suggestion,' I said, as the driver turned off his engine again, and we got out. We set off up the hill.

'Politics,' resumed Mr Khatib, as if the mosque of Sultan Hassan had never risen from the ground; and, before I could think of a way of diverting him, he continued:

'Not Egyptian politics, though. My interest is in English politics. I have a great admiration for your political institutions. That is why my studies, my writing, brought me no income. I began to write in the very year your hotel, the old Shepheards, was burnt to the ground by the angry crowd. It was very unlucky for me. Articles in praise of British institutions were unreceivable.'

'Would you do any better today?'

'A little, yes. Our countries are perhaps coming together. But my circumstances have changed. I am married, with a family to support. I became,

17

and remain, a guide.' He went on, 'You are married, sir?'

'Oh no.'

'Then you will not understand the difficulties. But I keep up my true interest. It is my good fortune to meet, in the course of my professional duties, an occasional English gentleman, with whom . . . '

We became separated by the people on the pavement. It was a moment or two before I again caught up with my guide. But he resumed, as if there had been no interruption:

' . . . with whom I am able to discuss the British institutions. You are not by any chance a peer of the realm, sir, or a Member of Parliament?'

'Alas, no' I replied. 'I am a poor' – and I emphasized the words – '*poor*, *junior*, civil servant.'

'Indeed!' he cried, in some excitement. 'A great profession in your country, and very knowledgeable. You see everything from the inside. Would you . . . '

'Unfortunately, Mr Khatib, the rules governing my profession debar me from taking part in political discussion.'

'Can that be so?' he exclaimed incredulously. 'You are exactly the people who know about these things. I should be delighted . . . '

But we had reached my third mosque, with its fine vaulted roof, gallery, and scores of lighted chandeliers. Squat in form, it had been compared – my guide informed me – to the 'Paris Opera House'. From the terrace we gazed at the view of the city with its infinite minarets, and looked past the Hilton to the farther bank of the Nile, as far as the Pyramids.

'I would suggest,' Mr Khatib said, 'that you end your day by seeing the *son et lumière* at the Pyramids.'

'I saw the Pyramids this morning from my bedroom window.'

'That was in daytime. You have not seen the *son et lumière*. It is a spectacle you should not miss.'

'I have to be up at four o'clock in the morning to catch my plane.'

'But it is not a late performance. You will return to your hotel by eight o'clock.'

'I don't think so, thank you.'

We left the mosque and Mr Khatib resumed his favourite subject.

'I should be delighted if you felt able to indicate what, in your opinion, is the future of the Liberal party.' (Mr Khatib's politics were a little old-world.)

Instead I asked Mr Khatib to point out to me the main features of the Citadel. Towards the bottom of the hill I gave him a story or two about Lloyd George, which took us back to the taxi.

The man who had received the currency note had kept hold of the door, but my guide dismissed him. My heart was beginning to warm towards Mr Khatib. Then he turned to me and said once more:

'And now a tour of the bazaars.'

'There is nothing I want to buy.'

'To look round simply. You will find them colourful. There is no need to buy.'

'I see no point in walking round bazaars if I buy nothing.'

'You will want to take some present home – perhaps to your mother?'

'I bought her one in the duty-free shop in Johannesburg.'

'She will expect something Egyptian – a souvenir from Cairo.'

Suddenly I thought of my god-daughter. 'All right, then. Just *one* bazaar, Mr Khatib.'

We took our seats in the taxi, Mr Khatib gave instructions to the driver, and sat back, a man with a weight off his mind.

'These drivers know their way about,' he said. 'And it reminds me. Is it true what your writer Bagehot once said: that in England the real centre of power is so concealed that if you tell a cab driver to go to 10 Downing Street he will not know where to take you?'

I laughed loudly. 'No fear,' I said. 'Prime Ministers go in for publicity these days. That address is one of London's tourist attractions.'

'Is that so?' said Mr Khatib. 'I wish I could drive up there myself. To think it is an ordinary house like any other. Has it window boxes?'

'Window boxes? I'm sure I don't remember.'

'I have always imagined it with geraniums,' he said wistfully.

Before long the taxi drew up at what seemed not a bazaar, but a small shop.

19

'You said just one bazaar,' said Mr Khatib, 'and I have brought you straight here, because it is the place you want. Absolutely no obligation, sir. But I can completely guarantee this shop – no fakes. You understand I have no connection with the business.'

'Of course not, Mr Khatib.'

We were inside. One glance round – at the sculptured figures, the silver-ware, the pottery, the ancient tapestries – and I was ready to run. But the owner, momentarily turning from a customer looking at necklaces, gave me a chair, and offered tea. When the customer left, the owner tried to interest me in the necklaces still on the counter, but I soon had those back in their drawers. Then I saw the camel on a shelf – stuffed, portable.

'For your mother?' asked Mr Khatib in surprise.

'My god-daughter,' I said.

'A fine male dromedary,' said the shop owner, wrapping it in mauve paper.

Outside, Mr Khatib returned to his suggestion for the evening. 'I would fail in my duty as a guide,' he said, 'if I did not stress the advantages of a visit to the Pyramids. It is a spectacle world famous. If we go now, we shall be in good time for the performance.'

'I am tired, Mr Khatib. I sat up all night in an aeroplane, and spent all morning in your museums.'

'But it will rest you. You will sit and enjoy. You are fortunate because this evening the performance is in English. I do not mind for myself, but I do not want you to regret afterwards that you missed the experience.'

Mr Khatib had sorrowful eyes. My affection for him was growing.

'What is this experience going to cost me?'

'The taxi fare will be one pound. I shall request another pound for my services, and there will be the entrance fee of course.'

'Of course . . . all right – I shall take your advice.'

My guide showed genuine pleasure, which he passed forward to the driver. We called at the hotel for my overcoat, at Mr Khatib's suggestion, and left the camel. We crossed the river, and took the road to the Pyramids, driving through swarming people in white robes, and past fruit barrows under their hard pressure-lights. We came to a large village, and Mr Khatib said:

'This is my village. I live here. All the people are my relatives.' It was still run on tribal lines, the headman settling all disputes. The village would stand by any member who was in trouble.

We reached the arena. I bought tickets, and in the darkness my guide led me to a front seat. A chill breeze blew from the desert, and I was glad of my coat. We waited. My companion wanted to talk, but I discouraged him. I felt a sense of mystery and awe. The sky was without a moon, but the stars, in the pure, desert air, were brilliant, innumerable. There were no lights yet, but I could trace the shapes of the Pyramids against the sky.

Music broke out from the loudspeakers, and the three Pyramids began to glow with a dim, blue-grey light. Then a ghostly effulgence illuminated the Sphinx, exactly in front of us; and this grew in intensity until the majestic figure held the stage, presiding over the whole solemn scene.

The music stopped, and a voice began:

'*Mesdames et Messieurs. Nous sommes . . .*'

French! I turned to Mr Khatib, in reproach.

'I am very sorry for this,' he said. 'I quite thought tonight it was the turn for the English language. The newspapers make many mistakes. I will translate.'

'No,' I said, 'I can understand.'

The narrator proceeded. Voices took up the tale from different corners, some speaking in the first person. The pungent French, inflated by the loud-speakers, rang out across the empty air. At intervals music played. The performance was dramatic and moving.

The Sphinx was speaking:

'Before history I was here. I have witnessed it all. Kheops I watched, as he built his pyramid. Khephron also I saw. They came and went. I watched the Pharoahs ride by, in their chariots. I know all. And I know the hearts of men.'

Mr Khatib sat close to me, listening intently, but shifting in his seat, as if a little uneasy.

Music; and then attention focused on the great pyramid on our right, and we heard from Kheops himself, and from the others in turn. Then again the Sphinx, the great brow dominating, the eyes scrutinizing:

MR KHATIB

'I see all. I saw Alexander, I saw Cleopatra. Julius Caesar came, Napoleon passed this way. And I see into the hearts . . . '

I dug my companion in the ribs. 'No mention of Lord Curzon.' I said. But there was no answer. He seemed most uncomfortable.

The voice came again, insistent: '*Je connais les secrets des coeurs.*' Then music again.

Mr Khatib turned to me. He said nothing; but he was almost – there is no other word – squirming. The performance ended. In the taxi, Mr Khatib spoke:

'You and I are friends. You trust me, I trust you. I keep nothing from you . . . the shop where you buy the camel, he my brother-in-law.'

I remained silent for a time, to mark my disapproval. We came to his village. I settled my account, and put him down. He was still worrying.

'Don't be concerned, Mr Khatib,' I said. 'I'm glad it was all in the family.'

It was a remarkably silly thing to say – but I meant it. It was true that we had become friends. And my god-daughter still treasures her camel. Naturally she calls him 'Mr Khatib'.

WILLIAM DALE

The Bridges of Florence

In July 1944 the British 13th Corps was making its way gradually north through Tuscany against an enemy who was staging a fighting withdrawal in that beautiful region. I was attached with my Phantom patrol to Corps HQ with the job of reporting the formation's progress to Army and Army Group. After some stiff opposition near Arezzo, our forward elements reached the southern outskirts of Florence around the middle of the month.

At this point there was a report circulating about the bridges over the Arno in Florence. It was said that an informal agreement had been reached between the Germans and the Allies whereby the historic bridges would be spared by the withdrawing troops, even though Florence would not, like Rome, be declared an open city. In any case the destruction of the bridges would hinder our advance very little, as in the height of summer the Arno is reduced to a trickle. There was some surprise, therefore, when one night there were loud explosions, and all the bridges of Florence were blown up at once – except one. The exception was the famous Ponte Vecchio, but the buildings at each end of it were destroyed instead, which prevented traffic from crossing it. Gradually the Germans withdrew to the heights around Fiesole, and on 4 August, the city was captured by 13th Corps.

I wondered why the German high command had appeared to change its mind, and some weeks later I was given an explanation. I was in Florence on leave, staying at the Hotel Helvetia. The manager was Swiss and had remained in the city while it changed hands. He and I were talking one day, and I asked him if he had any idea why the Germans had blown up the bridges. 'The explanation is perfectly simple,' he said. 'The German commander-in-chief in Italy, General Kesselring, had indeed agreed to leave the bridges intact. But the attempt on Hitler's life took place on 20 July. It was a failure and the reprisals were likely to be terrible. Kesselring was keen to prove himself a good Nazi and to that end decided to show no weakness in Italy, whatever promises had been made to the Allies. So he blew the bridges up.'

This explanation seemed to me plausible, though I was a little surprised that a Swiss hotel manager should be so well informed. I continued to brood on the event, and looked up every book I could find on the Italian campaign and on the plot against Hitler. I found no mention of an agreement on the bridges or of Kesselring's possible anti-Hitler sentiments. Then, in the summer of 1956, I was on holiday in Capri and met Herr Sigismund von Braun and his wife who were staying in the same hotel. He was a German diplomat in London and the brother of Werner von Braun, the rocket expert. He told me how in the war he had been interned in Addis Ababa when the British occupied Abyssinia, and then exchanged and sent to the Vatican while the Italian campaign was still in progress. I thought he might be able to shed some light on the question of the Florence bridges, so I told him the Swiss hotel manager's story. 'I'm sorry to disappoint you,' he replied, 'but there is no truth in the story. I knew of no arrangement being made between the British and the Germans about the bridges in Florence, and I am sure I would have heard about it as I was Counsellor at the Vatican at the time. What I can say is that the declaration of Rome as an open city cost the Germans dearly in lost ground, and it was decided never to repeat the experience.' That seemed to put an end to my speculations, but I still couldn't help wondering. Then I received some interesting information from the Imperial War Museum. They told me that, according to the US Army official history, General Joachim Lemelson, commanding the German Fourteenth Army, in late July 1944 ordered the destruction of all the bridges across the Arno except the Ponte Vecchio. That was against the wishes of the Italophile Kesselring, who was forced to acquiesce by the necessity of proving his loyalty to the Nazi régime in the wake of the bomb plot to kill Hitler.

So my Swiss hotel keeper was right.

ANTHONY FORSTER

The Other Travellers Club

In Paris there is another Travellers Club. Founded in the 1890s independently but in emulation of 106 Pall Mall, it is nevertheless very different in style. The clubhouse is the last mansion in the Champs Elysées surviving from the Second Empire; built for La Pavia, 'a Polish adventuress', it has interiors of stupefying ornateness. The exuberance of the heavy gilt plasterwork is only a little subdued by the passage of a hundred years, the chimneypiece in the salon is supported by immense caryatids and the grand staircase is of solid onyx. In short it is the ideal set for Flora's party in Act II Scene II of *La Traviata*.

In 1997 I was staying there for a visit to the Paris Air Show at Le Bourget. After the earth-shaking roars of the latest fighting aircraft of the world, it was a delight to spend a day savouring the extreme Frenchness of France, much more pronounced, one feels nowadays, than say the German-ness of Germany. I spent an improving morning in the Musée de Cluny and was then attracted to the nearby Brasserie Balzar because of its near-perfect resemblance to the ideal French eatery – the gleaming brass, the polished mahogany, the dignified waiters in their long white aprons and, indeed, the menu. Later reference to the Eyewitness Guide found it recommended as 'typically Left Bank in atmosphere and frequented by Sorbonne professors and students'. An animated party of just such sat down immediately next to me and enhanced the Left Bank atmosphere by smoking cigarettes before, between and during courses.

I was then ready for the Pantheon, the pediment of which proclaims *Aux grands hommes la patrie reconnaissante*, where I was awed by the grandeur of the central group of statuary placed where the altar would originally have stood. Depicting La Convention Nationale, it shows a group of Enlight-ened gentlemen gesturing ecstatically to the central figure of La Liberté, from behind which emerges the majestic mounted figure of the Emperor Napoleon accompanied by a contingent of the Old Guard. Ostensibly a tribute to the ideals of 1789 and La Liberté in particular, it ambiguously celebrates La Gloire Militaire. Of this secularized temple, the 1921 Blue Guide says, 'Visitors need not remove their hats'.

Returning to the Travellers (where no dinner is served in the evenings) I obtained a recommendation to a nearby restaurant, Chez André in the Rue Marbeuf, where I was soon tucked behind my little square table on a long banquette otherwise completely full. Parties of Americans from the big defence companies were in deep discussion about that day's military demonstrations at the Air Show. However, on my right I detected a strong presence of Left Bank atmosphere: a large elderly Frenchman dining alone seemed to be deliberately blowing his cigarette smoke in my direction. It also became clear that he intended to emulate the Sorbonne professors as he kept his cigarette going throughout his eating. Engaging him in conver-sation as far as my unpractised French and his previous drinks would allow, I asked him to desist from puffing in my direction. He explained thickly that a party of Americans (he used an uncomplimentary term) on his right had obliged him to do so. 'But I came here to eat and drink.' I said. 'Ah, monsieur, I came here to eat and drink and smoke,' he replied.

Grumbling, but more about the Americans than me – for example that they seemed to be taking over everything French – he agreed to stop smok-ing. Then apparently heartened in having found a companion for conversation, he launched into an account of how much he had enjoyed his time in England during the war when, as one of de Gaulle's Free French officers, he had been attached to the SAS. He spoke warmly of the charms of the girls of Reading, a town convenient it seems to his military base. Gaining in enthusiasm but also, alas, in incoherence, he recounted more of his military career. He had been in the Battle of Dien Bien Phu, that last great battle and defeat of the French army and empire. I was impressed.

'With your seniority, you must have been a colonel at least,' I ventured.

'A colonel? No, at Dien Bien Phu I was a general!'

'In that case, *mon général*, I insist that you resume smoking.'

I picked up his lighter and lit his cigarette for him. Harmony reigned.

I walked back to the Travellers, down the Champs Elysées with yet another monument behind me – the Arc de Triomphe – and reflected that Paris was full of reminders of past military glory.

MICHAEL ALLEN

Trouble with Bears

There is no doubt in my mind that the Yosemite Valley in California is one of the seven natural wonders of the world. I came to that heavenly valley from a city that is hell. It is called Tokyo, which means car-jammed, polluted and suffering from an epidemic of workaholism.

On the long Pacific crossing from Tokyo to San Francisco, I read about John Muir who was born in 1838 in Dunbar, some twenty miles west of Edinburgh, and then emigrated with his father to North America when he was only ten. Muir is a hero in America – a founding father of the National Parks movement. He lived in that century when the refugees from Europe were pushing west across America towards freedom; and in their freedom they butchered the buffaloes, degraded the Indians, decimated the forests and, locust-like, turned rich pastures into dust-bowls. He asked his fellow Americans to look around and observe the interdependence of all living things: 'Pollution, defilement, squalor are words that never would have been created had man lived conformably to nature,' he wrote.

That is what I learned as I flew high above the Pacific and then I landed in San Francisco and took a car to Yosemite, where I intended to walk alone for three days testing the prototype of a new walking boot which I had invented.

Next day I started late up the John Muir trail towards a beautifully-named mountain, Clouds Rest. Three miles later and 3,000 feet higher I came to the Merced river at a point where it plunges for thousands of feet over a granite lip. I lay down beside it and drank and remembered John Muir's words: 'no pain here, no dull empty hours, no fear of the past, no fear of the future . . . drinking this champagne water is pure pleasure – so is breathing the living air'.

As I climbed higher I was struck with awe that water, frozen into glaciers thousands of centuries ago, should have been the sculptor of so many massive, beautiful and natural works of art. And there is nothing more awesome that the face of Half Dome, which plunges down into the valley from that huge whale-backed mountain.

I knew I would not reach the summit of Clouds Rest, just short of 10,000 feet, that evening, and water was getting scarce so I filled my bottle from a stream, watched by a mule deer – so named because her ears are like a mule's. I went on into the evening, zig-zagging up the trail, searching for a campsite.

And there it was: a spur of the mountain, silver-grey granite, bare of trees – with a prospect of heaven. To the west, a red sun was setting behind Half Dome and the valley floor, now 5,000 feet below me, was a black pool of darkness. I turned and there, silhouetted against the eastern horizon, was Mt Lyell, highest of the Sierras, with a gleam of glacier ice between the outstretched ridges.

Here I made camp, building a fire against a smoke-blackened rock, warming my body against the sharp nip of frost. With food in my stomach, I thought about the bears and their hungry stomachs and went in search of a suitable tree.

These Americans leave nothing to chance – my 'backcountry use permit' was stapled inside a small folder which told me how to find a suitable tree and an appropriate branch, twenty feet above the ground, stretching at least ten feet from the trunk, and how I should divide my food into two bags of equal weight and fling them over the branch, which must be thick enough to support the weight of the food but not the weight of a bear cub.

It was all too complicated for me and besides there were no suitable trees, so I remembered what the author of a Yosemite guide book had said: 'I prefer to find a crack in the rocks and stuff my food deep down.' And that is what I did before crawling into my sleeping bag. No need for a tent for I was roofed by the stars. And then I slept.

Suddenly I was awake, every nerve sharp and alert to danger. It seems to happen to James Bond all the time but I have never experienced such an instant transition from sleep to complete awareness.

My eyes saw the stars, my ears heard the sound – the noise of a plastic shopping bag, full of food, being dragged out of a rock crack.

My brain said, 'You are not going to fight a big black bear in the middle of the night – let him have the food.'

I lay in my bag, very still, very quiet except for the loud pumping of my heart. Then I thought that without my food, my walk in the wilderness was over. I would have to turn back. A log cracked in the dying embers of the fire and I remembered that bears do not like fire.

My brain again: 'Slide quietly out of your bag, reach for the end of that long log that you were feeding into the fire and ATTACK.'

As I advanced, stark naked, on the huge boulder where my food was stored, a glowing log in my hand, my brain said, 'you've got a bare behind'. Ugh.

I peered round the corner of the boulder and slammed the log down into the crack and followed it with the beam of my torch. There looking at me was a small, furry yellow-bellied marmot with his mouth stuffed with my muesli.

I dragged the plastic bag out of its crack, put on a pair of pants and went in search of a tree. Now it was easy: tie stone to the end of the parachute cord, heave over a branch, replace stone with food bag and haul it up.

I built up the fire again, feeding long branches into it in case I needed another weapon. And then I slept again and did not wake until the sun had so warmed my bag that I was sweating.

There was only enough water to take the top off my thirst – not enough to dampen the muesli, not enough for a brew of tea. So I packed my rucksack and made for the summit of Clouds Rest.

I was sitting there, clicking my camera at the wondrous view, when a man and woman heaved themselves over the top. 'Had any trouble with bears?' he asked in an English accent. 'No, not really,' I said.

CHRISTOPHER BRASHER

The Professor on the Roof

Casa Cuseni, on the Via Rotabile above Taormina, had been the home of an Englishman well loved in the town during the twenties and thirties. The house became known as the Villa Kitson and Taormina became known about in England largely through the artists and writers who came to stay with Kitson. His shady house, set in a lush hillside garden, was filled with the collection of *Siciliana* that he had formed over the years – genuine pieces, not the fake, folksy stuff made for tourists since then. When the war came, Kitson stayed on. He hated the idea of abandoning his villa, and was the last foreigner eventually to leave as the Germans arrived.

At the war's end, the citizens of Taormina met to consider a programme of development. Development meant tourism, and tourism meant foreigners, about whose peculiarities they were uncertain. Their town was high and steep, had no beach, rising as it did above a pebbly shore. But it had its assets – a pretty Roman theatre, and Mt Etna itself in the window. The citizens recalled that they knew a foreigner whom they could trust to advise them. The commune of Taormina petitioned the British government to permit the return of Signor Kitson.

Kitson was elderly now and in frail health. He longed for the warmth of Sicily after the grey chill of austere England. But he was in no fit shape to go there alone. He worried over the problem. The Germans had been in Taormina *and in his house*! What would he find? How could he rebuild his life there, let alone do anything for Taormina? Then he thought of his niece, an admirably educated woman of independent character. Still better, she was a trained nurse, having served as one during the war. They struck a highly civilized bargain. The authorities permitted Kitson to draw upon his funds in Britain (not a small privilege at that time) and the two of them left England for Sicily and for good. Their welcome in Taormina was one of those occasions, happening rarely as they do, that redeem human relationships. After a civic reception, Kitson and his niece were escorted up the road to the Villa. There it was – the garden, luxuriant and abundant but groomed and kept together, the house uncobwebbed, its tiles shining, the ancient *amphorae* back in their places, the decorated Sicilian cart-boards, the paintings, the Roman glass – everything just as it always had been.

'But how can this be . . . ?' asked Kitson.

'We stripped everything out of the house and hid it from the Germans,' they said. 'Everything is in its place! *Everything*!'

And everything was. 'Except, of course, the car,' said Kitson. 'You couldn't hide the car!'

'But we did!' roared the butcher. 'I bricked it up in the back of my shop! It wasn't as if they left me any meat to hang there!'

Kitson was dead by the time I discovered his villa. One didn't have to be grand to get there, but it helped. Daphne was now obliged to make ends meet: so it had become the kind of guest-house for which one requires letters of recommendation from eminent persons if one wished one's application for lodging to be considered. Daphne Phelps gauged precisely the mix of guests she wanted beneath her roof. If there was a Member of Parliament in the garden cottage, it was either because he was a poet, had served with distinction in some bizarre wartime operation, or both. Were there to be an actor, it would be Gielgud; an author, it would be Greene. Only the oddest of the best: after all, D H Lawrence had written his 'Snake' poem while staying there with Kitson, and Frank Brangwyn had sung for several suppers by decorating the dining room. Changing times had changed old customs: the guests were now expected to *pay* as well as to be good company.

Daphne herself was now famous in a private sort of way. She had taken on her uncle's mantle and adorned it. She was learned concerning Sicily and fluent, not only in its language, but in deciphering the Byzantine code that still governed the conduct of the living. She had an understanding with the Church and with the Mafia, too, while she was also a friend to the anti-Mafia Danilo Dolci. If influence was needed she could draw support from one quarter or another.

I forget quite how it came about that my wife and I were elected, or selected, by Daphne Phelps. We were living in Malta at the time, and visiting Sicily. There was a letter of introduction, of course, but it was probably our mutual interests in other things that clinched matters. We were at the villa one afternoon when she arrived back after a foray into town where she had been speaking forcefully to a dealer in antiques who had been selling fake Roman pots to tourists. 'I would hardly be surprised if they went so far as to say "Cicero drank from this one!".' Her line of argument was that the inevitable exposure of everything of this kind expensively purchased in Taormina as faked was disastrous for the trade in more highly priced 'legitimate' antiquities. After going into all this at some length, she came, breathlessly, to a stop and then, pitching into an enormous chair with hungry lions' heads carved on its arm rests, asked,

'Have you met the professor on the roof yet? I encourage him to stay so that I can show him off . . . '

The room on the roof was well windowed and so light that it seemed suspended in air. Paul Wilkinson gave us China tea having gravely explained to us which specific tea it was. We were not used to this refinement. Our generation had not known any tea better than that obtainable on ration. In Mdina, the old citadel of Malta, I had occasionally been to tea parties in noble houses where a superior kind of tea was served in Sèvres china, but it was always with thick sweet condensed milk (fresh milk not being considered safe by old-fashioned persons). Wilkinson made his China tea with ritualistic care in a very special Chinese teapot, from which doses were poured into small cups without handles. Had I been on my own I might have pretended to have been perfectly familiar with all this. Then I would probably have given the game away by asking for lemon (as if a Chinaman would drink his tea with lemon!). But now I took a lead from my wife who made it cheerfully apparent that she was unused to teacups without handles or matching saucers. Fortunately, the fastidious Wilkinson humoured us.

He proposed to take us to the ruins of ancient Syracuse, and we spent a warm spring day clambering over the rocks while he made the history of the place alive. He did not need to carry a Thucydides or a Cicero – he could quote them from memory. We stopped to mop our brows at the Ear of Dionysius, and Wilkinson's account of its uses made us shiver.

Our liking for him grew over the next two or three years, between 1956 and 1959, largely through his correspondence with me. The first two or three letters in the series were between *Mr* Binns and *Professor* Wilkinson. Then, for eighteen months or more, we were Binns and Wilkinson. After that incubation we owned up, for ever after, to our forenames.

He came across from Taormina two or three times to stay with us in Malta at Villa Mompalao. He liked walking. 'Walk three miles a day and don't drink too much and you'll live forever!' he assured me. Walking with my wife in the north-western part of the island, near *Torre L'Ahimar*, the red tower, he suddenly stopped, put his finger to his lips. 'Can you hear it?' he whispered, 'the Snoring Snake!' They listened to the soft regular snore of it. My wife thought it was an old man, but there were no rocks big enough to hide one. 'There are no snakes in Malta,' she hissed, 'St Paul saw to that!'

'He only stopped them nipping,' said Wilkinson, 'but he let them go on napping!'

We learned more about Wilkinson – partly from Daphne Phelps, more exotically from Harry Luke and Stewart Perowne. Evidently Wilkinson had taken the collapse of his marriage badly and had felt the immediate necessity to make a dramatic gesture. He was distinguished in his field of medicine and, when he presented himself at the Colonial Office and asked to be given an appointment, at once, in the remotest, most impenetrable part of Central Africa, the response had been:

'But we have nothing good enough for *you*, Professor Wilkinson!'

The blue eyes blazed, the beard bristled, the long fingers curled, and of course they posted him to a job in a part of Africa not ordinarily visited. In due course, and in accordance with routine, the Colonial Office required him to pass an examination in the appropriate African language. Now Wilkinson was proficient in six European languages and Cantonese and Mandarin. But on this occasion he signalled back to London:

'I refuse to take this examination.'

The Colonial Office was unused to this kind of cable. They asked his reasons.

'Because it has no literature!'

The argument flew back and forth. The Colonial Office was insistent. Three weeks before he was due to sit the papers, Wilkinson agreed to do so.

'Merely recognizing a formality.'

Needless to say, he passed with distinction.

During one of his visits to Malta, Wilkinson proposed that he should show me Leptis Magna and Sabratha, which he had been shocked to learn I had not visited. We at once took a plane to Tripoli. In the pouches containing advice about the most hopeful things to do in a catastrophe, there were some leaflets about hotels in and around Tripoli. We decided that the best for our purposes would be the Del Mehari, or Camel.

It was an hotel oddly placed, in that the main road ran between it and the sea. But, having registered, we were escorted along a subterranean tunnel that ran beneath the road to the hotel bedrooms, which were built into the shore and directly overlooked the Mediterranean. We were shown to our separate rooms, rather small, but with lots of fitted cupboards. I unpacked, stowing away the few things I had brought, and then opened a latticed wardrobe to hang up my jacket. Wilkinson was doing the same in his room. We came face to face across a *bidet*.

The Del Mehari, we were told, had been built as a brothel for Italian officers, and had been used as such during the war, a kind of rest and recreation centre. The management were now coy about its past and endeavouring to create a new image. We appeared to be the only visitors they had. I went out that afternoon to hire a car. There were several to choose from, and I took what I thought to be the best bargain and most reliable, a Volkswagen beetle, and parked it outside the hotel. That evening Wilkinson gave me an inspired briefing on Leptis Magna, and we agreed to make that our first visit next morning.

When we walked out to the car after breakfast, I sensed a sudden tension in Wilkinson. He was a long lean man and, aside from the cultivated ferocity of his Shavian beard and bristling brows, he was generally relaxed. But now, suddenly, his whole body seemed to coil like a spring as he kicked the rear wheel of the Volkswagen, then, viciously, kicked it again. Odd, I thought, but we got into the car and, after I had driven ten kilometres or so, he seemed to recover his good humour and he told me more about Leptis. We stopped halfway at Homs for coffee. The car was parked along with others in the dusty square. When we had finished, I had to reverse it in order to get away. As I did so, Wilkinson pointed a long shaking finger forward and shouted 'Look out!', staring straight ahead. Distracted, I turned my head to the front to see what the matter was and we instantly collided with another Volkswagen, fortunately an empty one, parked behind us. I ran through the forward gears and fled from Homs as fast as the beetle could scamper. After we were safely away, I said, 'That was deliberate!'

Which it was. He sulked like a schoolboy until we got to Leptis Magna. But in bits and pieces he told me he had an intense and ungovernable distaste for things German that was beyond all reason. Then it came out that he had been one of the first doctors into Belsen. This had deeply affected him, and his loathing was sadly manifested in tantrums that were not worthy of him.

At the time, I did not take too much notice. Wilkinson's exposition of Leptis Magna had such extraordinary clarity that tantrums were forgettable.

Not long after our expedition, he left the roof-room at Villa Kitson and took a house at Lapathos, in Cyprus, that Lawrence Durrell describes in *Bitter Lemons*. He moved his exquisite china there and his library of rare books. Then the Turks came and destroyed all that. Wilkinson lost everything but his life.

I was in London while all this happened and did not know how much he himself had been shattered until he rang me up from the Savile Club. We met there, but he wanted to take me to lunch as a place that had been a favourite of his in the old days. We went to Rules. It was not as good as he remembered it, but it looked much the same and that pleased him. I was suddenly conscious that this was a farewell lunch. That afternoon he went

down, I think to Dorset, to stay with relatives, and then he died. He seemed
not to have anything more to live for.

GRAHAM BINNS

Never look a Gift Horse in the Mouth – at least not its Tail

Over forty years ago, before the inner desert of Libya had been opened up
by the oil exploration companies, I took a small military expedition to the
Oasis of Kufra, which lies deep in the Sahara desert, over seven hundred
miles from the north African coast. Its inaccessibility and remoteness had
long been a challenge to foreigners, for it is protected on nearly all sides by
the formidable sand seas – vast areas of soft shifting sands swept up into
dunes three or four hundred feet high. However, in the Second World War
it had been used as a forward base for the Long Range Desert Group for
their operations, often in conjunction with the SAS, against the Germans'
long lines of communication, which sometimes stretched from Tripoli in
the west to as far as El Alamein in the east. Kufra had also been the centre of
the Senussi resistance against the Italians in the 1930s. It was therefore a
place of both some mystery – having once been named 'the secret of the
Sahara' – and historical importance.

The journey from Derna and then Benghazi on the north African coast
to Kufra took us five days. We travelled via Jalo Oasis, the Serir or gravel
plateau, west of the sand sea, the sand sea of Kalanso itself (crossing it at its
narrowest point) and the moon country of the Jebel Hauaich – teeming, we
were assured, with scorpions and horned vipers! It had not been at all easy
and had involved many mechanical and water problems. We had been forced
to cross the sand sea and its knife-edge precipices in a vile and most atro-
cious *ghibli* (a hot wind) and we frequently got stuck in the soft sand; but
this made our arrival in El Giof at the centre of the Kufra oasis all the more
satisfying.

The navigator for our expedition, adept in using a sun compass by day and 'reading the heavenly bodies' with a sextant by night, was a young officer who, like a number of other Englishmen, was never happier than when he could identify himself, as far as possible, with the nomadic inhabitants of the desert in terms of dress, customs and etiquette. He had done a good job navigating us to Kufra, often over featureless desert and in poor weather conditions, and was now, since he spoke Arabic, the ideal man to enhance our liaison with the local people.

As we approached the oasis from the mountain to its north where the Senussi had made their last stand against the Italians, we were greeted at a small barrier post by a friendly Cyrenaican policeman, holding in his hand a large and magnificent fly-whisk, made from an Arab horse's tail. Without thinking I said, 'What a magnificent fly-whisk,' at which my navigator-cum-interpreter, absolutely horrified, said, 'Oh God, now you have done it'.

'Why?' I asked.

'Because,' he said, with barely repressed anger, 'he will now have to give it to you.'

Anyhow, nothing happened and we moved off into this story-book oasis with tall graceful palms, two salt lakes of the deepest blue and, on the hill above it, a Beau Geste-type fort in which lay buried one of the Senussi kings.

The whole oasis and its poor but friendly inhabitants seemed to be more or less self-sufficient, the only contact with the outside world at that time being the quarterly convoy of diesel lorries from the north and camel caravans from the Sudan and French Equatorial Africa. As one of the latter happened to be in Kufra at the same time as us, our navigator, liaison officer and interpreter was able to arrange a wonderful performance of dancing by moonlight by a tribe of nomads who came from the Tibesti mountains. The rhythm was hypnotic, the dancing virile and exciting and the girls attractive – that is what you could see of them above their yashmak face covering.

Carried away, I said to the young officer, 'The girls are lovely aren't they? I only wish they didn't have rings through their noses.'

'Why not?' he replied. 'When I marry, my wife is going to have a ring through her nose.'

After this, having, over the next few days, had tea with the mayor, bathed in the salt lakes and shopped and bartered in the covered souk, it was time to go. Reluctantly we said our goodbyes and set off to retrace our steps over the inhospitable terrain. As we came to the same small barrier police post which we had encountered on our way in, there was our friendly policeman. This time, however, he stood holding out in front of him, clearly for me to take, the splendid fly-whisk which I had admired. In confusion, I said, 'I couldn't possibly take it from you.' At which my young navigator friend almost exploded. 'Now, you've done it again,' he almost shouted. 'First you imply you want it, and now you reject it when you are offered it. How rude can you get!'

I knew when I was beaten and I am holding this wonderful fly-whisk in my hand as I write this over forty years later in south-east England. One lives and learns.

'DWIN BRAMALL

Road Rage in the Hindu Kush

The concept of Road Rage became current in our language in 1995, according to the *Oxford English Dictionary of New Words*. But I had my first experience of this fierce phenomenon some fifty years ago, at dawn one day on the road leading northwards from Kabul and over the Hindu Kush into Afghan Turkestan.

In 1951, I had been posted as Third Secretary to the British Embassy at Kabul. I had attended a wartime Persian language course at the School of Oriental and African Studies; Persian was the lingua franca of Afghanistan. My joining instructions stated that I would be well advised not to bring a car because Pakistan had imposed an embargo on the delivery of petroleum products to Afghanistan. Very little petrol was therefore available. This embargo was in retaliation for the vigorously pursued Afghan claim that Pakistan should cede the North-West Frontier Province so that it might become the new state of Pushtunistan incorporating Pushtuns on both sides of the Afghan-Pakistan border. In Afghanistan, the Pushtuns had long been the dominant majority.

Being car-less, I had to travel by local transport. Since there were, at the time, no airlines nor regular bus services in the country, this meant one of those brightly painted lorries with built-up sides which carried both freight and passengers. Of the passengers, the privileged two or three would have been able to buy first-class fares to ride in the comfort of the cab with the driver while the dozen or so of others would take their luck riding 'hard' on top of the freight.

In those days Afghanistan had only a few hundred yards of tarmac road. These led to the Prime Minister's office. All other roads were dirt and, despite the work of pick and shovel brigades, their surfaces were always uneven and generally corrugated. Snowdrifts, landslides and flash floods were common occurrences. It therefore seemed reasonable that a two man crew was required to pilot a lorry through these conditions. The captain was, of course, the driver. His job was to keep the show on the road. If this meant driving fifteen hours at a stretch, so be it. Quite a few of these drivers took opium to keep themselves awake.

The second crew member, the apprentice, had a most dangerous role. It was to cling to the back of the lorry. When the lorry stopped on an incline – it often had to on the curves of a mountain pass – his task was to jump down and thrust wooden chocks under the lorry's wheels to prevent it sliding down the hillside. Burnt by the heat of summer and frozen by the winter snows, the life expectancy of an apprentice was short. Some would fall from their lorries as a result of fatigue or hypothermia. Others would die young from lung cancer.

It was on such a lorry that I embarked on my first journey north of the Hindu Kush. We travelled all night, crossing the range over the 9,800 feet Shibar pass and, early next morning, the lorry put me down in Baghlan. Here, there was one of the few industrial units in the country, a Czech-built sugar beet plant which provided a market for several hundred small beet farmers.

The provincial governor was an eagle-nosed Pushtun while the chief executive of the sugar beet enterprise proved to be a broad-faced, smiling

Uzbek called Nazer Qull dressed in a padded silk robe. That night he invited me to dinner. We sat on a Bokhara carpet and, after a pilaff of rice, lamb and vegetables, drank tea. He spoke affectionately of his teenage daughter who excelled in raising silkworms on leaves from the local mulberry trees. A year or so later, a visiting UN Food and Agriculture sericulture expert was much struck by the skills of this girl and arranged a scholarship for her to study sericulture in Japan. But this offer had to be referred to the Afghan government, who did not approve of young women travelling abroad, much less so if they came from one of the minority (non-Pushtun) races. The scholarship had to be declined.

To return to Kabul, I caught another lorry driven by a Persian-speaking Tajik called Gul Agha. But I had to travel 'hard'. At first, I enjoyed the ride slouched on top of the load of cotton bales with half a dozen other passengers. That night, crossing the Shibar with snow on the ground and the wind knifing down from the Pamirs, I had never felt so cold. A fellow traveller helped me through with a gift of dried mulberries which, being rich in sugar, are a pick-me-up for anyone 'crossing the pass'.

By dawn, we had reached a point only a dozen miles from the capital where the road narrowed to one lane. Here, we happened to meet an oncoming jeep which hooted at us to pull aside. But there was no space for our driver to do so and backing a three-ton lorry loaded to five tons on a pot-holed road is always a hazardous business. So Gul Agha waited hopefully for the jeep to reverse. However, the jeep's passenger, an arrogant young Pushtun, leapt out and came storming up, shouting abuse and waving a pistol. Our driver got down, his apprentice joined him and we passengers climbed down too, but the Pushtun maintained his offensive. His frequently repeated punchline was the shouted question, '*Shoma Afghan hastid?*' (Are you an Afghan?) This was, in fact, a declaration of racial supremacy since, for the past two hundred years, the Pushtun majority had ruled over the other minority races (Aimaq, Hazara, Uzbek and Tajik) and made the name Afghan synonymous with that of Pushtun. Gul Agha was therefore not a proper Afghan but only a wretched, snivelling, second-class Tajik and would have to back down. In silent, resentful sympathy, we helped him reverse the heavily-laden lorry.

At the journey's end when I said goodbye to Gul Agha, he took my hand and replied: 'Sir, thank you. You understand our destiny. Next time let me drive you to my home in the Panjshir valley.' Thus began my association with this valley (*see page 258*), the one which Eric Newby and I were to visit, the heartland of the Persian-speaking Tajiks. Later, the Panjshir was to become the pivot of resistance against the Soviet occupation forces and, from 1996, against the fundamentalist Islamic and Pushtun Taliban.

HUGH CARLESS

The Romans had a Word for it

Despite unjustified assertions to the contrary, this is not an anti-American story.

Washington, July 1976. I was a mere First Secretary with only one ambition. How could I escape 3100 Massachusetts Avenue even if only for a day? Any excuse would serve. Happily, we diplomatic prisoners could usually pray in aid the Ambassador's instruction that we accept every invitation to speak to local audiences: Britain was soon to be in hock to IMF and needed good American friends wherever they could be corralled.

So it was that I jumped at the invitation to address the Kiwanis in 'Xville', West Virginia, a pleasant town some sixty miles north-west of Washington, my theme, inevitably, being 'Britain Today'.

A particularly hot and humid Wednesday morning found me turning off the Beltway at Exit 10, then on to Route 50 for Winchester, Romney and beyond. I recalled the relevant section of the Washington *Weekender's Guide*: 'In 'Xville' one can see several historic buildings. The Old Jail antedates the Civil War. The Edith Kuykendall House on River Road is not open to public inspection except by prior arrangement with the occupiers or owners. Worth seeing is Sycamore Dell, where Lew Wallace wrote part of *Ben Hur*.' I looked forward to sampling these delights.

The Kiwanis did not fail me. Their chairman, Mr Theodore James the Third, the very model of a modern rotarian, insisted that we tour the town in his impressive silver Cadillac. The Edith Kuykendall House proved to be almost as interesting as advertised although there was no sign of a chariot at Sycamore Dell. After this strenuous afternoon's sightseeing, I was interviewed by a magnificent lady (38+ and I am not referring to age) who was, I gathered, a student of journalism from a nearby university, temporarily employed by the local newspaper, the 'Xville' Sentinel.

Formal introductions dispensed with, we bonded immediately. I handed over my c.v., which she stowed away without a second glance in a capacious satchel. She had never had the pleasure of meeting a real diplomat before. Could she take my photograph? 'Of course.' Was this my first visit to 'Xville'? 'Yes, and I'm very pleased to be here. It won't be my last.' Where did I come from? 'London.' She frowned delicately. 'London, Ontario?' I paused for reflection. 'No, London, England. The original one, you know.' And so we went on, pleasurably exchanging significant data. She finally fled with a parting message about the need to file quickly before the paper was 'put to bed' for the week.

Came evening and a splendid dinner at the Lost River Motel far from the centre of town, attended by thirty amiable Kiwanis and their ladies. I talked of my distant island. Facing temporary difficulties? Yes. But permanently down and out? Emphatically not. Told my usual story about George Washington's grandfather, who had left my college at Oxford (Brasenose) early in the eighteenth century owing the college seventeen shillings and sixpence, a sum not finally repaid until 1920. Moderate laughter but perhaps a little incomprehension. I desperately threw in a few statistics. Referred to a 'quiet revolution' going on in Britain beneath an apparently unpromising surface. Threw doubt on *Time*'s capacity to report anything overseas accurately. Evoked the 'Dunkirk spirit' and at last sat down to encouraging, if hardly overwhelming, applause.

After a good night's sleep, I returned to Washington and promptly dismissed 'Xville' from my mind.

I was therefore surprised several weeks later to be telephoned from reception in my office by someone describing himself as the Editor of the *Shenandoah Recorder* (or some such title) the weekly newspaper published in a town a few miles east of 'Xville'. The words came floating up the telephone: 'You will not know me. But I have something with me, Sir, which I think you will be interested to see.' How could I resist? I asked him to come up.

The Editor turned out to be a courtly, slow-spoken, southern gentle-man, perhaps a bit-player in a real-life version of *Gone with the Wind* (University of Virginia, 1940?). His carefully-cut seersucker suit shone on a languid frame. He drew from his pocket a cutting, evidently from a recent issue of the '*Xville*' *Sentinel*. I noted a rather grainy photograph at the head of a paragraph of print. Could that be me? Yes. Above the photograph floated a puzzling caption: 'Curriculum Vitae'. Curiosity intensified. My visitor smiled gently: 'Maybe you would like to read what the *Sentinel* has to say about your talk?'

I squinted at the text: 'the Honorable Curriculum Vitae addressed the 'Xville' Kiwanis at a fine dinner hosted by their Chairman, Mr Theodore James the Third, at the Lost River Motel three nights ago. Most of his speech was devoted to the financial troubles of the grandfather of our nation's founder. Mr Vitae is a native of London, England.' Silence.

Is there a moral to this story? I cannot answer with any confidence. But it may have something to do with avoiding beautiful young students of journalism; using English at all times; and never telling stories that seem amusing in Oxford but may not, perhaps, fit the bill in solid Kiwani coun-try. Whatever the case, I vowed to be more careful in future.

MICHAEL PIKE

Hunting with Falcons

The author allowed us to take any piece from his published writings. With Sir Wilfred's very kind permission (and that of his publishers, Harper Collins), we have selected this passage from Arabian Sands.

Sir Wilfred tells us that those years with the Bedu had been the most formative of his life and that, seeing them fifty years ago, he was just in time before the area was 'opened up' to oil exploration, motor transport and other side effects of modern 'civilisation'. Falconry was one of the noble skills of a fast vanishing way of life.

[EDITORS' NOTE]

We were hungry before we arrived at Zayid's fort and were looking forward to eating meat that evening. We had not bothered to take a spare camel on this short journey, and, being anxious not to tire our riding camels, had taken little food with us. For the last two days we had been living on milk. There was plenty of this as the sands here were full of camels. Just before dinner four Bani Yas visitors were brought into our room to share the meal with us. As we sat down to feed, each leant forward and took a leg of meat off the dish before us and put it on the mat in front of him before starting to eat the rice. The rest of us were left to share the head and some other scraps. I was struck once more by how uncouth and selfish were these Bani Yas and Manasir who lived on the fringe of the desert, compared with the Bedu from the interior.

After dinner the room filled up with Zayid's retainers, several of whom had falcons on their wrists. I have been told that in England it takes fifty days to train a wild falcon, but here the Arabs had them ready in a fortnight to three weeks. This is because they were never separated from them. A man who was training a falcon carried it about everywhere with him. He even fed with it sitting on his left wrist, and slept with it perched on its block beside his head. Always he was stroking it, speaking to it, hooding and unhooding it.

The room was packed with people, some disputing over the ownership of a camel, others recounting a raid or reciting poetry. The air was thick with smoke from the coffee hearth and from guttering lamps, and heavy with the pungent reek of locally grown tobacco. Yet a tiercel, blinking in the lamplight, sat undisturbed on the leather cuff which protected my neighbour's left hand. I asked him how long he had had it, and he said, 'A week. He is a fine bird. You will see, Zayid will prefer him to the other ones', and he stroked the bird's head. All the birds in the room were peregrines, which the Arabs call *shahin*. I asked my neighbour if they used the *hurr*, or saker falcon, such as I had seen in the courtyard of the Amir's house at Laila. He said, 'Yes, if we can get them, but they are difficult to come by, and expensive. They are worth twice as much as a *shahin*, which you can get for a hundred rupees.' I knew that this was about eight pounds. He went on, 'In the Najd they prefer the *hurr*, since they have better eyesight than the *shahin*, and, as you know, the Najd is all open gravel plains. I myself would rather have a *shahin*. They are swifter, bolder, and more persevering.' He held up his falcon for me to admire and called its name, 'Dhib! Dhib!' which means 'wolf'.

I asked him how he had got the falcon, and he said, 'Zayid sent me with a message to Shakhbut and on my way to Abu Dhabi I saw a *shahin* on the salt-flats. Next day I went back there with a friend. We took a tame pigeon with us. I had tied a length of string to its leg and fastened the other end to a stone. Then we sat and waited and at last when we saw the *shahin* I threw the pigeon into the air and hurried away. As soon as it had taken the pigeon we returned and drove it from its kill. We quickly dug a shallow pit downwind of the dead pigeon and about as far away as that wall opposite us. I got into this hole and my friend covered me over with some salt-bushes and then walked off. When the *shahin* came back to the pigeon I slowly pulled it towards me with the string. Do you understand? Good. When it was within reach I caught it by the leg.'

I asked him why it did not see his hand, and he said, 'It is easy. A *shahin* always faces up-wind, and anyway it was busy tearing at the pigeon.'

A little later Zayid came in, everyone rose, and after we had settled down again and Zayid had been served with coffee, one of the Bani Yas said, 'Zayid, I saw two *hubara* near bu Samr this morning', and someone else said, 'I saw three last week.' *Hubara* are MacQueen's Bustard, a bird the size of a hen turkey; they arrive in Arabia from Persia, Iraq, and Syria at the beginning of the winter and most of them leave in the spring, although a few breed there. Zayid had told me that his men had found three nests the year before. Now he asked about falcons, and someone said, 'Hiza is sending up two more which they caught last week. They should arrive tomorrow.' Falcons are caught at this time of year on the coast while they are on passage, and Zayid needed a few more before he went hawking. He said, 'Good – we will get away in four days' time if God wills', and then, turning to me, 'You must come with me.' I willingly agreed, having always wanted to go hawking.

In the morning Zayid was busy checking saddle-bags, ropes, and water-skins, giving orders about the food to be bought in the local market, and the camels to be fetched from the pasturages, and inspecting his falcons. He said that one of them looked off-colour and was to be given a purge of sugar, while another was thin and was to be fed on an egg mixed with milk. He watched a falcon being trained to the lure. It had only been taken ten days ago, but everyone agreed that it would be ready to go with us. Later, three Arabs arrived with the two birds which Hiza had sent. One of them still had its eyes sealed. A piece of cotton had been threaded through its lower lids and tied at the top of its head, drawing them up so that the bird could not see. As it had begun to feed, Zayid told the men who carried it to remove the thread. The other, a tiercel, had a broken flight feather which Zayid now mended with a splint made from two slivers of gazelle-horn. He then branded both birds on the bill with his mark.

Four days later, Zayid said, 'We will get away this evening. I expect we shall be away for about a month. We will hunt in the Sands to the south-west of here where there is plenty of grazing and lots of wells. The Bedu say that there are bustard there.'

Later that afternoon we rode away from the fort, past the palm-trees. Zayid had sent the baggage camels on ahead with orders to camp on the edge of the Sands, and now we trotted across the gravel plain accompanied

45

by twenty-five of Zayid's Bedu retainers, some of whom carried falcons on their wrists. They sang a *tagrud*, a marching song to which Bedu trot their camels. They were in high spirits, for they had been looking forward to the beginning of the hawking season as people in Scotland once looked forward to the Twelfth.

We reached camp as the sun was setting. The dunes were already dark against a flaming sky where cirrus clouds floated like burning vapour. The slaves had collected bushes and piled them into windbreaks behind which large fires were blazing. We soon gathered round them to warm ourselves, for the evening air was chill. We sipped coffee, while the rhythmic ringing of the brass coffee-mortar invited everyone to draw near. A Bedu family had already joined us, and soon their camels drifted across the darkening sand towards us, followed by ragged long-haired boys. A couple of goats had been slaughtered and cut up, and large cauldrons of rice were simmering on the fires. A little later the herdsboys came into the firelight. One of them was carrying a bowl of milk, capped with foam, which he handed to Zayid before sitting down in our circle to wait for dinner. They told us that they had found the fresh tracks of five bustard round the well, and tracks, two days old, of others in the Sands near by. Zayid turned to me and said, 'God willing we will eat bustard tomorrow.'

We were astir early next morning. Someone fetched the camels and couched them beside the fires, round which we huddled in our cloaks, for it was still bitterly cold. Zayid called out to ask if I would care to ride Ghazala and I eagerly accepted. Bin al Kamam said to me as he tightened the girth and adjusted the saddle-bags and sheepskin, 'You have never ridden a camel like this', but I told him that I had ridden her on my way to Sharja in the spring. Then as the sun rose we picked up our rifles and camel-sticks and prepared to mount. The falconers lifted the eight peregrines from the blocks on which they had been perched, looking wet and bedraggled from the drenching dew, and called to the three salukis. We stood behind our mounts. Zayid looked round to see that I was ready, and then placed his knee in the saddle. Instantly his camel rose, lifting him into the saddle, and we were off across the sands. We expected to find the bustard on the flats between the dunes rather than in the dunes themselves. We walked our camels while we scanned the ground for their tracks. I had expected that we would be quiet, but I might have known from experience that no Bedu can ever keep silent. Everyone carried on a noisy conversation and anyone who got left behind and trotted to catch up broke automatically into song. Suddenly an Arab on the left of the line signalled to us that he had found fresh tracks, and as we turned our camels towards him a bustard rose about four hundred yards away, the white bands on its wings showing up clearly against the red sand. A falconer unhooded his bird and raised it in the air; then it was off flying a few feet above the ground; the bustard was climbing now but the peregrine was fast overhauling it; now they were faint specks not easily picked up again once they had been lost sight of; then someone shouted, 'It's down!' and we were racing across the sands.

As we slithered down the dune-faces and climbed out of the hollows and then galloped across the flats, I realized what an exceptional camel I was riding. I was fully occupied staying in the saddle, but the falconers who rode beside me carried their falcons on their wrists, held by the jesses.

We came upon the peregrine in a hollow, plucking at the lifeless bustard. One of the men slipped off his camel, slit open the bustard's head and gave its brains to the falcon. He then heaped sand over the corpse to hide it, and lifted the puzzled-looking falcon back on to his wrist. We had all dismounted. Zayid pointed to some oily splashes on the ground and said, 'Do you see that muck? The *hubara* squirts it at its attacker. If it gets into the *shahin*'s eyes it blinds it temporarily. Anyway, if it gets on to its feathers it makes a filthy mess of them, and you cannot use the bird again that day.' I asked how many bustard a peregrine could take in a day, and he said, 'A good bird might take eight or nine, but they will take seven on the wing to every four they take on the ground. Do you see where they have fought?' and he pointed to a trail of feathers for twenty-five yards across the sand. 'You can see what a battle they have had. Sometimes a *hubara* manages to stun a *shahin* with a blow of its wing.'

We went on again, and flushed a bustard from a hollow in the sands. It landed as soon as the peregrine overtook it. The peregrine stooped at it twice, and then landing beside it jumped at it, trying to seize it with its talons. The bustard spread out its tail and struck at the falcon with its wings.

The salukis, which, whenever they saw a falcon loosed, raced along behind it, now arrived and helped the falcon to kill it. The falcon then drove the dogs off, and when we arrived they were lying down beside the dead bustard at which the falcon ripped and tore.

We killed two more bustard and several hares before Zayid stopped for lunch. I have been told that wild peregrines will not take hares or rabbits, yet Arabs find it easier to enter a newly-trained peregrine to hares than to bustard. Generally one of the salukis caught the hare, but during the next three weeks I frequently saw a peregrine bind to a hare which the dogs were coursing.

While we were baking bread and roasting two of the bustards by burying them in their feathers in the hot ashes, a raven circled round croaking. Zayid said, 'Lets see if a *shahín* will kill it. I had one last year which killed a raven', but the peregrine which he loosed only made a few ineffective stoops, easily countered by the raven turning on its back. We went on again as soon as we had fed, and a little later put up a bustard within fifty yards of us, but the peregrine which Zayid had unhooded refused to fly. Zayid looked up and, pointing to four eagles high above us, said, 'It is afraid of them.' Shortly afterwards we put up another bustard and this time the peregrine took off. Almost immediately it dashed back to Zayid and thumped against his chest as an eagle swooped down at it with a loud swishing noise, rather like a shell going through the air. I was surprised that the eagle had gone for the peregrine and ignored the bustard. Stroking the frightened bird, Zayid said, 'That was a near thing – it was lucky it did not get her. Well, we shall have to go on – it is no use hanging about here with those eagles overhead.'

Late in the afternoon we saw eight bustard flying up a valley between the sands. We watched them alight, and rode slowly and, for once, in silence towards the spot, after having tied up the dogs. One of the falcons was unhooded and evidently saw the bustard on the ground, but when loosed failed to find them, although it flew backwards and forwards low over the ground. It was then brought back to the lure. Two bustard rose together a couple of hundred yards ahead of us as we moved forward. Another falcon was loosed, overhauled one of them, drove it to the ground and killed it. We remained where we were while its owner went over and collected it.

The remaining bustard lay very close, but one by one we tracked them down and flushed them. The salukis were untied as we flushed the last bustard. Each time it landed, the dogs arrived and it took to the air again, until at last it seemed determined to outfly the peregrine. Round they flew in a great circle, the falcon swooping and the bustard dodging it. The bustard seemed to be flying quite slowly with unhurried beats of its great wings, yet the peregrine was evidently flying its fastest. As they passed directly over our heads the peregrine made one last swoop, missed, shot up into the air and then swung down to us.

We rode singing into camp long after dark, tired and bitterly cold, but well content with our opening day. As we sat round the fires and went over the kills again, and later as I lay awake under the blazing stars and listened to the restless moaning of the camel herds, I was glad that we were hawking in the traditional way and not from cars as they do nowadays in the Najd.

WILFRED THESIGER

Not a Gentleman

It was that period of the year when clubs were closed for some of the time, and several members from another club were having dinner at the Travellers. At the end of my meal, I got up to pay and in front of me, waiting to pay his bill, was a well-known judge, one of the visitors from the other club. While Mrs Savoury was adding up, he addressed her saying, 'Mrs Savoury, you are just the type of Club servant we would like to have in the — [and he named his club]. Would you consider coming to join us?' She thanked him for his kindness. He paid the bill and left the room and then she turned to me and said, 'That man is not a gentleman. You don't pinch Club servants like that.'

PETER WORDIE

Visiting the General

I was met at Istanbul and escorted through a crowded customs hall where Russian and Ukrainian traders were sleeping next to mountains of baggage containing televisions, tumble dryers and ghetto-blasters. On the tarmac outside was a rickety old Tupolev, which still had its Aeroflot markings despite the fact that it was now supposedly part of the personal flight of the so-called 'President of the Chechen Republic of Ichkeria'.

It was a cold, clear November night. There was no heating on the 'Presidential flight' and, apart from two Chechen 'bodyguards', I was the only passenger. As we set off over Anatolia, trying to dodge the Russian air blockade by travelling via Baku, the warmth and camaraderie of the House of Commons lobbies, where I had voted only twenty-four hours earlier, seemed long ago and far away. Most of my colleagues were already back in their constituencies – relaxing, advising, arguing, entertaining, doing all the usual things MPs do at weekends. I had set myself a different agenda, however.

The Caucasus had long held a beguiling fascination for me. It had the drama of a history set in the eye of the storm between the competing empires of Russia, Iran and Turkey. Its remoter valleys and passes were home to dozens of small tribes and nations, each of whom spoke a different language, often unrelated to each other. And it had a cultural significance in ancient legend and modern literature – I knew its wild, romantic beauty from Pushkin, Lermontov and Tolstoy. By late 1993, the Caucasus was beginning to assume its old pre-Soviet strategic significance and the newly independent Transcaucasian states on its southern rim were the focus of particular interest. Their independence and the prospect of securing the vast energy resources of Azerbaijan were threatened, however, by a number of messy local conflicts, fuelled by Russian interference, in Nagorny Karabakh, Abkhazia and Ossetia.

Yet Russia had a problem in its own backyard too. In the northern Caucasian republic of Chechnya, whose warlike people had resisted Russian tsars and commissars for centuries, a former Soviet air force general, Dzhokhar

Dudayev, had seized power and declared unilateral independence. To the outside world Chechnya remained a part of the Russian Federation; to Moscow it had become a pariah republic run by gangsters and criminals which would have to be blockaded and crushed. I had asked to visit Chechnya and to meet this Dudayev who was so ready to risk the wrath of the Kremlin. So he had sent his rickety Tupolev to Istanbul and I was off for a long, bitterly cold weekend in the Chechen capital Grozny and my first meeting with the General.

There was one hotel in Grozny and it was hardly de luxe: there was little food and no heating but I was provided with extra blankets and the disturbing privilege of two armed guards outside my bedroom door. Central Grozny in the snow looked much like any other Soviet city: dingy, poorly-constructed blocks of flats and back streets where straggly fruit trees peered over painted wooden fences from the gardens of ramshackle cottages. On the outskirts of the city, however, there were larger, more opulent buildings – the property of Chechnya's new rich. Russia's economic blockade was clearly working well for some people.

There was an air of unreality about everything in Grozny, a sense that things were not quite as they seemed and an ever-present undercurrent of menace. Rumours were rife about who was getting fat on the embargo and there were stories that Dudayev and his cronies had linked up with senior figures in Moscow to turn Chechnya into a convenient entrepot for dodgy arms dealing. The Russians were said to have left behind a vast stockpile of weapons, some of which had been exported, some used to equip Dudayev's militia.

Whatever the truth of the rumours of Russian arms deals, there has always been a 'gun culture' in Chechnya. A Chechen's first priority, I was told, is his weapon followed by his horse or car and then his house. Last of all comes his woman. My introduction to this macho 'gun culture' came when I heard shooting in the streets and turned to find a group of youths dancing and firing semi-automatic weapons at the sky. They were celebrating a wedding.

When I arrived at Dudayev's Presidential Palace, formerly the local Soviet, the 'gun culture' was more evident than anywhere else. I stepped out of the lift on the wrong floor and found a large crowd of bearded Chechens, brandishing every conceivable type of weapon, all shouting loudly and trying to push past each other into the lift. The effect was of a scene from a Marx Brothers film. I closed the doors and went up a floor.

As I entered General Dudayev's office, it occurred to me that the size of a leader's study is often in inverse proportion to his respect for democracy. Dudayev's was large and empty. It was also cold and unlit because a bomb blast at a nearby electricity substation had cut most of the city's power. A lean, wiry man with dark eyes and a black pencil moustache, Dudayev was sitting under a large Chechen flag – green with a white and red stripe and the sinister shape of a wolf reclining on it. I asked about the wolf.

The Chechens were wolves, he said, wild, free and untamed. He became even more melodramatic as he described the current political situation. 'If the Russians come to Chechnya again, they will never leave,' and he clenched his fists, somehow simultaneously cracking the knuckles of his fingers. I stifled a laugh at these amateur theatrics but there was no doubt that his hatred of Russia was genuinely raw and uncompromising: the Caucasus was not part of a legitimate Russian sphere of interest Although I considered myself a Russophile, I had some sympathy – the entire Chechen nation had been deported under Stalin, after all.

Yet Dudayev seemed no less hostile to other foreign influence in the region The resources of the Caucasus should not be exploited by foreign adventurers and rapacious oil companies seeking easy profits. The only outside assistance he needed was from other Muslim countries: he was determined to create a pan-Islamic Federation which would help to unite and defend the Muslim peoples of the Northern Caucasus. As if such a dangerously destabilising idea were not enough, with a mischievous grin flashing a glimpse of wolf's teeth across his sallow face he added that he had just been to Baghdad to discuss the matter with Saddam Hussein.

As I listened to his rambling monologues, I thought that he was more than a little mad and certainly dangerous. Yet, when I took my leave of him after a gloomy lunch with a dozen grey-faced goons in the Presidential dining room, I noticed that the trousers of his oddly cut suit were at 'half mast'. He seemed absurd rather than dangerous, a pantomime villain making blood-curdling threats like Captain Hook. No doubt he would soon be removed in a coup or a civil war.

When I saw him again two years later he had changed. It was late in the autumn of 1995 and the Kremlin had finally lost its patience. Its increasingly indiscreet attempts to remove Dudayev by engineering coups and even a civil war had failed, leaving him stronger than ever. When Moscow ended its proxy war and decided on direct intervention with a brutal assault on Grozny, the Russian army was tied down in a protracted guerrilla campaign. Grozny, a city the size of Oxford, was reduced to rubble and Dudayev's fighters took to the mountains. By the end of 1995, despite hundreds of thousands of troops in and around Chechnya, the Russians controlled very little of the country outside its capital. They were taking heavy casualties and public opinion was strongly against the war. I realized that direct intervention was exactly what Dudayev had wanted.

I stayed in a village outside Grozny from which, every evening, rebel fighters would depart to attack Russian positions around the city. During the day, Russia's bewildered conscript soldiers ventured onto the main road nearby to establish checkpoints but they did not stay for long and never after nightfall. In order to avoid the Russian patrols, however, I was taken in a jeep through snow and mud across open countryside to the foothills of the Caucasus. First I waited in one farmhouse, then another, then a third before being moved again when it was dark

When finally I saw the General, he was no longer a pantomime villain but the military leader of a national liberation struggle. He was clearly. focused and energetic He paced the room in his neatly pressed combat fatigues and highly polished boots, declaring confidently that Russia's attempted 'genocide' of the Chechen people would fail. 'This war will not end in the subjugation of Chechnya but in the destruction of Yeltsin and the Russian Federation,' he said. This time, there was no hint of melodrama. On the flag behind him I noticed that the wolf was no longer sitting but standing and ready to attack.

We talked for hours and when, late at night, I returned across the snowfields, I realized that Russia's war had turned an obscure oddball into a national hero. Its brutality had legitimized Chechnya's claim to independence and Dudayev had become a symbol of resistance to the oppressor.

Perhaps it should have been obvious that his final transformation would be from hero to martyr. Russia needed to save face before It could leave the killing grounds and, a few months after my departure, Dudayev was killed in a rocket attack as he talked to an intermediary about the conditions for peace. Even in death he remained an enigma, though, and many Chechens insisted that he was still alive. After all, someone said, he was seen only a few days ago in Istanbul.

HAROLD ELLETSON

Maybe you do it all the time

What is the best way to say thank you to one's hostess? I suppose that flowers are always acceptable but I recall one occasion when it did not quite work out as I planned.

In the fifties I took a slow boat to China and I stopped off while it docked in Singapore. Joan and Michael Wilford were then at the High Commission and had me to stay for three blissful days.

The day before I left I went to the flower market to order a present for my hostess. I had been studying Chinese on the boat and was eager to practice. I soon discovered that a wide range of dialects were spoken so it took me some time to find a seller who understood Mandarin. Eventually, after a lot of bartering, most of which I thought I understood, I arranged for delivery the day after my departure. They seemed quite expensive but I had no idea of Singapore flower prices and anyway the Wilfords had been very kind.

Some two weeks later, I arrived in Peking where a letter from Joan Wilford awaited me. She wrote:

'Maybe you do it all the time. But we were somewhat surprised the day after you left. We were awoken by a knock on the door to find a coolie with a box of magnificent flowers on his head. We went in and unpacked them. A few moments later there was a further knock, another coolie, another box. We had barely unwrapped these when there was a third knock and we were amazed to see a line of coolies with boxes stretching over the hill to the golf course.

'We filled every vase, filled the bath, hung them from the bushes in the garden and were still able to send boxes to all our friends.

'Maybe you do it all the time.'

My knowledge of Chinese had improved by then and I had learnt the importance of more of the monosyllabic particles the Chinese frequently used. It dawned on me that instead of ordering three dozen flowers, I had bought three dozen gross or over five thousand. I thought that they seemed quite expensive.

Many years later I stayed with the Wilfords in Tokyo where Michael was then Ambassador. Joan recalled my Singapore stay and begged, 'maybe you do it all the time', but that I should not do it in Tokyo.

So I bought her a single orchid. I am sure that it cost a lot more than the flowers in Singapore.

But what does one give one's hostess?

JOHN MORGAN

Shamshuddin – a Tribute

Arriving at Bareilly railway station in October 1941, a newly-commissioned subaltern on my was to report to the 9th Jat Regiment, Indian Army, I was immediately surrounded by the usual hordes of would-be porters all clamouring to carry my bags. Elbowing his way to the front arrived a rather consumptive-looking character in a sweat-stained tarbush, who enquired if I was Second Lieutenant Francis. On receiving an affirmative reply he immediately took charge, furiously drove off the crowd, armed himself with my valise and, inviting me to follow, beat a passage through the densely-thronged platform to the outside of the station where he had commissioned two tongas, one for me and another for himself and my baggage. On asking for his identity he replied, 'I am your bearer, Sahib – Adjutant Sahib sent me'.

Privately I thought this a trifle presumptuous as I had envisaged my

interviewing a number of applicants for the post and making my own selection. I thought I would sort this out on arrival at the mess and perhaps
engage a rather more robust and presentable individual.

How wrong I was. The question never arose. From that moment onwards Shamshuddin, for that was his name – but I always called him 'Bearer'
– assumed complete responsibility for all my domestic affairs and served
me, until my eventual departure from India five years later, with a devotion
and loyalty the depth of which I find hard to describe.

I suppose during those five years I employed him for a total of no more
than eighteen months – most of the time our battalion was on active service,
and I only returned to Bareilly at intervals. But whenever I appeared
Shamshuddin would immediately present himself and return to my service.
I would remonstrate with him regarding the inconvenience this would cause
to his current employer. That would be brushed aside as irrelevant. 'Captain
James Sahib [or whoever],' Shamshuddin would say, 'knows that I am *your*
bearer.'

His primary duties were, I suppose, that of valet-in-chief. Such as looking after my clothing, cleaning and ironing my uniform, keeping my quarters
tidy and serving me in the mess. But his services extended far beyond these
basic functions. Nursemaid, counsellor, news purveyor, messenger, keeper
of the purse – his rôle covered every aspect of my welfare outside purely
military duties. One of his more taxing chores was to arouse me in the morning and ensure that I presented myself fully dressed on parade at daybreak.
No easy task, especially after a late mess night. But Shamshuddin developed
this to a fine art – always ready with cups of hot tea, or alka-seltzer if more
appropriate, he would entreat, cajole and badger me until I had arisen from
my charpoy, shaved and dressed. Due to his efforts, I don't think I was ever
unpunctual.

I always entrusted Shamshuddin with my petty cash. On the first of each
month he would pedal off on his bicycle to down-town Bareilly and present
to the bank my cheque for a hundred rupees. Deducting his wages, he would
retain the balance and make minor disbursements on my behalf – reporting
when the money was finished. He would then pedal off for a further replen-
ishment. In the early days, I would ask him to account for the money and he

would outline expenses accurately to the nearest anna. After that I never bothered. Such was his stewardship of my affairs that on many occasions before going out for the evening I would ask him for a sum of money. 'Too much, Sahib,' he would say, 'you will only need this', and would hand over a lesser amount. He was usually right.

Shamshuddin was never slow to protect my person against unexpected perils. For example, one evening, before changing for dinner, I heard the *bhisti* entering the bathroom to pour the usual kerosene-tin of hot water into my bath-tub. A moment later with a bellow of alarm he bolted outside with cries of '*Sanp hai!*' Peering round the bathroom door, I was startled to observe that the object of his terror was a black cobra coiled inside the bath. Being allergic to snakes, I retreated hurriedly. Not so Shamshuddin. With great daring he seized my hockey stick and so belaboured the wretched creature that it was quickly rendered unconscious. Whereupon he hurled it into the garden, poured in the hot water, mixed it with the cold, and returned to me blandly announcing, '*ghusal taiyar hai Sahib*' (your bath is now ready, sir) in the tone of one regretting a minor inconvenience.

Pre-war residents of Indian cantonment stations will readily recall the efficiency of the 'bearer's grapevine'. Shamshuddin was well tuned in to the network which was often used to my advantage. For instance, the giving of private dinner parties by junior officers to repay local hospitality was somewhat difficult as we rarely possessed proper crockery and effects. No problem for Shamshuddin. With the assistance of other bearers, my table would be adorned with an excellent dinner service, high quality glassware and cutlery and other decorations. The trick, of course, was to ensure that the owner was not among the guests (the 'borrowed' effects were instantly returned after use). I recall my embarrassment when the wife of a senior official complimented me on my floral arrangements which, she said, bore an astonishing resemblance to flowers in her own garden. Shamshuddin while serving us maintained an entirely impassive countenance, but I thought I could detect a distinct gleam in his eye.

Missions of a more delicate nature were often effected on my behalf. Making up a party for the Bareilly Club Annual Ball, I penned a note to Nurse Jones at the General Hospital and asked Shamshuddin to deliver it and wait for a reply. Realizing its contents, he respectfully informed me that he believed Nurse Jones Sahib would be accompanying Captain Thomas Sahib to the Ball, but it was his belief that Nurse Robinson Sahib was still free. In due course Nurse Robinson was pleased to accept my invitation.

I don't think humour was Shamshuddin's strongest point. He would tolerate but remain unmoved by the horseplay and practical joking of young officers in the mess. In fact I don't think that laughter played any great part in his life. His greatest problem was the seemingly inexorable increase in the size of his family – there was always an addition to report whenever I returned to Bareilly. I think that the total came to eleven by the end of the war. He would seldom accept my congratulations but would dolefully comment that this was just one more mouth to feed. When I lightheartedly offered various but impracticable solutions to his problem, he would dissolve into a sort of agonized helplessness which was the nearest he ever came to demonstrating mirth.

I have never really understood the underlying reasons for this selfless devotion to duty on the part of a non-combatant bearer. My time in India was clearly limited and I would depart at the end of the war. Shamshuddin must have realized this and, with his own career to consider, it would have been quite understandable for him to have sought employment giving him longer-term security.

I think I was a fairly 'average' employer. On many occasions I must have thoughtlessly kept him hanging around unnecessarily when I could easily have dismissed him to go home earlier. But on the other hand, I never took advantage of my position to exploit him. I think I was firm, but not unkind. I took a credible interest in his welfare and usually granted minor requests for a small advance of money or a day off for family business. We treated each other in accordance with the tenets of civilized behaviour, conversing solely in Urdu, and never entering into familiarity. On his part Shamshuddin, although a servant, was never servile. Respectful, never obsequious. It was a man-to-man relationship – we both understood the rules and abided by them.

But these traditions of the dignity of service can only partly explain why I should have been so privileged to gain this man's loyalty. It wasn't the money. I never paid him more than the going-rate – nor did he ask for it. I suppose status played its part. There was a certain social standing attached to being the Bearer of a British Officer. In his spotlessly white *kitmutgar*'s uniform, with the regimental badge and colours on his turban, he stood proudly in the mess dining room savouring his position. (If he thought I was imbibing a little too freely on mess nights, he would lurk in the bushes outside to a late hour, ready to help me back to my quarters if it should be required. Although typical of his solicitude, I am glad to say that only once was I obliged to avail myself of this assistance.)

There is much more to it than all this, because his interest in my welfare was wholly genuine. Shamshuddin, through the grapevine, kept a careful track of my movements beyond Bareilly and of the various actions in which I took part. He took a real pleasure in my modest achievements and in my promotions to more senior rank. When I returned from the eastern front stricken with malaria, he was genuinely upset and posted himself close to my hospital ward throughout my illness, ready to provide what services he could.

I could recount many more examples of Shamshuddin's devoted service, but I still cannot explain why I should have received so much more than that required by the call of duty. All I do know for certain is that between us two men of different races, different cultures, of widely differing ages, there was forged a bond of mutual respect and friendship – one that we both cherished – and which for me will remain to the end of my days.

Eventually the time came for me to leave India. I dreaded the moment of parting and suggested this should be at Bareilly Station, where we had first met. Shamshuddin wouldn't hear of it and insisted on accompanying me all the way to the transit camp outside Bombay. There he attended to me while I waited for embarkation. Then the day arrived and I had to go. I summoned Shamshuddin, who guessed why I had called: already the tears were staining his cheeks and he could see that my own eyes were moist. Words were inadequate and for once I broke the rules, putting my arms round his thin shoulders and embracing him closely. I walked off and couldn't bear to look back. But I know that Kipling's parting salutation came to mind.

'You're a better man than I am Shamshuddin.'

PETER FRANCIS

Teach yourself Socotran

Socotra lies, nearer Africa than Arabia, in those blue-green waters south of Aden that romantic Arabists call the pink Arabian Sea. Thousands of travellers to and from the East, from p.o.s.h. P&O fares to those with assisted passages, have sailed by and sighted the island on the horizon. But, with few exceptions, no European was known ever to have landed there by choice. Only a few had done so perforce, when their ships fell foul of the island's rocks and left them there stranded but thankful.

Very little scientific research had been done by this latter class of traveller. On many parts of the island no Western foot had stood. It was Socotra Incognita, and called out for exploration.

In the spring of 1967, the Army mounted a three-month expedition to Socotra. It was organized and led by Major Peter Boxhall, with the Lord Shackleton as patron. I was then Second Secretary at the Embassy in Baghdad, and was asked along to help the late Tom Johnstone, then of the School of Oriental and African Studies. Middle East Command was to 'establish second-order planimetric control of the island': we knew that their real plan was to map it. With them went the Civilian Element – a small SCR-size gathering of adventurous academics, eager to study the Socotran and his speech; press his plants and catch his flies; feel his spleen and auscultate his bosom. The average Socotran took this in remarkably good part.

My job was to gather as much as possible of the Socotri dialect spoken by the mountain troglodytes, a little-studied people whose way of life was frankly Stone Age. I set off with a camel-load of kit and two dozen cheap lighters for communicative locals. The terrain in the Haghier – the main range on Socotra – was tough, but the work should have been easy: simply get myself into the mountains, find a family of hospitable cavemen living near a palm-grove by some idyllic pool, and talk to them for a week or two.

After two days of assault-course climbing I had not seen a single Socotran. They were there all right: from high on the mountain sides they would spot us and send down whooping noises. Once, a local wise to Westerners howled 'Give me some matches' from a distant hill. 'Give me some matches' echoed round the valleys.

I scaled cliffs and found cave-dwellings with stoned-up mouths and fresh dung. But no inhabitants. I came down again and saw lonely huts of stone wall and palm-frond roof. Abandoned. With so sparse a population the proportion of Socotran residences to residents must be amongst the world's highest.

I was slowly accepted into this non-society. One by one the aborigines started appearing. I was glad they came one by one as it was usually at mealtime. I would halt on some waterless plateau or barren valley side and be looking for firewood to cook. Suddenly and silently a half-naked male was there. He would step up and snap his fingers, a summons to shake hands. Then he would sit down by the fire and wait for service.

The first to come I pounced on like an academic panther. He was quite promising; he spoke a little Arabic.

'I'll point to some things,' I said in that language, 'and you tell me their names in Socotri.' He looked blankly at Ali the Camelman. Ali the Camelman said in the selfsame Arabic words: 'We'll point to some things and you tell us their names in Socotri.'

'But that's what the Sahib wants,' our guest replied. 'Surely I haven't got to tell you both?'

This was what we came to know as Socotri Logic. I had had a foretaste on the first day at base: 'What's the Socotri for coffee with milk?' I had asked a camp-servant. 'We don't say that in Socotri,' he replied, 'We drink coffee black.'

Our lunch guest's promise was not fulfilled. I pointed to the track: 'Oorem,' he grunted. I elicited five more words: tree, rock, bee, cup and one that meant 'I trust that nothing adverse has befallen you during the night'. Then he stood up and said, 'Must be off now. Long way to go before sunset,' He crossed the five yards to where Ali was squatting, squatted beside him, and was still there when I finished a siesta a half-hour later.

I travelled on through the fantastic land: over twisted, misshapen hills; past the aborted cucumber trees, all bole and trunk and almost bald of leaves, and under the fleshy green cupolas of the Dragon's Blood tree.

My soles and my patience wore thin together, for there were days of unadulterated idiocy.

'Hello, Good Morning!' I would cry in Socotri as odd aborigines suddenly materialized from behind rocks.

'Hello, Good Morning!' they would call back.

'How are you?' I would ask breezily.

'How are you?' they replied.

No use insisting. I could see how they were anyway undernourished and overexposed. Let's try to find some place-names at least.

'Where are you going?'

They would grin – splendid teeth – and say:

'Where are you going?'

They're obviously keeping their cards close to the chest, so I'll give a little:

'I'm going to Has Hus.'

'I'm going to Has Hus' was the reply.

I tried again, asking where they had come from. Again the same echo and, when I said 'I've come from Hadibu', the same response. It was all too much: all of them coming where we had come from and making for the same place. And all of them walking in the opposite direction.

I consoled myself with other things. The expedition botanist, with the help of a knowledgeable native, had discovered and identified a list of Socotran plant-names. The terrain they preferred was botanically the best, viz. the most impenetrable.

'Arrr,' would cry the West Country botanist: 'I do believe there be a *Tamarindus indica*.' And he was off up the cliff face. Eventually he would come down again with a collector's piece for Kew and his shirt ripped open. Ali the Knowledgeable would examine the specimen and pronounce it something in Socotran. This I noted phonetically.

'And what's this to you?' I would then ask the botanist.

'—' he would reply, 'or commonly known as the Penis of the Plains.'

Frequently, as we set off again, we would hear Ali repeating the Latin names to himself. Days later we found that he had retained them almost all.

I should like to see the face of the future explorer who, venturing in the remoter regions of Socotra, meets Ali: 'You want go see *Punica proto-punica*? Give me matches, you see very good *Dendrosicyos socotranus*,'

Then there were the place-names. These were particularly important: the Expedition's surveyors with their 'planimetric control' needed a phonetic list of geographical features.

The existing map had quite a number of names, but such as gave rise to an expedition game. We would visit a village named on the map and ask the inhabitants what they called it. This usually produced two names for each village. With our rapidly expanding experience of Socotri Logic, we at first, concluded that the villagers did not know where they lived. But the discrepancy occurred so often that I began to suspect the map. Suspicions were confirmed once I knew the meanings. The linguistically handicapped cartographer had clearly elicited his 'place-names' by pointing and asking a Socotran guide. Sometimes he had been given the true name; but equally often he had carefully transcribed an unintelligible answer which meant 'That's where my cousin lives' or 'How should I know?'. It was howlers like this that made navigating by the map such a challenge.

Here too, Socotri Logic was no help. We would be labouring up one of the 500-foot dunes that the monsoon winds had thrown up against the cliffs.

'What's the name of this cliff?' I would pant at Ali.

'Didum Didum,' he would grunt back.

A half-hour later with the dune behind us we would stop for breath and chlorinated water. I got out the notebook.

'Now, Ali. What did you say that cliff was called?'

'Momy Momy.'

'That's funny. I don't remember exactly, but didn't you say it was something like Didum Didum?'

'You never asked me.'

'Yes I did. About half an hour ago.'

'How should I know whether it was half an hour or not? We don't have watches here, you know.'

And then a long Socotran diatribe about my giving him my wrist-watch so that he could tell the place-names better.

For all this, the lists steadily grew, those of the plant-names and place-names, that is. The indigenous dialect stayed frustratingly inviolate. And the camel waned visibly. (Although but for its now frequent attacks on the camelman I should never have learned how to swear in Socotran.)

We toiled over mountain passes and on into verdant palm-groves; down cliff paths so steep that the camel had to be held back by its tail, and along coasts so contorted that these cave-dwellers had both open-plan and multi-storey residences. But the Reasoned Linguistic Response was just not there. The two dozen cheap lighters were going on guides and bowls of dirty goat's whey.

So it stayed till I came to Irihin. By then I was almost resigned to replacing 'linguist' on the expedition rota with 'second camelman'.

Irihin was perched on the easternmost point of the island, and quite different: neat stone-walled houses roofed with the beams of plundered wrecks and these topped with tortoise-shells. The women in their bright orange smocks did not flit away like the usual gazelles, but stood and watched, smiling. As ever, the men and boys materialized when we lit the fire for dinner, but the moment the warmed army stew smelt its least unappetising they asked leave to go.

One invited me back to share his *ta'am*. A mess of boiled maize-husks is no match, however, even for tinned army stew, so I declined. 'Your wives won't be expecting me,' I said.

Next morning they came again. The men drew their brown sackcloth longhis up to their knees and squatted round my camp-bed. The boys were allowed to form a larger ring around them; outside these sat the children. It was like an inverted onion, the tenderest layers outermost.

'You know some Socotri' volunteered one youth. 'I'll teach you some more. I'll write it down so you won't forget.' He took my Parker and the Public Service notepad and started a list of that long-sought, yearned-for Socotri vocabulary.

I remembered the tape recorder. I showed them how it worked, recording and playing back their talk.

'In the name of Allah the Compassionate the Merciful,' said the old men in awe.

64

'Easy,' said my newly-acquired scribe, and proceeded to operate it perfectly.

They all pooled their words, beautiful clear pure Socotri words in undiluted dialect. They brought drums and played wedding-beats, at ten o'clock in the morning. They shrieked a fearful chant which they said drove out spirits. I didn't doubt it.

I somehow felt it was cheating. More words were collected, more songs, chants and mock-serious conversations recorded in that one morning than in all the fortnight previous. And I wasn't even there. I left them to it and went off to telephoto the women.

Why the village of Irihin should have been so different one can only conjecture. They were seafaring folk and lived on fish . . . but that's an old wives' tale. And it was on the rocks of Irihin that the more spectacular wrecks had occurred: Victorian governesses marooned and married here perhaps? . . . Nuns or nabobs gone native? Or . . . As the plunder-lusty locals of Irihin run amok through the staterooms of the sinking SS *Whatsit*, the ship's crew equally lustily swims to shore, where the women of the village, by nature hospitable . . .

We shall probably never know; though I might have asked the Irihin ladies had I learned a little more Socotran.

MICHAEL TOMKINSON

A Great Little Tailor

It seems to me that the European Man of the late twentieth century has a problem, sartorially speaking. Wherever I travel I meet someone who has made a deal for a suit to be tailored in the back streets. Savile Row's roll of dishonour is marked with the names of those who have jumped ship, rushing into the open arms of Ah Man at the Mandarin or Lacksman of Calcutta and Delhi.

As the world becomes smaller, more and more exotic towns are appearing on this sartorial map. Jakarta has double-breasted suits pat, but remember to take your own 'London' cotton thread, as otherwise the sleeves will tend to detach. Shirts are better in Manila than farther north, and at a fraction of the price, but beware the cuffs: if ordered for cufflinks, they are often too tight.

There is one last wrinkle to us latter-day Beau Brummells, and that is that we keep our tailors' identities a closely-guarded secret, only referring to them in hushed whispers. Whether this is to remain one up or whether it is from embarrassment at not buying British is a mystery even to me, and I am one of the worst culprits.

Few towns, however, could be so off the beaten track as Lhasa, capital of the semi-autonomous country of Tibet. I could have felt almost safe from temptation, sartorially speaking at least, as Michel Peissel, four others and myself boarded the Chinese Boeing in Kathmandu for a six-week stint along the valleys of the Salween and the Mekong.

Moreover, the amount of our baggage alone should have precluded any additional purchases along the way. China South-West Airlines like to soak their passengers in the overweight department, one of what may be Bamboo Communism's last digs at the materialist imperialist.

However, as we took our seats, I heard Peissel utter the fatal words, 'I know a great little tailor, just off the Barkor.'

For the first few days, as is written so often, the rarefied air of Lhasa made heavy activity impossible. After the initial euphoria of oxygen depri-vation has worn off, it is a struggle to walk the five hundred feet from the hotel room to the 'Yak Café'. Any movement exacerbates a constant headache. Sleep is fitful and fevered. The idea of shopping is necessarily sidelined.

All good things must come to an end. Four days after we arrived, feeling a little restored by a breakfast of scrambled eggs and yak sausages, our con-versation once again turned to the great little tailor. In hushed tones (since no one likes to give away such intelligence) we decided that, having a few more days in the capital, we would be fools not to take advantage of this *unique* opportunity. He aparently cut like an angel with a laser-eye for detail and was Tibetan to boot. All concerns of overweight, with the next flight a month distant, were now conveniently forgotten.

The first stop for any expedition leaving Lhasa is the Barkor. It is the street around the Jokan, the holiest shrine in Tibet and the destination for thousands of pilgrims from all over the country. For this reason, rather as Solomon's Temple, every inch of space had been occupied by merchants, selling everything from religious paraphernalia to what we were searching for – saddles, bridles and stirrups for the six of us. This is a tricky negotiation even for the fiercest Kampa warrior, let alone a group of wide-eyed gasping tourists from the lowlands.

The bargaining was lengthy and aggressive: 'Get out of here!'. 'Who are you kidding? After all, it's as plain as the huge noses on your dog-faces that you could afford to take a Jeep!' and so on. All said and done, of course, in the open, surrounded by curious onlookers, some dressed in traditional costume; others were in crumpled army uniform, decidedly out of date even by PLA standards, forced at the seams by woollen sweaters, lending the Tibetan police a teddy bear aspect that is quite misleading. Security is apparently loose but omnipresent.

After hours of bargaining for our tackle, with nothing yet decided, we broke for lunch. The route to the Momo and beer haven that is Tashi's restaurant led straight past an elegant if rather ramshackle old monastery, three-quarters abandoned by the orders, now only with one monk in residence, the rest of the building having been given over to the homeless laity long ago. As we walked by, Peissel pointed it out with a wink and a conspiratorial nudge; these were the premises of his great little tailor.

We made hurried excuses after lunch to the rest of our team, for after all . . .

Off we darted as if to meet Harry Lime. In all seriousness, we even considered a quick double-back to shake off our cameraman, who was too clothes-conscious by half from our point of view.

Into the monastic courtyard we went, and up and around creaking staircases as steep as ladders, closed off with hatches, along a tumbledown gallery leading to the far north-western corner of the building. The door cannot be mistaken, but who am I to give away tricks of the trade.

We knocked.

The room itself was full, four people crammed into a single monk's cell. Every corner piled to the ceiling with bolts of cloth and remainders. The air filled with the chatter of sewing machines.

The tailor was not in, but expected back at any moment. The assistant took us in hand and in no time at all we were being fitted for waistcoats, congratulating each other on a ruse well played.

The door opened behind us, I thought blown by the wind.

'*Go cum tsang*,' I heard but turning I saw no one. Then I noticed Peissel looking at the floor, face lit up with a huge grin, arms outstretched in welcome. I followed his gaze down to where I saw a man, all of twenty-seven inches high, levering his twisted and deformed frame across the floor. His legs folded up underneath, more hindrance than help, he still moved with deceptive speed, climbing onto a stool in the centre of the room.

Our tailor had arrived.

In a moment his mouth was full of pins and the air full of calming banter. Like a groom with a horse, a good tailor can fill you with a sense of well-being in any language; he was no exception, and his order book filled accordingly.

Upon leaving, I had to say that, in this case, although we could claim to know the ultimate waistcoatery in the Orient, 'my little tailor in Lhasa' was near the knuckle, to say the least, however 'great' he may be.

SEBASTIAN GUINNESS

Like Magic

You may like to hear my story about the Sudanese cook. He was not my cook, nor is it, strictly, my story. I had it from the lips of my banker friend in Beirut, Rupert Scales, chief witness to the events described. He was a good *raconteur*, and probably others heard it too. But I thought it such an amusing story that – before Rupert and his wife disappeared to South Africa I wrote it down, with his approval. So you can imagine that from now on it is Rupert himself speaking.

When I began my job with the Anglo-Orient Bank in Cairo I was a bachelor.

The bank provided me with a flat, on the ground floor of a converted two-storey house, and the flat above me was occupied by Tom Scaife, who was running a travel agency. We each had a Sudanese cook, and both of them were called Hassan. They were well-trained servants, and we left the house-keeping entirely to them. They got into the habit, in true Middle Eastern fashion, of regarding our belongings as common property, borrowing as the occasion arose. Some of our friends, confused by the identical table appoint-ments, the fact that the man in the *qalabiyeh* was always 'Hassan', and by the similarity of our surnames, were under the impression that we were one household.

On my marriage that was to end. The Hassans were instructed to make a final division of the property. We also gave them distinguishing names. Tom's Hassan, a quiet Moslem, came from the northern Sudan, and we called him Hassan North. My Hassan was older, taller, and a more forceful character. He came from the mysterious, pagan South; and we named him accordingly.

When my wife and I arrived from London, Hassan South was standing at the door of the flat to welcome us. He was gripping a posy of pretty flowers which he presented to Cecile. Inside, on the dining-room table, were a few objects, such as toasters, and a large silver dish-cover.

I looked at Hassan for an explanation. He had curious hair, curly, the black chequered with white, giving him the appearance of a jester, or a wiz-ard, you weren't sure which. He lifted the cover, and revealed a number of small objects – napkin rings and that sort of thing. He had unwrapped all the wedding presents and thrown away the wrappings, the cards with them

Cecile was aghast. 'How are we to tell who they are from?' she exclaimed.

'Mam,' said Hassan, 'I remember.'

Cecile looked incredulous; it was the first time she had encountered the formidable memory of Hassan and his kind.

I asked him who the dish-cover was from. 'From me,' he said, 'for dinner parties.' Cecile protested at the magnificence of the gift. I was a little dis-turbed, but all I said was that we should expect some good dishes under it.

While we were examining the presents, Tom Scaife came down to greet us, and invited us to dinner that evening.

Next day I decided I had better tell Cecile something about Hassan.

'Occasionally there is a strange happening involving him. There seem to have been two yesterday.'

'What happenings?'

'The flowers he gave you . . . I've never seen violets in Cairo before. How did he come by them?'

'*Interflora*? There's a branch here, I know.'

'They work the other way round. The *flora* should be here, Hassan elsewhere.'

'They could fly them in.'

'It was a small bunch for international traffic.'

'What else?'

'The dish-cover. *Interflora* doesn't supply them. They come from the Portobello Road. I suppose it might be old Army property – officer's mess, you know.'

'Perhaps he stole it.'

'Hassan is not a thief.'

'Then what's your theory?'

'Listen,' I said, dropping my voice, 'it's not *my* theory. I'll tell you what's said. Hassan is reputed to have magical powers, to dabble in witchcraft.'

Cecile's brown eyes opened wide. 'You don't say? What does he do?'

'Conjure objects out of thin air; cast spells; that kind of thing.'

I repeated one or two stories, including Hassan North's tale about the embassy wife they both once worked for, who bullied the servants to such an extent that Hassan threw a spell over her; she rushed from the house, and was killed by a passing car.

'How awful!' said Cecile. 'But it might have been an accident.'

'That's just it. One never knows. A rational explanation always seems available.'

'Have things happened to you?'

'Never before. Perhaps I'm not subject to them.'

'It may be like ghosts,' suggested Cecile. 'Only certain people see them. Do you think I attract the supernatural?'

'You would attract anything,' I said. 'Now that I've told you about our Hassan, do you mind?'

'Mind? I think it's splendid. I'll keep on the right side of him.'

Nothing unusual happened for some weeks. I don't count numerous occasions on which Hassan retrieved objects thought to be lost. My wife was a great one for leaving essential belongings – sunglasses, gloves, keys, almost anything portable – about the town. She had only to say, 'Hassan, have you seen my address book?', and the missing article would be restored. But we did not put this down to magic: Hassan South had links by bush telegraph over a wide area.

There did come one episode: merely a conversation we overheard. But it left us uneasy.

We were having lunch when we heard in the kitchen the voice of an angry woman, saying:

'You did this. You are medicine man.'

Then came Hassan's even tones:

'Always knock, please, before entering.'

'I very ill, very ill. I not leave the bathroom three days.'

'I not discuss with you.'

'That chemist, he is good chemist, he give me fixative. He say medicine perfectly okay when he put it in bottle. Then it turn into the opposite. Who could have done that? YOU!'

'It nothing to do with me. I not interfere with no medicine bottle.'

'Then how else? You have powers.'

'I not waste them on your fat belly.'

'I go to the police. You be sorry for this.'

'You not go to the police. You feel too big fool.'

After we had heard the woman go, I called Hassan in.

'I don't know what that was about,' I said, 'and I don't want to know. But I don't want to see you in trouble, either. Tell me, just between ourselves, can you do these things?'

He turned away for a moment. Then he replied:

'Master not ask me that. If I have strange powers, I never say. Nobody say. If I have no powers, never say either.'

I had to leave it at that.

Shortly before Christmas, I received a cable from London to say that the Chairman of the Bank, Lord Aldermanbury, was visiting Cairo with his wife. I told Cecile that on such occasions wives were marked as well as husbands, and we planned a special dinner for them: Kuwait Bay prawns in paprika sauce, roast turkey with chestnut stuffing, cheese (I was against cheese, but Cecile insisted on it), pineapple mousse. We wanted to borrow Hassan North to help, but Tom was having people in to dinner himself; so we invited only two other guests. Hassan South leapt about the flat, scouring, dusting, polishing the tiled floors.

Cecile had not met the Aldermanburys, and when the evening came she felt nervous, but the champagne restored her confidence. The dinner began well, the prawns came and went smoothly.

Then Hassan, with that slightly jaunty air he sometimes had, brought in the turkey, but he slipped on his highly polished tiles, and fell down sideways. His dish-cover crashed to the floor, followed by the turkey, which turned a somersault, slid along towards the Chairman, and came to rest at his feet. Some of the stuffing came out on the journey. To cries of commiseration from the company Hassan rose, scraped up the stuffing with a long forefinger and poked it back where it belonged, replaced the bird on the dish, put on the cover, and took our dinner away.

Cecile went white under her tan. She got up from the table; but there was nothing she could do, and I told her to sit down again. It was one of those social occasions when nothing appears possible but an awed silence. I passed it offering up thanks for the cheese. It was little enough, to fill the void; but to go from prawns to pineapple mousse would have been unthinkable, an end to my career.

Hassan came in again. To my utmost horror, he was bringing the turkey back! Before anyone could speak he set the dish in front of me, with a superb flourish swept off the cover; and there, standing boldly, was a sirloin of beef, accompanied by roast potatoes and Yorkshire pudding.

A gasp went up from the table, then shouts of applause. Hassan brought in Brussels sprouts and – if I may say it in the same breath – Savigny Les Beaune 1961.

After that, conversation was brisk, continually returning to the subject of Cecile's resourceful housekeeping. The Yorkshire pudding especially seemed to impress our guests. 'It was like magic,' said Lady Aldermanbury, when they left at the end of the evening.

Cecile could hardly wait to shut the door on our visitors.

'That clinches it,' she said in triumph. 'He is a magician, and of top rank. Prime beef, out of nothing.'

'Let's have him in,' I said.

'He'll have gone home by now, to his family. I thought he deserved tomorrow off.'

The next evening we dropped in on Tom, intending to give him an account of our dinner party But, like most bachelors, he preferred to talk about himself. Pouring some drinks, he told us about his evening.

'I'm rather peeved,' he said, sitting down. 'Something went wrong at the meat stage. Hassan North served us with bits and pieces – he had some nice prawns there – and went back to the kitchen for the second course. Suddenly we heard a fearful howl, and the door bang. I went in, the oven door stood open, and there was no sign of Hassan. He has disappeared. It seems I have lost a perfectly good servant.'

'What was in the oven?' we both asked at once.

'A turkey'

'What should there have been?'

'A turkey, I suppose. How should I know? I leave the catering to Hassan, as you are aware.'

Cecile and I each took a long drink. I saw it at once: all the wizard had to do was pop upstairs into an empty kitchen, open the oven door, and change the dishes.

Tom spoke again. 'Why not stay and help me eat up? That is, if you like turkey?'

We reassured him about that.

WILLIAM DALE

An Innocent Abroad

It is easy to forget today how rigid we considered the Iron Curtain in the very early 1960s. To go beyond it was to disappear into *terra incognita* spiced with danger and mystery. The matter of getting a visa alone was a major and almost insuperable undertaking.

The most important annual gathering of book publishers in the West is the Frankfurt Book Fair. It has a long history. Already in 1628 William Harvey's book on the circulation of the blood was rushed through the press (using three different kinds of paper because that was all the printer had in stock) so that copies could be distributed at the Frankfurt Fair.

Most British publishers went each year to display their wares, but the most important and beneficial factor was to meet and chat to a myriad publishers from other countries with whom one could negotiate deals about rights in one's books, and about selling – or buying – books with a strong colour-plate element which would serve equally well in any edition, whatever the language. These became known as 'co-editions'. In Harvey's days it had all been a lot easier: an author wrote his book in Latin, a language universally understood by scholars.

The Eastern bloc countries were always represented at the Fair – but well away from their Western colleagues – by a curious mixture of a few highly intelligent intellectuals and a much larger contingent of burly minders in ill-fitting suits, who usually only grunted when one asked a question or left a message. Contact between us from the West and *them* from the East was, therefore, rare and hesitant: the linguistic barriers alone were something of an obstacle.

Despite these handicaps, my firm had made tentative approaches about buying a Polish/English dictionary from a Warsaw publisher, for which we thought, among our range of other dictionaries, there seemed to be a reasonable commercial need. The Polish firm in turn was most anxious to buy rights in some of our scientific and technical publications. But there was a major problem: the Poles could only pay in blocked *zloty*, that is a form of currency that could be used nowhere else but in Poland itself. The proffered holidays in Cracow did not appeal to our accountants.

There was, however, it was pointed out to us, another route: we could attend the international book fair held every two years in Warsaw, and pay for our stand and expenses there in the blocked *zlotys* issued to us. Only a few academic British publishers had ventured there before, such as Longmans and the two university presses of Cambridge and Oxford. So we decided that my own doughty marketing colleague, Piers Raymond, and I should venture to Warsaw to represent our firm.

In due course we left Heathrow in a half-empty LOT plane. Our first surprise: we were not served a meal on what was a fairly lengthy flight, but only a glass of weak lemonade and a piece of dried-up cake. The major impact on arrival in Warsaw was the overwhelming greyness of everything: the airport building itself, the long, cobbled road into Warsaw, all the streets, the apartment houses, the cars, the very clothes people wore: there was a total absence of colour such as we had never seen before.

Once established in our hotel – the newly refurbished Hotel Europejski – Piers said he would go to bed, even though it was quite early. I felt that I wanted to explore Warsaw, not only to see this new environment but also to get a meal. The piece of cake was not very sustaining. In the end, Piers decided to come too. Then came another surprise: there seemed to be no restaurants, or we could only be served a meal if we had some special sort of ration card. After three hours of looking round the city and searching for food, we finally got sausages and mash in a stand-up eatery in the centre of the city. We also remarked at once, and continued to do so throughout our time in Poland, on the curious lassitude among the population and the absence of rush and tension. This was emphasized by the surprising lack of traffic on the broad and spacious main streets.

However, the book fair was exciting. It was held in the mammoth, cathedral-like Palace of Culture and Science, a central landmark in Warsaw and a monster of an edifice, 'a gift of friendship' from the Soviet Union to the Polish nation, built some ten years earlier. To us it seemed like a constant reminder from Stalin that Big Brother was watching what the Poles were doing. The crowds attending the Fair were huge, particularly in the foreign section in which we were sited. The questions we were asked – usually in German but often in excellent English – were intelligent and many people seemed surprisingly well informed about our books in various scientific fields. Orders were thin on the ground but then we had undertaken the whole exercise more as a case of showing the flag than as a money-making venture.

Serious negotiations continued with Polish publishers; these were held in little kiosk-like chambers where there was room round a table for no more than six people. We were told (by other publishers) that this presented an opportunity for recording the discussions on concealed microphones.

A deal was eventually concluded over our Polish/English dictionary. We decided, cautiously, to buy 1,500 copies. The Polish publishers expressed themselves very disappointed by our parsimonious attitude. But the entrancing girl who had been attached to us as our official interpreter and guide proudly showed us the major local newspaper on the next morning, where a front page headline read, in big bold type: 'London publishers buy Polish Dictionary'. We learned early that there were two sorts of reality.

We were dog tired after our long days inside the poorly ventilated building, but there was no let-up in the evening. We moved to a nightclub called 'Krokodyl', in a square of rebuilt seventeenth-century houses, for an exceedingly slow meal and endless dancing. I danced more in two and a half weeks in Warsaw than during the rest of my life. This was the cheerful side of life in Poland.

Another amazing factor worth recalling was that almost every person we wanted to meet had two full-time jobs. They didn't earn enough money with one. So making appointments – an essential part of any book fair – was fraught with difficulties.

I too had been given a second task while I was in Warsaw. My brother was at that time working for the *Illustrated London News*, then still owned and edited by the redoubtable Sir Bruce Ingram. When he heard that I was off to Poland he asked me to lunch and suggested that I should take photographs of Warsaw for the paper. He had been trying endlessly to get some since the end of the War. I was the proud owner of a new German, single lens reflex camera, a Retina S, and was doing a lot of photography work at the time, so the idea appealed to me.

I agreed, but thought it would be politic to find out whether there were any rules against photography. On enquiry to the Fair authorities in Warsaw, I was assured that I could photograph anything I wanted, as long as I kept clear of military installations. The difficulty was when to find the time to do the necessary walking about. As Sir Bruce was principally interested in my showing the architecture of what had been rebuilt after the War, and what had been left in ruins, I decided that it was best to get up early in the morning, to leave the hotel at 6 a.m. and to be back for the rather pathetic breakfast at 8.30 a.m.

The first morning I didn't venture far. After all, almost everything looked strange to our western eyes; for example, the old ladies in long skirts who swept the streets in the morning with long-handled besoms; the amazing paucity of traffic, except for bicycles; the marked lack of goods in the shops; the crumbling fabric of the buildings that had survived the war. I moved around, snapping happily.

The next morning I discovered that I was being followed at a discreet distance by a little man in a light grey suit and a brown raincoat. He made no effort to conceal himself and trotted behind me wherever I turned. It was a disconcerting scenario, something straight out of the many spy films then current. But I carried on, though my heart was beating faster and not every shot I took was wholly in focus. In fact, I exposed an entire film twice, with remarkable consequences.

I was a bit daunted on the third morning: should I venture out or not? A glance out of the hotel bedroom window showed that my 'shadow' was already waiting opposite the hotel entrance.

He was obviously expecting me to carry on. So I sallied forth once more. It should be said that by then the Poles had confined reconstruction of what the war had destroyed in two ways. Surprisingly, their first priority had been to rebuild the historic monuments and ancient houses that had all been gutted. They had done so from plans that had been preserved in museums and archives. Only when that phase was complete did they begin to erect huge, monolithic, barrack-like blocks of tiny apartments in order to house the impoverished population who had lost their original abodes, and were

living in excessively crowded conditions. The authorities had made considerable strides with this phase of rebuilding.

As I wandered round the city the little man continued to follow everywhere. He must have been thoroughly puzzled by what I thought worth
photographing, though he probably approved of my concentrating initially
on the University; the Old Town that overlooked the Vistula; the gigantic
new opera house in mid-construction; the charmingly provincial market
place that looked old, but had only been rebuilt in 1953; and the churches,
like that of the Holy Cross in the pleasant street of many bookshops, the
tongue-twisting *Krakowskie Przedmeiscie*.

After five or six mornings I was waving to my 'shadow' as I left the hotel.
He, of course, never responded. Then I discovered that I could slip out of
the back of the hotel through the slumbering kitchen quarters. I thought at
first that I had given him the slip, but after some twenty minutes I suddenly
saw that he had caught up with me. Even though he had not once interfered
with what I was doing, I felt my photography would improve if I was on
my own for a change. And in any case, I wanted to go further afield to the
outskirts of Warsaw, rather than concentrating purely on the centre of the
city. After all, Bruce Ingram had said he wanted a true reflection of the soul
of the city, not just the glamorous bits. I got up an hour earlier. I caught an
early tram and discovered that I was *alone*. It was bliss. I found new churches,
factories, warehouses, parks I hadn't previously seen. I decided to make it
my final outing – and I was late for breakfast.

At the end of the Fair I had an anxious moment as we passed through
customs at the airport, when all our luggage was thoroughly searched and
we were even forced to buy local cigarettes to use up the last few *zlotys* we
had left. But fortunately the prying hands didn't open the shoe bag which
hid my films.

Back in London we had a lot to report to our publishing colleagues. I
culled from my half-dozen films a good selection of photographs that gave
a true picture of Warsaw at that time. Bruce Ingram was very pleased with
what I sent him, though I had quite a job working out the correct captions.
After much discussion it was decided that my efforts should be published
anonymously. I agreed, though a bit reluctantly, and wrote under the heading

of 'Our Correspondent', when my double-spread appeared in the ILN. A cutting of my piece disappeared into a drawer; so did the actual photographs. Two or three years later a college friend, who had become a nuclear scientist of some distinction, came to dinner. Conversation turned to my little photographic foray because he had just come back from Poland where he had been on a Government mission He looked at all the photographs quite casually, until he came to a subject at the end of my selection with which I had been particularly pleased. It was of a huge, half-ruined entrance arch, part of a gutted early nineteenth-century building, covered entirely in ivy, with an anonymous factory-like building behind it. The ivy-clad ruin exuded a sense almost of the romantic. 'You took that?', he asked. 'You photographed that? Was there no one about at the time?' I explained that it had been very early in the morning and that I had given it a vague, totally innocuous caption. He looked at me quizzically. 'Don't you know what that building is?' I responded by saying that I didn't know, and simply thought it looked rather romantic. 'That, dear boy', he said 'is the Polish nuclear research institute. People have been arrested simply for trying to peer inside.'

From that moment onwards I was very relieved that my article had appeared anonymously.

FRANK HERRMANN

Karachi

I doubt I am alone in that peculiar schizophrenia which affects me abroad, an incomplete mixture of nostalgia for home, and a distinct loathing for most compatriots. This nostalgia is self-editing. Flanks of Wiltshire chalk down arrive in the memory conveniently shorn of Swindon town. Lakeland hills lose their trodden scars and sodden orange camp-sites. London shrinks to a handful of the smarter, cleaner squares and parks, with Fulham or Islington conveniently dissolved to a grey sludge, just out of sight. The most notable deletion is the Great British People. They seldom exist in my memories of home. Where they do, because they are necessary to lend realism to an occasional urban scene, they appear as those water-coloured line figures that an architectural draughtsman might employ to demonstrate human scale and perspective.

I do not suffer unduly from this antipathy to my compatriots when at home: I appear to have less of an inclination than most to assault my fellow Londoners on the Northern Line. In clement weather, I can even smile at passers-by in St James's Park. But put me six months out of London, in a small hotel lobby in Phnom Penh, within earshot of a pair of British journalists discussing their expenses, and I am overcome by a form of paranoid anxiety. At times it seems to me that my fellow Englishmen have followed me to some distant country with the clear, though deniable, aim of embarrassing me. I fear that either they or worse, a local, will look at me and suddenly *know* – he's English too. The outcome is that I either pretend loudly and unnecessarily to be from Iceland, or plot wildly to have them denounced to the secret police for sedition, and taken out of earshot.

The worst fear is that one might be co-opted, on grounds of nationality, into their lives. A few years ago, younger and less defensive, I arrived from Peshawar into a mauve dawn at Karachi airport. I had learnt that the easiest way to navigate the airport was to treat passengers, pickpockets, porters, customs officials, police and taxi touts with indiscriminate, good-humoured menace. So it was that I bulldozed through a final, superfluous passport check, deliberately heedless of a pair of small men in nondescript uniform who pawed excitedly at me, pointing at my British passport, before I emerged into the main concourse, and they fell away under the shins of a pack of taxi touts.

I had selected a tout, been passed to a driver, checked the approximate number of wheels on his Morris Minor and turned down the offer of the attentions of his sister's friend before the officials caught us up, and stopped the car at the kerb.

'British,' they gasped, one lying across the bonnet. 'Sharing taxi.' They pointed behind them at a Viking in a safari suit, a good six foot six and built to last, who stood looking uncaringly around him. Whatever their excitement, he appeared not to share it. Upon further discussion with the officials, it appeared that the two security officers had chanced upon this Englishman and had selflessly set themselves the task of helping him get into town. I gathered that he was unfamiliar with Karachi, and I was exactly the sort of fine gentleman needed to share a cab with him. And we could talk to each other, which was an added bonus.

Maybe I had not, in those days, developed my current antipathies, but it seemed such a simple request, and this silent, gentle giant was a better prospect as a companion than the frequent louts whom taxi-drivers tried to force upon their passengers at the airport gates as extra, sharing passengers.

I am not small; he was enormous, and the two of us filled the back seat of the car, with a couple of spare limbs extended into the front. I was relieved that he had no luggage. I pointed out that this was unusual. 'Lost it,' he said, 'in Karachi.' I asked if the airport officials had been helpful. His answer suggested that they were too involved in sexual activity with close relatives to have given the matter as much attention as it deserved. The airline staff, who reportedly shared the officials' personal habits, had been similarly diverted, in spite of the fact that he had only had one beer on the entire flight from Europe, and they were all liars.

This diverse information, blended with olfactory data that my nose was beginning to collect, suggested that my friend was steaming drunk. I determined to lose him as soon as possible.

I asked him which hotel he was going to. He replied that there was a small Danish-run brothel on Soi 8, which he told the driver to take him to. The reply was that the driver did not know the road, but was willing to follow directions. I added that the only Soi 8 I knew was in Bangkok.

'Right, well *you* tell the driver.'

'But that's no good. This is Karachi.'

The subsequent exchange made it clear that my companion not only had thought himself in Bangkok, but continued to do so. It was also explained to me that I was deceitful to suggest otherwise, and a certain amount of violence was proposed to encourage me to agree.

'Look out of the window. Does that look like Thailand?' I asked. Sind was a particularly fetching khaki that year, and the soap-powder hoardings were emblazoned with Urdu.

81

'Of course it's Thailand.' He gestured towards a dusty bullock. 'Look at that bleeding water buffalo.'

I appealed to the driver, who confirmed nervously that we were in Pakistan, not Thailand, but that if my companion felt strongly about it, his sister had a friend . . .

His suggestion tailed off, as the Viking wrapped his hands round the driver's throat, and applied pressure. The response had apparently been insufficiently imaginative and the driver was required to confirm that we were in Thailand. With a desperate look at me, he coughed out his agreement that this was indeed Bangkok, and that he himself was Thai, very much so, and would remain so as long as required. We set off for Soi 8, with a massive paw resting on the back of the driver's neck. Occasionally he would be encouraged to greater speed by playful blows around the ears. The Viking indicated a willingness to take control of the car by force if the driver chose to stop, and demonstrated his competence by occasionally leaning further over to assist with the steering when we came to a 'tricky bit of the road'.

Then, as fast as it arose, my companion's hostility evaporated, and he gradually explained that he had had an argument with the staff on the plane. He was unaware that he had been marooned, though he admitted to having slept a bit, somewhere. He was a regular visitor to Bangkok, but had found the officials particularly obtuse on this occasion. He had drifted round the airport, been relieved of all his money, his passport, and tickets. This had distressed him, being hardly fair, so early in his trip. But after a few arguments and some limited violence, the officials had suddenly fixed up this taxi ride. Indeed, I had been so helpful he wanted to buy me a drink. And the driver. And why not go back to the airport and invite the officials from there as well? I explained that he needed both money and passport to get a drink in Karachi, which was dismissed as an irrelevant observation.

The taxi-driver was whispering at intervals, begging me not to leave him with this giant lunatic, and meanwhile was combing Karachi for Soi 8, as if a Thai side street might through need alone be conjured up on the shores of the Arabian Sea. He refused to drive to a police station; he felt that they might fine him for his trouble, and the mad Englishman looked expensive.

So it was that we made our way to one of the only places to serve alcohol to drunken foreigners, an international hotel in the city centre. My maudlin colleague fell gently into the road, while I explained to him that I would assist the driver in parking the taxi. Then we would all have a drink. Meanwhile, he was to tell his entire story to the hotel manager, and ask for a consul, in case we were a bit late. As we fled down the road, I looked back to see him swaying on the steps, hugging a startled doorman.

Early the next morning, with a pang of guilt, I called at the hotel, to check that he had been dealt with. The grave concierge explained that he had indeed entered the hotel, but had attacked a palm tree which had been staring at him, and had gone out in search of beer and Thai women, of which he had found a shortage in the hotel.

I turned and left; he was someone else's unpleasant problem, I told myself. The concierge tapped me on the shoulder.

'That gentleman was disgraceful. Disgraceful. British, I think. A disgrace. Maybe the British people should deal with him. Are you from Britain?'

'No,' I said, with a slight lilt in my voice. 'I'm from Iceland.' Somewhere, faintly, I heard a cock crow.

CHARLES WEBB

Munich Crisis 1938

Everyone remembers their first trip across the Channel. Mine was probably not much different from hundreds of others, but it did occur at a particularly poignant moment of twentieth-century history; and it shows how much less sophisticated some of us were at that time.

At the end of summer 1938, I had successfully completed the first half of my final dental exams. I was due to take the second half one year later. Some friends of mine had been travelling on the Continent and I knew that they were going to be in Paris on their way home. With very little money I decided to take off, pick up the Paris contingent and then go on via Brussels to Germany. Würzburg in Bavaria was my eventual aim: my mother's forbears several generations ago had been one of the ruling families in those parts. Furthermore, a cousin of my mother's had been a student in Brussels just after the last war (1914–18) and had kept up with the family with whom he had lodged: he gave me a letter of introduction.

When I arrived in Paris and found my friends, I learned that they were hurrying back to London in view of the 'international situation', but I was not to be put off.

I went by train to Brussels (rather surprised to find that a certain degree of black-out was already in force). My uncle's friends, to whom I had an introduction, were obviously in no mood to welcome a young British student and were packing up to get away to the country. I found a cheap little hotel near the Gare du Nord – largely patronized by railway workers. I was very pleased to find that with a mixture of English, German and French I got on well with everyone. They were, of course, mostly Flemish-speakers.

The international news was getting more worrying and I was advised to go to the British Consul (initially I went to the Embassy). The young official in the consulate was clearly unimpressed that this rather callow dental student was thinking of travelling on to Bavaria: I was summarily advised to go back, at least to Paris.

As it was my last night in Brussels, I decided to go down to the Place de Brouckère to have a coffee and a drink and 'watch the world go by'. By this time I was really slightly concerned that several shops were closing and putting up rather permanent-looking shutters. I was approached by a very personable and respectable-looking young woman who asked if we could have a chat – she knew of a nice little bar round the corner. I suggested that she should join me where we were, but she said, 'No, business girls do not drink on the main boulevard.' Foolishly I did not get the full implication and in a couple of minutes I was in the back room of a very sleazy bar and had been joined by another girl. Something of a bruiser waiter brought a tray of drinks, firmly pointing to one in particular. Having read some of the well-known travel spy stories, I firmly chose one of the other drinks, whereupon the 'lady' in question tasted the indicated drink to reassure me. Then, to my embarrassment, these two girls attempted to remove my jacket and even (horror of horrors) my trousers. Fortunately, discretion suddenly became the better part of valour and, risking the beefy bartender, I beat a hasty and only just dignified retreat. I was thankful to be on the early train back to Paris. I had had my first experience of a brothel.

I think my main concern was my passport and my extremely limited amount of cash. As far as I knew there were no such things as travellers' cheques.

Back in Paris, I realized that it was very stupid hanging around in France since my friends had gone. I decided that I would have a last morning and be extravagant with my few remaining francs. I took myself off to the Champs Elysées, found a table outside a very grand café, Le Claridge, bought a copy of *The Times* and ordered a Dubonnet. I noticed a rather odd couple sitting at a nearby table: a youngish man who was obviously English, wearing real country tweeds, and a very glamorous young lady companion. Was she a French woman? Was she his secretary or mistress?

She looked across at me and gave me a half-smile and then the man came over and asked if he could have a look at my *Times*. Before long, I had joined them and we were getting on very well. The lady was also English, and spoke French, though the man did not. Suddenly he looked at his watch and said, 'Come on, I have a wireless in the car, we can listen to the London news, there is to be a special broadcast.' It was in fact the arrival back at Croydon aerodrome of the Prime Minister, Neville Chamberlain. I heard the famous 'piece of paper' speech but just at that time there was considerable police activity on the boulevard – it was the French premier, M. Daladier, arriving back in Paris from Berchtesgaden.

My two new friends insisted I lunched with them in the very grand restaurant. They were delightful: we had pink champagne and I realized they were on honeymoon, supposedly on their way to the South of France. He was a potato and beet farmer from Lincolnshire. I stayed on in Paris for another two or three days: they insisted on lending me £15 (a fortune for me in those days). As is so often the case with such first-time acquaintances, we became very good friends for many years.

PETER MACKENZIE-YOUNG

Untrodden Territory

The Embassy's first reaction to my arrival in Bangkok in 1955 was, 'What, here already?' Perhaps not so surprising, as it had taken me six weeks to get there on board a Danish cargo-liner, by way of Genoa, the Canal, Aden, Penang and Singapore. Nobody had bothered to tell me that the journey could have been cut short by disembarking at Penang and taking the over-night train to Bangkok. Nor, callow youth that I was, had it occurred to me to find that out for myself. Not that it really mattered one way or another, as the first purpose of my arrival was not actually to work in the embassy, but to spend eighteen months studying the Thai – or, as it was then known, to us, the Siamese – language (on account of Churchill's stubborn refusal to accept any modern forms or spellings of foreign place-names; he is said once to have asked, when faced with the capital of Turkey, 'Whoever heard of an Ankara cat?' The consequence for us in Bangkok was that, although we were permitted to use the name Thailand when writing to the Thai authorities, we were strictly enjoined to stick to Siam in all internal correspondence).

In retrospect the relative remoteness of Thailand in 1955 seems almost incredible, now that the temples of Bangkok and the country's various sea-side resorts have long been part of the mass tourism circuit. Bangkok itself, though already a large city (with perhaps two million inhabitants; no one knew for sure) still had something of a village atmosphere, light years re-moved from today's polluted and traffic-ridden megalopolis. The Oriental Hotel, which now vaunts itself as one of the best (the very best?) in the world, was then a rather run-down establishment, living on its memories of Conrad and Maugham and other similarly intrepid travellers. Two of them during the fifties were the then Duke and Duchess of Argyll. It fell to me, as a very junior Third Secretary, to drive the then Duchess (Margaret) round the temples, where she took her photographs with a Box Brownie, assuring me that it produced better results than the expensive cameras of all her friends.

As for the country outside Bangkok, it was untrodden territory for the ordinary tourist. Even Chiengmai, the northern capital, seemed almost as remote as Shangri-La. Soon after my arrival, I had the chance to experience this for myself, as it happened that our consul in Chiengmai went on his leave and a caretaker was needed for the period of his absence. Not that I could have attempted to fill his shoes; he was a former army officer and accustomed to tour round his consular district barefoot, swearing that it was the most comfortable way to travel in those remote parts. But it was felt by my superiors in the embassy that a period in the north, away from the fleshpots of Bangkok and the temptation to rely on English, would benefit my study of Siamese.

In the event, there were still all too many opportunities to speak English even in the Chiengmai of the mid-fifties, partly because the northern climate had induced several ancient Britons to settle there in their retirement. They were very kind to me; no doubt the spurious grandeur of my position as acting consul served as well as a letter of recommendation. Two in particular are still vivid in the memory.

One of them, himself a former very distinguished member of our consular service, put me neatly in my place at our first meeting. He asked me how I had travelled to Chiengmai, to which I replied, thinking proudly that this showed the proper pioneering spirit, that I had come not by air but on the overnight train (the road in those days was abysmal and few were brave enough to attempt it). 'When I first came here,' he told me, 'it took me six weeks – on an elephant.' Indeed, the elephant stables were still there in the consulate compound, but by that stage no longer occupied.

The other of the two had spent his career in one of the British timber companies, supervising the extraction of teak from the northern forests. He was good enough to invite me to lunch and on to watch some Thai boxing, my first experience of that spectacular sport, where we saw one of the contestants knocked out by a straight right foot to the jaw.

These two, both in at least their late seventies, living in the same remote corner of south-east Asia and liable to run into each other on a day-to-day basis, were not on speaking terms. Whenever the name of one was mentioned in the presence of the other, the invariable reaction was, 'oh, that madman!' They must have known each other all their adult lives and had presumably once been friends, but something – nobody could tell me quite

what – had gone amiss between them during the war. It was thought to
have been to do with the property of one, which had been left in the care of
the other during the Japanese occupation. But whatever it was had created
a total blockage in their mutual relations. And yet both were kindly old
gentlemen; Maugham would have chronicled their story.

There are still now, I believe, some newer ancient Britons sitting round
their drinks at the Chiengmai Gymkhana Club but, for those of us privileged to have been there before all the modern hotels were built, the place
no longer holds the magic it once had.

JUSTIN STAPLES

Recognizing the Talent, but not the Man

I was Commercial Counsellor at the British Embassy in Seoul from 1976 to
1980, during the unfolding of the great Korean 'miracle'. As what is now
termed 'deputy head of mission' I had several quite long spells as chargé
d'affaires *ad interim*. One of these periods put me in the unique position of
being a chartered accountant authorized to sign an international double
taxation agreement on behalf of Her Majesty's government.

But the real benefit from being 'in charge' came, both for myself and my
wife Margaret, at the time of visits to Seoul by the Royal Ballet and the
Royal Opera. The former provided the opportunity to meet many members
of the company and to entertain to lunch not only Margot Fonteyn but also
her mother, Hilda Hookham, a delightful personality with whom Margaret
got on particularly well. The friendship with Margot Fonteyn led to a later
occasion when we dined in Houston with both Margot and her husband,
the man who would almost certainly have been president of Panama but for
an assassin's bullet that paralyzed him from the neck down. In spite of his
disability, which meant that he could not speak and had to rely on Margot
to feed him and interpret what he was trying to say, we came away with an
impression of a man whose eyes would twinkle at a humorous remark and
who had somehow projected himself as a delightful dinner companion.

The visit to Seoul by the Royal Opera gave us a chance to see the company in rehearsal as well as at repeated performances before enthusiastic Korean audiences. There was also the occasion to extend hospitality to John Tooley, Colin Davis, Geraint Evans, Jon Vickers and others; but, more unusually, the pleasure of getting to know Laurence Olivier over a period of several weeks.

Prior to the arrival of the Royal Opera, a film company visited Seoul to make a film about General MacArthur. The star was to be Laurence Olivier. The film also included my younger son as an extra, playing the part of a GI landing on a Korean beach. He played the part for one day only, however. A young Korean boy foolishly stepped in the path of a heavy tank, leading the production company to discover that there were laws against employing people under the age of sixteen. In any event, the film, rumoured to have been financed by the Moonies, was a commercial disaster. When eventually given its première in New York under the name *Oh Inchon*, it received such a dreadful panning that it disappeared without trace and we have never seen it.

It was during the time of Laurence Olivier's stay in Korea that Lord Mountbatten was murdered by the IRA. A member of the then very small British community asked if we might arrange a memorial service, a proposal to which I readily agreed. I took on the responsibility for organizing the service, to be held in the crypt of the Anglican cathedral, which is sited immediately outside the gates of the British Embassy compound.

It seemed appropriate that I, as British chargé d'affaires, should give the eulogy. It seemed equally appropriate that the first lesson should be read by the Defence Attaché, while to demonstrate my progressive, politically correct, non-sexist credentials, I asked the wife of the manager of the Chartered Bank, Thora Medley, who was also chairman of an informal British women's group, to read the second lesson.

A notice of the service was circulated to all known members of the British and other Commonwealth communities, numbering some two hundred at that time. I sent several copies of the notice to the Hyatt Hotel, having heard that Laurence Olivier had just joined the film production party there. This was not generally known, as the producers were concerned to maintain tight security for him and to provide their valuable star with as much peace and quiet at possible.

Shortly after the circulars went out, the Ambassador's secretary passed a telephone call through to me. I heard a rather frail voice say, 'It's Larry Olivier here. Thank you for the notice of the memorial service. Dicky Mountbatten was a good friend of mine and I should very much like to play some part in the service.'

My immediate response was to suggest that my caller take over the responsibility for giving the address.

'No, no. I would lie awake all night worrying about what to say.'

'What about reading one of the lessons?'

'Yes, that I should like to do.'

I undertook to send him a clearly printed copy of the chosen text. Having settled that particular piece of casting, I rang the Defence Attaché to tell him that he had been upstaged by Laurence Olivier. I did not, however, tell anybody else. I wanted to be sure that members of the community came to the service because it was a memorial for Lord Mountbatten, not because they expected to see the great actor, Lord Olivier.

On the day of the service my wife and I arrived at the cathedral, flying the flag in the official Daimler, the large and impressive model, ideal for formal occasions. Koreans were sure the car was a Rolls Royce – a mistake about which neither I nor anyone else in the embassy did anything to disillusion them. On taking our places in the front pew, I could see Laurence Olivier and a couple of 'minders' already seated across the aisle. His hair had been darkened for the part of MacArthur. I would not have recognized him if I had not been expecting to see him there.

The service went well. Instead of Laurence Olivier staying up most of the night composing the address, that task had fallen to me. I thought it was rather good and I have the text somewhere among my souvenirs. But the only comment I received afterwards was from a businessman who asked, 'Did London write that for you?'

As we were standing in the cathedral courtyard introducing our distinguished lesson-reader to a few very surprised members of the congregation, a member of the community came up to me and asked, 'Where did you get that marvellous preacher to read the lesson?'. No one in the congregation had recognized the person of Laurence Olivier, but they had no difficulty in recognizing the talent!

RICHARD TALLBOYS

On Sakhalin

There are two surprising things about reindeer, aside from their wholesale lack of red noses. The first is that their horns are very soft and covered with thick fur. And the second is that if you ride them expecting them to be like your basic horse, they will promptly and inevitably collapse under you. Or at least they will if burdened by the fourteen stone that I consider my fighting weight.

I discovered these curious facts in a moment of surprise and brief but bearable pain in a larch forest recently, on the far eastern Russian island that Anton Chekhov once declared was the absolute worst place, the ghastliest dump, in the world. Yet despite the brief deer-related drama I have to say that the island didn't actually seem a bad place at all: it was a brilliantly sunny afternoon, with a warm breeze blowing off the Pacific; there were two rare sea-eagles perched on a branch nearby (I had it in mind that I might ride over to look at them, but the reindeer had other plans); the deer's herdsman was a splendid looking man who was member of an exotic tribe called the Nivki, but who nonetheless had once been Russia's cross-country ski champion; and when Rudolf did eventually toss me off his back I tumbled onto a carpet of moss and blueberries that provided the softest landing of any equine trauma I can remember.

My dignity suffered, but nothing else; and once I had remounted and had been instructed that you sit on a reindeer's shoulders, and not over his waist, we trotted off quite briskly and happily into the woods. Sea-eagles are evidently birds that bore easily, because they were both gone by the time the deer and I trotted up to their tree. But otherwise, with the herdsman giving me handfuls of blueberries and strawberries every so often, and then reaching over with a flask of cloudberry-flavoured vodka, it seemed a pretty idyllic afternoon.

My reason for recounting this small adventure is to make the point that once in a while, travel can be an extraordinarily redemptive experience. Normally it is quite the opposite: you go somewhere that is touted as being magnificent, delightful, spectacular or whatever (Versailles, the Spanish Steps, Tahiti) and it turns out a disaster – either tediously just as you imagined, or expensive, ugly, dull or, most likely, filled to bursting with tourists. But once in a while the very reverse is what happens: you fetch up somewhere that has a reputation for being simply dreadful, a place where you wouldn't send the absolute worst of all your mothers-in-law, and it turns out that you have a stunning experience, and leave thinking that the place truly is the stuff that dreams are made on.

Such moments happen all too rarely. I once went to visit the remote West African republic that by general agreement is the worst country in the modern world (guesses welcome, on postcards) staggered away after a month of eating bananas and stewed rats and doing voodoo, agreed it was indeed the direst of places, and then fell almost terminally ill with the cerebral malaria I caught there. But I have remained optimistic over the years, believing I can find truth in the axiom about redemptive travel experiences being the very best. One needs only to go to a place that has at least an equally bad reputation as the African hell-hole, and yet somehow manage to fall in love with it. It has to be a place that has bad, bad karma, and you have to adore it for being so.

It has to be, in other words, a place much like the island where I rode the collapsing reindeer: the far eastern Russian hell-hole-that-was, Sakhalin. 'I have been to Ceylon,' wrote Chekhov, 'and it is Paradise. And I have been to Sakhalin Island, and it is utter hell.'

The famous first line of the epilogue to *Crime and Punishment* reads: 'Siberia. On the bank of a wide and desolate river stands a town; in the town there is a fortress; in the fortress, a prison.' Siberia is a cheerless place, a land of the ruined palings of Tsarist prison camps and Stalinist gulags, a land of perpetual frost, amply deserving of its fearful reputation. Not for nothing is

Siberia called *the land beyond the sun*.

But Sakhalin island lies beyond even this. It is two thousand miles beyond Siberia's hugely wide eastern frontier river, the Lena; a thousand further
than the Amur and Black Dragon rivers and the borders with bleak Man-
churia; way beyond the terminus of the Trans-Siberian Railway; well beyond
that other heartbreak railway built by the starving convicts and today called
by that most gently innocent of acronyms, the BAM. They call it *the island
at the end of the world*, and people shudder when they hear that you're going
there. 'Sakhalin?' said a Muscovite, peering at me queerly. 'Rather you than
me.'

It is an elongate island six hundred miles from tip to toe and some imaginative cartographers say it looks like a fish. Specifically, a salmon. It can be
seen, just, across the Strait of Tartary from the hills of the Russian mainland
– or what the islanders call 'the continent'. It looms like some vast sea-mon-
ster behind the eternal fog-banks; low scrubby hills, coal-streaked cliffs, the
ruins of Tsarist forts and the almost equally ruined but newly built Border
Guard stations of today, with whirling radars and armed sentries to keep
people out, where once they kept people in.

The island has been known, above all, for its prisons. This is where, from
1860 onward, the tyrant-emperors of Petersburg sent the most incorrigible
flotsam of society, the persistent murderers, the spies, the morally deformed
and the officially-mutilated. Tens of thousand of Russian prisoners, deemed
vile enough to send well beyond Siberia, fetched up on Sakhalin, faraway
and forgotten – a melancholy situation that drew the young and then unknown playwright Chekhov to the island, to write journalism, to do a book
that exposed the excesses of torture and brutality, and gave him the kind of
Muscovite fame and confidence he needed. His digs remain, the wooden
house a small museum, rarely visited.

The prisoners were sent as colonizers too, of course, and their contribution to the gene-pool lives on. In the streets of Yuzhno-Sakhalinsk and
Alexandrovsk and Due and Nogliki today, the convict faces can still be seen,
just as they can be seen in Sydney and Melbourne and Perth, on that other
more southerly Pacific island, of rather kinder climate, that was once used
for much the same purpose. Incarceration, and criminal colonizing.

The Russians came east to an island that was far from deserted, however. As with the Britons who came to New South Wales, so the Russians who came to Sakhalin displaced thousands of their own aboriginals – Aleut hunters and herders, scores of the hairy Ainu (whose womenfolk painted bright blue moustaches on their faces, and thought themselves not at all unusual-looking), the fish-skin-wearing Ulti and Evenki and the salmon-worshipping Nivki, all of whom had for centuries clung to a precarious existence on the island. And they all grumbled mightily at their displacement then, and they still do today, a constant background threnody.

Exile remained a dominant force in twentieth century Sakhalin too. Beria sent his traitors there in the early Bolshevik days, Stalin sent his enemies there in the thirties, Brezhnev sent those whom the state considered useless, right up to the seventies. And world politics intruded as well: the island see-sawed between the competing suzerainties of Russia and Japan – the latter who, since Sakhalin is a geological extension of Hokkaido, believing they have some right to claim the island as their own.

First the island was all Russian, then it was shared, then divided half and half with a latitude-line down the centre separating the frosty imperium of Petersburg from that of Tokyo. And finally, following a decision taken in 1945 at faraway Yalta, it became all Russian once again, as it is today. But flotsam washed up as a result then also: tens of thousands of Koreans, stateless slave-workers for the Japanese, were forbidden by the Communist Russians to return home, and they remain there still, Russian-speaking and sullen, roundly and endlessly cursing their lot.

Add to this potent mix of gloom the discovery of coal (and consequent environmental ruin, in places) and then of huge quantities of oil (with the same results threatened), and the breakdown of communism and the growing influence of the Mafia and the collapse of the rouble . . . a deeply bad karma, one might say, hangs over Sakhalin like the thickest and clammiest of winter fogs.

And yet. And yet. I have been there twice now. I have spent a total of about one month on the island, and, together with almost all other westerners who make a habit of going there (of whom there are an ever-increasing number, mainly from Texas and Louisiana, now that Russia is allowing Americans to exploit her island oil) I find myself becoming helplessly enchanted with the place. It turns out to be unutterably beautiful; its people are as friendly as any one can find; one seems to have experiences there that are quite unrivalled; and, perhaps best of all, though Sakhalin is easy enough to reach by air or by sea, *virtually no-one goes there*. It is, in short, a splendid secret, its treasures protected by the cloak of its vile repute.

The reindeer-day was a classic of its kind. Deep berry-rich woodlands, kindly deer-herders living in tents made of skin, Malamut dogs as guardians of the camp, tiny lakes, fresh-running streams, cups of strong tea brewed over a birch-twig fire – and the talk of this tall, rangy cross-country skier who, though a Nivki tribal, had taken a degree in anthropology thirty years ago, but in a moment he had never once regretted had decided to leave city life and spend the rest of his years driving reindeer across the Russian tundra. He is one of the happiest and most remarkable men I have ever met.

But there were other days, of equal joy. I once went with a boatman out towards a sandbar that separates the Sea of Okhotsk from the river-estuary near Nogliki, in the north of the island. There is always a two-mile patch of dense fog to negotiate, and the skiff has to steer blindly through the mudbanks, following a course of small trees that have been stuck into the flats as markers. Once through, the sandbar is a place of wind and wild grasses and dozens of small wooden dachas, from which families venture out to fish for salmon – which they hang to dry in the gales, and which they then smoke, and sell at about fifty cents a fish. To stand on the sand in the teeth of an Okhotsk gale, to be drinking a beer and taking fresh smoked salmon dipped in fresh-pressed seal-oil – an experience, once again, like few others.

A Nivki family took me in for a couple of days – they were far from isolated, since the most beautiful of their three daughters had married an Italian merchant seaman, and lived in Calabria – and fed me on roast reindeer and salmon caviar and newly churned butter and home-made bread and fresh lingonberry jam. And vodka, of course – raspberry and blaeberry and blueberry flavoured, and flowing endlessly, to the point of forgetfulness.

But perhaps the best day of all was when a group of us decided to walk from Yuzhno-Sakhalinsk to the summit, four thousand feet, of Mt Chekhov.

We rose at dawn, strode through long muddy lanes, turned up a narrow path through forests of birch and Japanese bamboo, then ever upwards to where the trees gave way to low grasses and rocky plains alive with wildflowers. We made the summit after four long hours, and ate caviar and salmon and drank beer, and watched while the girls collected berries, and then made blinis over the fire, and let us drowse tipsily in the autumn sunshine.

Lena, who had come as my interpreter, was a small and pretty woman, whose husband was an oceanographer. She was also fiercely nationalistic, and kept telling me how much greater Russia still was than America ever could be. And more so, naturally, than Britain ever was.

And on the day we reached the summit of Mt Chekhov, and looked over at Mt Pushkin a mile off to the east, and over at the wild, wild Sea of Okhotsk to the east, and the still blue waters down towards Japan, and as we gazed over at the jet planes landing at Yuzhno-Sakhalinsk airport and talked about the enormous impact all the new-found oil was about to have on the island, so Lena rose to her full five feet and, with immense pride, spread her arms at this astonishing panorama and said simply: 'Watch out West! Russian bear is leaving its den!'

And while I still do not quite believe her, I am glad she said it; and that there is pride and optimism and beauty to be found, and shared, on a place that Russia's greatest playwright once thought of as hell, but which clearly isn't anymore.

SIMON WINCHESTER

On resuming Diplomatic Relations with Persia

In October 1952, following his bitter dispute with Britain over the nationalization of the Persian oil industry the previous year, Dr Muhammad Mossadeq, the Persian Prime Minister, broke off diplomatic relations and expelled all British diplomats. The last such break in relations had occurred a century earlier when, in December 1855, H.M. Minister, the Hon Charles Augustus Murray, second son of the Earl of Dunmore and a Fellow of All Souls, Oxford, in acrimonious personal dispute with the Shah and his Prime Minister, quit Tehran with his staff and a hundred-strong train of baggage mules for Baghdad, where he proposed remaining until the Persians made amends and apologized. This personal feud, in which the self-righteous Murray was far from blameless, was prolonged and exacerbated the following year by the Persian seizure of Herat – regarded by the British as a gateway to their Indian empire – and the consequent brief and one-sided Anglo-Persian war.

On both occasions diplomatic relations were duly restored – in July 1857 after an interval of nineteen months and in December 1953 after fifteen months, but the manner of doing so differed greatly. Both stories are worth telling.

Murray's departure for Baghdad on 5 December 1855 troubled the Persians, who quickly sought to settle the quarrel through the good offices of Stratford de Redcliffe, our Ambassador in Constantinople. There they agreed to accept a number of humiliating demands to mark Murray's return, including a 21-gun salute when he hoisted the Union flag over the Tehran Legation, but they jibbed at British insistence on the dismissal of their Prime Minister. Negotiations came to a halt after the outbreak of war over Herat and were only resumed as part of the peace negotiations in Paris. Article Ten of the peace treaty signed in Paris in March 1857 stipulated that the British Mission would return to Tehran immediately after the treaty's ratification 'when the Persian Government agrees to receive it with apologies and ceremonies specified in the separate Note signed this day by the Plenipotentiaries of the high contracting parties'.

Palmerston was then Prime Minister and there were few concessions to Persian feelings in this Note, which spelt out in cruel detail the necessary 'apologies and ceremonies'. The Persian Prime Minister was to write, in the Shah's name, a letter to be delivered to Murray in Baghdad by a high-ranking Persian and copied to all foreign missions in Tehran, withdrawing the offending letters etc. about Murray written by the Prime Minister, the Foreign Minister and the Shah himself; a further letter would invite Murray in the Shah's name to return to Tehran with his staff; another high Persian official would then be sent to Baghdad to act as Murray's mehmandar or escort officer; on Murrary's arrival in Tehran, the Prime Minister would himself 'go in State to the British Mission and renew friendly relations with Mr Murray'. Next, the Foreign Minister would call and escort Murray to the Shah's palace where he would be received by the Prime Minister and conducted into the royal presence; finally, the Prime Minister was to call on Murray again the next day at noon and the call returned by Murray the following day.

The defeated Persians had little choice than comply with these demands and on 18 July 1857 Murray with his staff and a large retinue of servants, guards and muleteers entered Tehran.

The story of the resumption of diplomatic relations in 1953 is very different. It began with the toppling of Dr Mossadeq on 19 August 1953 (28 Mordad 1332 in the Persian calendar) in a coup in which both the British and Americans had a hand. His replacement as Prime Minister, General Fazlullah Zahedi, the pro-German general kidnapped by Fitzroy Maclean in 1942 and held in Palestine throughout the war, was now *bien vu* by both ourselves and the Americans. In Whitehall hopes ran high for an early resumption of diplomatic relations.

I was then head of the Economic Relations Department in the Foreign Office and a day or two following Mossadeq's fall was summoned by William Strang, the Permanent Under-Secretary, and asked to be ready to fly out to Tehran as chargé d'affaires as soon as this could be arranged. Meanwhile

John Henniker, head of the FO's personnel department, began recruiting staff for me. I was, of course, delighted to have been chosen for this exciting assignment but surprised, as I knew very little about oil which was then handled by a single desk officer (Peter Ramsbotham) who reported direct to our superintending Under-Secretary (Roger Makins); and I knew even less about Persia.

However, hopes of a quick return to Tehran were disappointed. The Persians wanted an oil settlement first fearing, not without reason, anti-British feeling whipped up by Mossadeq. Eden, the Foreign Secretary, insisted that diplomatic relations must come first. It took over three months before the Persians gave way. Eventually, on Saturday 5 December (the very day ninety-eight years earlier that Murray had broken off relations) a painstakingly drafted communiqué was issued simultaneously in London and Tehran announcing the resumption of diplomatic relations, to be followed 'at the earliest mutually agreed moment' by oil negotiations. The unusual procedure of issuing so important an announcement on a Saturday afternoon ahead of a statement in Parliament was for fear that the Persians might change their minds!

I was now all set to fly off to Tehran and left my job in the FO, as did the others who were to accompany me. But once again there was disappointment. When the Swiss Minister, Alfred Escher – then in charge of British interests – handed our names to the Persian Foreign Ministry, he was reminded of the decision that no British diplomat who had served in Persia should be allowed to return. The four senior members of my team were all old Persian hands.

This was a bombshell. Would HMG bow to Tehran's ruling or not? A decision on so politically sensitive an issue could only be taken by ministers and both Eden and Churchill, the Prime Minister, were in Bermuda conferring with President Eisenhower. Telegrams were exchanged and I was instructed to see Eden the moment he returned. This I did on the morning of Saturday 12 December, when Eden said that provided I had one old hand who knew his way around our two large compounds in Tehran, he would agree to replace the others. I opted for John Fearnley, who had been in the embassy's commercial department at the time of the break and was keen to return. In place of those dropped I was given Charles Wiggin (later to be ambassador to Spain), Dick Franks (a future head of MI6) and D W Pierotti. I could not have asked for a better team.

Close though we were to Christmas, there was no question of delaying our departure. A small Viking was chartered to fly us – a party of fourteen men and women but no wives – to Tehran, there being no commercial flights from London then. We were due to take off from Bovingdon in Hertford-shire before dawn on 18 December, but fog delayed us for twenty-four hours and we did not reach Tehran until the afternoon of 21 December after over-night stops in Athens and Baghdad, where we were again delayed by bad weather and had a very bumpy flight over the Zagros mountains. We were met at the closely-guarded airport by the Swiss Minister, the deputy head of the American Embassy, the assistant *chef de protocol* and a few journalists, British and Persian.

There was no question of my having to follow any prescribed ritual such as had marked Murray's return a century earlier. Escher, the Swiss Minister, accompanied me to the Embassy and the following morning escorted me to Abdullah Entezam, the Foreign Minister, to whom I handed my credentials in the shape of a letter signed by Eden. I disappointed Escher, who enjoyed the limelight, by cancelling a hand-over ceremony he had arranged with press and photographers, as I thought we should keep our heads down and move forward cautiously.

In his volume of memoirs *Full Circle*, Eden states that I was armed with 'formidable instructions'. They were certainly lengthy but in essence quite simple – namely to establish good relations with the Persian authorities, as-sess the possibilities of an oil settlements, prepare the way for an ambassador, and maintain a united front with the American embassy.

Before I could get on with the job I had some trouble, at arm's length, with the Shah who tried, through intermediaries, to deal with me behind the back of his ministers. Apart from this, all went well and full diplomatic relations were restored with the arrival of Roger Stevens and the formal presentation of his credentials to the Shah on 25 February 1954. Eden's first choice had been Robin Hankey (the late Lord Hankey) but as he had served in Tehran it was wisely decided not to seek his *agrément*. Stevens, brought in at short notice from Stockholm and knighted for the occasion, proved an excellent choice.

DENIS WRIGHT

The Dieppe Raid

It was a memorable one-day visit to France, memorable because the date was 19 August 1942 and there was no friendly welcome from those on the other side of the English Channel. I spent the whole day on the bridge of the headquarters ship, HMS *Calpe*, and I was in company with Major General Roberts, the army commander, Air Commodore Cole, the RAF liaison officer with 11 Group, and Captain Hughes Hallett, the naval force commander. I was on the port side of the bridge. On the starboard side was a young anti-aircraft gunner and, also on the starboard side in the bow of the ship, was a midshipman controlling the numerous motor launches picking up men from the water and later the many wounded being transferred from other vessels – the two hospital ships having left the scene for Newhaven with a full complement. We were properly the last ship to leave and, in a typical British gesture of defiance, shelled the German heavy gun battery on the clifftop to the east before withdrawing. The midshipman had done well as we took with us some two hundred wounded. The *Calpe* herself had lost over a quarter of its complement. The young air gunner was dead and Air Commodore Cole was wounded. So much for a very necessary visit to France from which lessons were learned that saved many men who took part in the subsequent Normandy landings.

In peace time my wife, formerly my WAAF driver at Biggin Hill for more than two years, and I travelled extensively, and some thirty years after the *Calpe* had returned me safely to Portsmouth, we were on one of several visits to South Africa. We were staying with two very old friends, the Doctors Dawson, whom I had met in Kenya in the days of the Mau Mau troubles. One evening two friends of theirs who lived, as they did, in Natal came round to have drinks on the veranda. On being introduced to the visiting husband and wife, I was told that the former had gone to England in the war to volunteer. 'But,' said my hostess, 'you would not have met up as you were in the RAF and he was in the Navy.' I asked him where he had served and he told me that for most of the time he was in destroyers based in England. I said that I had been engaged with the Navy on several occasions during the war. Some surprise was expressed and I was asked when and where. I said I was with Admiral Ramsay in the Naval Operations Room at Dover Castle when the *Scharnhorst*, *Gneisenau* and *Prinz Eugen* went through the Straits; I had sailed in a destroyer escorting a coastal convoy to Portsmouth and in another to Dieppe and back in one day. He said, 'That sounds like the Dieppe Raid. I was a midshipman on the *Calpe* getting some of your chaps and others out of the water.' We had been within a few yards of each other all through that day. With one accord we raised our glasses in silent gratitude to fate which had preserved us unharmed and, after more than thirty years, had brought us together again in the peace of a South African summer evening and in the good company of friends.

GERALD LE BLOUNT KIDD

Medical Trifles

My father, though far from stern in most respects, utterly forbade any discussion of medical matters in his hearing, for he was not a doctor but a Scottish economist and a fellow-delegate of Maynard Keynes at the Bretton Woods conference in the autumn of 1944, when I was just beginning to dissect frogs and dogfish. He was an ascetic man with a profound distaste for all things medical; there was a complete embargo on any mention of diseases, doctors or bodily functions at the family table.

My father having made his point, I never spoke of medical matters at home, nor did I do so at Merton College for the subject, with others like the mention of a lady's name or discussion of the portraits in Hall, was an offence to be punished by sconcing. Such breaches of etiquette meant that the culprit had to drink $2\frac{1}{4}$ pints of ale without removing the tankard from his lips or taking breath before it was finished under pain of paying for the others' beer in the event of failure. The culprit could appeal in Latin to the Warden and if this was flawless the penalty was lifted. My Latin was rusty as I had given it up after achieving the credit in School Certificate then necessary for entry to Oxford; I never got beyond the wretched Labenius who was constantly running around the Roman Empire with news of victory or defeat in the Gallic Wars. Had the messenger paused occasionally to drink 2¼ pints of beer, I'd have been better placed to appeal, but my vocabulary was inadequate and after a fine opening – 'Parce nos, Custos' (Spare us, Warden) – of which I was proud, my appeal was full of errors of grammar and syntax and so a curt note was sent back to me from High Table by Warden Mure, the great Hegelian scholar, which simply read 'Poena stet' (the punishment stands).

Nor should the doctor assume that medical tales are of general interest. When I joined the Travellers, an elderly member whom I had known since my childhood told me he didn't sit at the Centre Table as he felt 'vaguely threatened by all those sleek lawyers'. Sure enough, on the first occasion I sat there, two elderly barristers were discussing esoteric points of law and made no effort to draw me into the conversation. I was forcibly reminded of the well-known anecdote of the judge who said to the barrister in court, 'Presumably your client is conversant with *de minimus non curat lex*?' , to which counsel replied, 'My Lord, in Chipping Norton they speak of little else.'

So, steering neatly between the Scylla of discussing subjects that distress or bore the layman, and the Charybdis of committing an 'indiscretion', doctors tend to congregate in the same clubs. At the Travellers medical men are comparatively rare, but I can think of at least sixty fellow doctors at the Garrick without referring to the members' list; and I suspect that there are a good many doctors at the Athenaeum and the Savile. But at the Travellers there are so few that within a few months of joining well over thirty years ago I found myself acting as the Club Doctor.

This was an unofficial appointment, without fee or contract, which started in curious circumstances. I was dining at the Club one evening, eating the 'Guinea Dinner' which was served in the 1960s, when the tranquil atmosphere of the Coffee Room was shattered by loud shouts from the kitchen. An ashen-faced House Manager asked me to accompany him thither without delay. There had been a serious altercation caused by an unhappy affair of the heart; tempers were running high; fisticuffs appeared to be an ominous possibility and there were carving knives lying about. Valium was then a new sedative of which we had great hopes; I administered it freely to all the parties concerned and to most of the onlookers before returning to my limp toast and kipper paté. It was a baptism of fire.

Thereafter, the duties of 'Club doctor' were not onerous. Once a year I examined Alfred Gilbey to pass him fit for beagling in Yorkshire. He remained extraordinarily well, even into his nineties, an example of the health which often follows naturally from a regular routine and the self-discipline imposed by faith.

Two or three times a year I would be called to the Club bedrooms, quite often for acute gout, a disorder natural to clubland; Thomas Sydenham noted over three centuries ago that it was commoner amongst wise men that fools. Occasionally these calls were in the wee, small hours, and I relished the atmosphere of the empty Club at night, its silent, deserted rooms like seaside towns in December. Once I had difficulty getting in as the temporary night porter was engaged in the worship of Bacchus. He took as long to answer my knock as Macbeth's porter and was in a similar state when he appeared. On that particular occasion the visit was to a member of a reciprocal American club, a Harvard professor, who had eaten too freely of the Travellers' Pie – the only person in my experience to have consumed three portions at a single sitting. 'To eat is human, to digest divine,' I murmured as I left him with a beaker of bicarbonate. For years thereafter the professor sent me a Christmas card portraying a groaning board of gourmandise.

The Club's valet was always a great help in deciding whether I should be called: he had an uncanny aptitude for recognizing a hypochondriac. He sometimes consulted the hall porter for a second opinion for he, too, was shrewd. If they decided I should visit the patient, they were generally right.

These random reflections are scarcely 'Travellers' Tales'. 'Anecdotage' would better describe my nostalgic glance at a jealous waiter, a beagling priest and a flatulent professor. They are the very essence of general medical practice.

We often see humanity at its most vulnerable, at its best and its worst; at birth and at death and at the crises in between. It is no accident that the territory where medicine and literature meet is densely populated; but I am no Somerset Maugham nor Conan Doyle. I shall hang up my stethoscope and devote myself to all those hobbies which I forsook when I married medicine. As Oscar Wilde so caustically observed, 'Some doctors take life very easily'. I shall now join their ranks, though I hope in only one sense.

DAVID HAY

The Number One Twister

There was a sound of revelry by night. Cambodia's capital city had gathered her beauty, her chivalry and her diplomacy in one of her great and gracious palaces. Fireworks cascaded across the indigo midnight sky, illuminating the wide waters of the mighty Mekong river and the fringes of sugar palm trees which stood along the banks. Tropical flowers released their slow perfume upon the balmy breeze. The chandeliers shone over fair women, brave men and rotund ambassadors. A thousand hearts beat happily as the Head of State, His Royal Highness Prince Comrade Norodom Sihanouk, the former (and, as history was to tell, also the future) king, dressed comfortably in an impeccable dark-blue silk tuxedo, conducted the Palace orchestra as they played a dance number of his own composition.

Then, a change of mood, a different sound struck like a rising knell. Hush! Hark!! Was it the remote thunder of a B52 bombing raid across the Cambodian frontier with Vietnam? Happily, that night, not so. The Prince handing over his baton and withdrawing to mingle with his guests, and the normal conductor taking over, the band had struck up an entirely novel, even alien, rhythm, fresh from the West: Chubby Checker's 'Let's twist again, like we did last summer'. The elders and chamberlains froze, the generals looked to their aides, the young Cambodian lords and ladies glanced around them for a lead, the cabinet ministers and parliamentarians seemed puzzled, the diplomatic corps hesitated politely, taken by surprise. It was my cue, my only moment of greatness, ever.

Quite the loveliest young woman at the Royal Cambodian Court was the prima ballerina of the Royal Corps de Ballet. I had often admired her, in traditional head-dress and costume, dancing at the head of her troup – on one magical occasion, in the open air against the backdrop of the floodlit temples of Angkor Wat. A favourite daughter of the head of state, Bopha Devi was a royal princess over whose petite figure and bejewelled but diminutive fingers the giant figure of General de Gaulle was to bow low during a forthcoming state visit to Phnom Penh. But this moment was mine, not the General's.

Like most intellectuals, and some theologians, I am a disco devotee. A habitué of Hélène Cordet's 'Saddle Room' at the bottom of Park Lane throughout the early sixties, I was well up to speed in these matters. The Palace soirée had hitherto proven rather stilted, and one at which – a self-conscious and slightly worried chargé d'affaires of 33 summers – I had been zealously over-doing the diplomatic hard graft. In a moment of recklessness and release, I set aside my champagne glass, nodded briefly to His Highness this and Her Excellency that with whom I had been struggling in my fractured French, crossed the ballroom to the Princess and swept her wordlessly onto the floor.

After a minute of bewilderment, she caught my rhythm; after two minutes was twisting elegantly but with enthusiasm; and after five minutes found herself alone with me in the middle of a wide circle of spectators – some agape and agoggle, others smiling cheerfully, yet others (mostly the Eastern bloc heads of mission) envious and disapproving.

When the music stopped, the Princess giggled and withdrew, while I struggled to recover my breath. On the MC's mike, the unmistakably regal voice of 'Monseigneur' cut through the speculative murmurs of the court, declaring that Mr Fielding was then and there awarded the title of 'The Number One Twister of Cambodia'. The orchestra broke into a ragged fanfare, and a chamberlain was sent running for a token prize which the Head of State immediately handed over, in the shape of a small silver Cambodian cockerel in a crocodile-skin box bearing the gold crest of the Khmer monarchy. I bowed and withdrew with appropriate self-deprecation into the surrounding throng, where enemies offered me reluctant congratulations, friends slapped me on the back, creeps ingratiated themselves, and two newspaper editors asked me for my view of the foreign policy implications.

The apotheosis of the (admittedly slightly pseudo) so-called playboy chargé d'affaires was thereby complete. It was December 1965, twenty-one months after my first arrival in a less than welcoming Phnom Penh. The dog-house was now behind us: for active British diplomacy, the ball was once more out of the scrum. Time to move on. Within twelve months, I was to be en route for Paris. In that latter city, in 'La Cabane', a favourite little disco on the Île St Louis, life resumed very much the tenor it had known in Park Lane. But it was Sihanouk, not Checker, that I had to thank. Government edicts sending foreign embassies to Coventry are rarely rescinded; they tend to peter out, with a whimper rather than a bang. So the end of the story had a twist to it.

LESLIE FIELDING

All Change in Arabia, and yet no Change

Manchester United, Arsenal, Stanley Matthews. This was all that I managed to decipher from the string of excited words that flowed from the smiling mouth of the ten-year-old bare-footed rascal playing in the sand. He was as keen to communicate and show his knowledge of British football as I was to seek his assistance in finding the house of Tarish.

I had recently moved into Abu Dhabi from the desert and the year was 1966. Roads, urban or country, were much the same, rutted tracks through the sand; one had to keep the Land Rover moving or one would become bogged down. If we had to get out to push the car, we would soon find that the metal body was too hot to touch, while the burning soft sand flowed over toes foolishly exposed in sandals.

I knew Tarish from my days in the desert, three years earlier; and now I wanted to visit him in the maze of sandy streets between the small new cement-built 'people's houses', each with little to my unaccustomed eyes to distinguish it from another.

Tarish and I used to sit together on a dune to enjoy the tranquillity of the desert far enough away from the clatter of pipes and the roar of the engines of the drilling rig. The red sand dunes, rising hundreds of feet one on top of the other, rolled away as far as the eye could see. The silence was broken only by the happy tune of the desert larks and by our halting conversation, each speaking a language that the other hardly understood. Tarish was young and keen, he was more intelligent than some of his compatriots working around the drilling rig, so he was given a job with greater responsibility. His task was to wash and sort the small rock cuttings that were brought up by the drill from thousands of feet below the red desert sand. Under the microscope these cuttings might give the first indications that oil, the black gold, was to be found deep down in the rocks.

We had already discovered a large field and completed two prolific wells. On that day, we expected that our third well in the field, located to the north of the other two, would confirm that the discovery was really large, a giant by any standards in the Middle East. Some said, 'Abu Dhabi will have more oil even than Kuwait.' Neither Tarish nor I had been to Kuwait, but we had heard stories of the immense wealth there.

Possible oil wealth in years to come meant little to us; we had work to do and we enjoyed the challenge of the desert. Kuwait was wealthy on oil, but they did not have the Hamra sands bordering on the awesome Empty Quarter, where men could hunt for weeks without meeting another human. Abu Dhabi was blessed because the *hubara* – the bustard – and the gazelle were still plentiful in the desert, or a hare could be relatively easily trapped for the cooking pot. In distant Kuwait they were not so blessed; they did not have the sweet water in high red dunes, water that was adequate for date palms, modest agriculture and a few animals. We saw little purpose in their Rolex watch and Cadillac car way of life, but we were interested in their schools and their medical facilities.

Tarish's cuttings showed oil. We were excited at the prospect of another prolific well; we would flow the oil and gas mixture down a long burning pipe, both to clean up the rock formation eight thousand feet down in the earth, and to estimate the flow rate. Probably thirty or even forty thousand barrels a day, ten times more than most other Middle Eastern wells. We would light a flare, the smoke would be visible in daytime, and the flame at night for fifty miles. The desert sand would be fused into glass flowing down the side of the burning flare pit and be coloured blue by the dirt coming out of the well. At night-time, thousands of moths would perish as they flew towards the light, their bodies turning the hollows of the wind ripples in the red sand white for a hundred yards around the flare. I prepared my gauges and sample bottles, placed a small rag burning diesel oil at the far end of the pipe and Tarish slowly wound open the valve on the well head to release the expected enormous pressure. Usually the oil rushes up so fast that it has no time to cool and is as hot as boiling water.

Alas, the well produced a miserable trickle of water dirtied with dark streaks of oil. No amount of coaxing on our part could produce the expected roar of oil and gas: we were facing disgrace! The truth was that the rock formation containing the oil did not extend as far north as we had believed; our hole was nearly 'dry'.

I reported the great disappointment, news of which rapidly reached London (that is, after about twenty hours, such were communications in those days). Everyone recognized that original estimates of the size of the oil field had to be drastically reduced. Grandiose development plans had to be re-evaluated.

Tarish returned to his rock cuttings, saying quietly that God is generous, more oil would be found; and indeed only God could know what would happen in the decades to come in Abu Dhabi.

I did eventually find Tarish in his new house in 1966. Sheikh Zayed bin Sultan Al Nahyan had recently taken over the leadership in Abu Dhabi, the oil wealth had begun to flow and was being applied for the benefit of the people. We wondered at the scale of development, the speed of construction, the vitality, hard work and dedication of the few nationals who were ready and capable of shouldering responsibility. Tarish's life was changing too: his father took a foreign wife, causing dissent in the family, but Tarish was fortunate to escape to England for education. He returned several years later to find the first changes dwarfed by the new developments on a scale no one could have foreseen. Thanks to his intelligence, hard work, and good fortune, for which he praises God, Tarish is in 1998 a very wealthy and successful businessman. He has a number of good agencies looking after foreign companies. He imports goods from many countries of the world. He has property in London and Munich.

In 1998 Tarish's father died, so once again I went to call on him, this time to express condolences. Several years ago, the father had moved to Dubai and set up house near the palace of the Ruler. I did not know the house so I telephoned for directions. I was told that I would never find it unaided so I should go to the Ruler's palace, wait there and telephone for a guide. Dubai is now a city as modern and well endowed as any with all the expected services and facilities. But there is an area behind the Ruler's palace where many houses, both grand and modest, are distributed without a thought for planning. The dusty tracks, as of old, meander between the houses and children still play in the sand, totally oblivious of the busy broad highways and high-rise urban development that surrounds them only few miles away.

I arrived at the palace but, instead of telephoning, I called to a ten-year-old bare-footed rascal playing in the sand. He knew Tarish's late father and without hesitation eagerly leapt into my car with a broad grin and, after introductions, said what I understood to be Manchester United, Gazza and – was it Linaker?

DAVID HEARD

El Tatio and the Atacama Desert

We lived in Chile for nearly six years working for an international company. They were very interesting and significant years covering, as they did, the three Presidents, Eduardo Frei, Salvador Allende and Augusto Pinochet – 1968 to 1974. Apart from the upheavals of politics, we also survived an earthquake and a volcanic eruption (*see page 187*). But this was a more peaceful journey.

We had the opportunity to use a small plane, a Cessna seating six people, to fly us from Santiago to the north, Antofagasta and San Pedro de Atacama. The first part was uneventful, Pacific to the left, Andes to the right and endless Chile ahead. It was the Easter weekend and the charter pilot was delighted to come on this particular trip – and teach me to fly!

Once we left Antofagasta for San Pedro, everything became more interesting. The colours of the desert were superb. Orange, beige, purple, mauve, sandy and even bright yellow. Lumps of sulphur could be picked up from the side of the road if one did the journey by car. And the floor of the desert sounded hollow as you walked on it – the Chileans call that part the Valley of the Moon.

The other striking element was a series of ghost towns, remnants of the nitrate era when enormous wealth was generated. We were told Galeries Lafayette had opened shops in these towns, a company from La Scala Milan toured, leading singers appeared. Then suddenly, almost overnight, it all disappeared. The Germans invented artificial nitrates and everyone left. The nearest equivalent to the appearance of the towns is Pompeii. People left furniture and possessions where they were. Slowly, of course, the looters took their toll, but the graveyards, with their wrought-iron tombs and crosses, tell of significant and affluent populations. In Calama an imposing theatre façade is still visible and from the air each town looks like a collection of open match-boxes.

We flew on to San Pedro over this amazing landscape, every now and then flying really low to see more detail. Arriving at San Pedro we circled and waggled our wings to tell the inhabitants we were landing and please keep off the strip. They came out to greet us and brought rusty old oil barrels of petrol for us to refuel. While there was still daylight, we flew up to El Tatio to see it from the air. It was 14,500 feet up and we got there in about twenty-five minutes. Too quickly for some of our passengers, who got altitude sickness. We flew back rapidly down to San Pedro – an oasis village with a smartish hotel and a church with cactus wood beams dating to about 1524.

While the pilot, San Martin (a famous name in Latin America) went to negotiate road transport to El Tatio, we went to the museum. Small but fascinating, it was run by Padre Lepège. He was a Belgian missionary priest who had served in the Congo. Being an anthropologist, archaeologist and eccentric, he had rather fallen out with authority. He was 'banished' to the Atacama desert where he was in his element, discovering much about the Atacama Indians. He had found some mummies buried upright in the foetal position, a unique flint matrix – the start of a series of tools – and numerous pots and other artefacts. He spoke no English, limited Spanish but fluent Swahili. He was an excellent and enthusiastic guide – in French.

San Martin found us in the museum and told us he had secured a lorry for the morning. We would start at 4 a.m. Why? Because the hot springs at El Tatio did not gush – they gave off columns of steam which would disappear once the sun came up. The hotel, accustomed to mad English visitors, gave us breakfast at 3.30 and some sandwiches for lunch. The driver, the two women in the party and our daughter crowded into the cab. This was nicely heated by the engine as we climbed steadily. The pilot, our male guest and I got into the back. It was open and though we were wrapped up warmly and covered by a tarpaulin, we froze gently for three and a half dark, bumpy hours, crossing streams, ice sheets, and mountain tracks until we arrived at 7.30.

The Chileans call them geysers but, as I said, they do not gush. Nevertheless they are spectacular. At that altitude, as dawn breaks, the air is very cold and these still, solid columns of steam actually look like fountains. For a time we forgot how cold we were and just gazed and gazed. But reality intervened and we jumped off the lorry and tried to warm up by 'running' to get close to the pools. At that altitude and over treacherous ground it was more a stagger. But we were rewarded. The pools were of varying sizes, many quite small, two or three metres across. The water in them was boiling, but at well below 100° Centigrade because of the altitude. The colours just below the surface from the minerals looked like enamelled jewellery – mostly greens and reddish browns, but there were also blues, mauves and yellows. Round the edge of the pools grew short, fine grass, about an inch high. The steam settled on the blades of grass and then froze, giving the appearance of a frosted silver setting to the jewellery in the pool. Quite beautiful.

Slowly, the sun came up and we started to thaw out – our male guest had been literally blue with cold and not at all well at first. As the air warmed, the columns of steam disappeared, and we returned to our coffee and sandwiches. It was about 8.15. The show had been relatively brief!

Although the columns of steam had disappeared, there was plenty on which to feast the eye. We were on the Bolivian border and high in the Andes. The views were breathtaking and, as the mists cleared, we saw the peaks very plainly.

At about 9 o'clock we climbed back onto our lorry. The journey back, being downhill, was quicker and certainly warmer. We could also see more of the landscape. We stayed in San Padre another night. This gave us time to explore the oasis, admire the church and revisit the museum. The desert beyond the oasis showed its beautiful colours and we learned that it was so dry that nothing lives there at all. On a four-hour road journey to Antofagasta going about sixty miles an hour, you will not collect a single fly on the windscreen.

The plane refuelled in Antofagasta and we saw the port and the railway developed by the British. Chile was still very Anglophile. Then we flew back to Santiago – this time with the Andes on the left and the Pacific on the right. Navigation is fairly simple. As we drove home from the airport, reflecting on our adventure, we saw the Andes making a magnificent backdrop to the city.

Chile is certainly a spectacular country.

ROBERT ELY

The Tsar's Wine Cellar

How often at the Travellers Club Centre Table the topic turns almost imperceptibly to wine. 'Did you ever taste a Margaux '25? They do not make them like that any more.' And so on and ever on.

In the fifties I was Private Secretary to the Ambassador at Moscow – Sir William Hayter. He announced to me one day that he wanted to visit the Crimea and would I seek Foreign Ministry approval. Much to my surprise, it was forthcoming. No western ambassador had been allowed there since the war. I happened to be the only foreigner to have a Soviet driving licence and, even more to my surprise, the Ambassador asked me to drive the Rolls. It was a heady experience doing a hundred miles an hour on deserted roads on the site of the Kursk Salient battlefield to the amazed stares of passing collective farmers.

We arrive at Yalta. After a day or two showing us the usual things, the Soviet authorities were at a loss what to do with us. They had never had such visitors and we could not be left to our own devices. They proposed a visit to the Tsar's Wine Cellar. This turned out to be a series of tunnels like adits into the hillside at Massandra.

We were taken along what seemed miles of wine racks. How they survived intact the Bolshevik turmoil was a mystery never explained. Our guides would occasionally stop and produce a bottle: 1905 pink champagne, 1805 Napoleon brandy, 1793 Madeira. From time to time Sir William murmured some word of appreciation.

At long last we returned to the director's office. On the table from end to end were a long line of bottles and a few small plates of macaroons. It became clear that whenever Sir William had uttered even a grunt of approval, the bottle had been extracted. We then went through the lot one after another, 1793 Madeira and all. Eventually the Ambassador asked me to make an appropriate speech in Russian. At the time I thought it most beautiful and eloquent paean of thanks that I had ever heard. I was horrified when it was greeted by our hosts with total dismay. They explained that we had clearly misunderstood the purpose of the occasion. The aim was to show us that Soviet power was able to produce wine as good, if not better, than in Tsarist times. A line of waiters then appeared and placed the Soviet equivalent alongside its historic counterpart. There was no way out but to go through the lot, and we did.

I think that the Ambassador asked me to make another appropriate speech. We learnt later than we had paid a subsequent visit to the Botanical Garden.

JOHN MORGAN

Bishop Reporting

Following several sweltering months in British (or should I say Bookers?) Guiana, I was relaxing for a few days in Barbados when, emboldened by rum, I invited an almost equally tall woman to dance at a coconut grove night spot as music and blood began to warm up.

Somewhat north of my 30 or so in the early 1950s, she appeared to be unescorted and was attractive in the travelled way that impressed me at the time. After we had returned to her table she introduced herself: 'I am Princess Pearl of Sarawak but I don't suppose that will mean anything to you.'

'Oh, but it does.' As we danced and talked until it was almost time for flying fish for breakfast we learned much about each other. She and her sister, Princess Ruby as I recall, had grown up in Sarawak, daughters of Sir Charles Vyner Brooke, the last White Rajah. The link between us was that, as Japan surrendered in 1945, I had paddled a Catalina flying-boat dinghy to the Astana Besar, her father's palace on the bank of the Kuching river.

Next night we met again and as we dined and danced, distancing ourselves sufficiently from the intoxicating music of a Barbadian steel band, talked another night away. This is what I told Princess Pearl:

After Hiroshima and Nagasaki had been atom-bombed in August 1945, I was cooling off with an iced beer in the La Ha Paint House (a building belonging to a company of that name which we had requisitioned for our mess), across the road from the office of *The Statesman* daily English language newspaper in Calcutta, when I was joined by an enormous and rugged man somewhat reminiscent of John Wayne.

Frank Owen, known also as the 'Hereford Bull', a former Liberal MP, editor of the London *Evening Standard* and protégé of Lord Beaverbrook, had created SEAC Newspaper as an inter-service daily at the personal request of Admiral Lord Louis Mountbatten, Supreme Allied Commander in South East Asia.

How I came to be in Calcutta is a tale in itself. Suffice it to say, I had joined SEAC Newspaper in *The Statesman* building after serving in a Hunt class destroyer and was messing in the La Ha Paint House.

Frank said he had been ordered to launch an edition of SEAC in Singapore once it had been re-occupied. Hitherto our main task had been to provide the troops in Burma with a daily. A Singapore edition was now essential. He slackened his bush jacket belt and refilled my glass. 'I've scrounged a Dakota from the RAF and we're all flying down tomorrow, barring you. Sorry, you are the youngest and most junior of us and there's no room. Catch up under your own steam.'

Under my own steam! I took a cab up to Calcutta docks where merchant ships which had been preparing for Operation Zipper – the expected opposed landings in Malaya and Singapore – were raising steam for our nuclear-sent, bloodless return to the mainland peninsula and island. It was one of those Calcutta afternoons when sweat stains a jungle-green bush jacket and collects in the small of the back. I walked to the docks. Some of the ships, their officers melting beneath crisply starched white tunics, seemed too grand to be accosted by a hitchhiker.

And then there she was. The *Fort Stager*, a rusting workaday coal burning tramp. Cupping my hands to improvize a loud-hailer I addressed a grimy figure at the head of the gangway. 'Are you bound for Singapore?' I yelled in competition with the clatter of a forest of cranes and the high-pitched chatter of the coolies.

The mate spat into the filthy flotsam idling between the tramp's rusting plates and the dockwall, and called, 'On the morning tide'. Perhaps my hunch about this tramp had been right? 'May I join you?'

The mate in grubby singlet rubbed his stubble. 'Skipper's drunk in his bunk. He's out of Scotch. Come back by 0600 with two bottles.' I made all haste to the La Ha Paint House to plead my cause with the one man in Calcutta who seemed to have access to limitless alcohol.

It was sundowner time and the Hereford Bull was already well into his second burra peg. 'Well young feller-me-lad, we're flying out at dawn.' I produced my trump: 'And I'll be joining you in a few days.' He seemed surprised I had obtained transport so quickly. 'And how is that?'

I wriggled uncomfortably in the itchy wicker mess chair. In my anxiety to confront Frank, I had not yet showered for the evening. The prickly heat was torture. I qualified my optimism. 'Well, it's like this. I'll be joining you if I can rustle up a couple of bottles of Scotch.'

Frank responded swiftly in that urgent, mid-Atlantic accent he had made all his own, a barked blend of growling Beaverspeak and the soft undertones of his friend and political patron, Lloyd George. The Beaver was written all over him, as indelible as the endearments of a Tiger Bay tattooist.

Before the war intervened the Beaver had driven Frank mercilessly until – tanked up or sober – he had written brilliantly for the *Daily Express* and as a youthful editor of the London *Evening Standard*, clubbed the night way, returning always with his hair water-combed to pass the first edition at Shoe Lane.

'Alright sailor,' – an alternative for young feller-me-lad 'give me your beer coupons. The Yanks across the road are short of beer but OK for Scotch.' Frank heaved his starched figure past the *chokadower* (guard) and through the mess entrance. Seldom entirely sober and less so once the sun had passed over the yard-arm, yet always close-cropped and smart, Frank had square-bashed at an OCTU (Officer Cadet Training Unit) before being raised overnight by Supremo from second lieutenant to lieutenant colonel. He returned with two bottles of Haig.

I drew a large sum in advanced expenses – SEAC Newspaper was Fleet Street east of Suez – and returned to the *Fort Stager*. The grimy mate, dawdling where I had left him, was laconic. 'OK. So no Scotch.' I stood at the foot of the gangway with a bulging kitbag, rolled-up jungle canvas camp bed and a green canvas slops (naval store) issue suitcase. 'No Scotch, no passage,' the mate said.

Triumphantly, I passed an imaginary wand over the suitcase, opened it and displayed the Scotch as a Cup Final captain might loft his team's trophy. Invited aboard, I was conducted to the grizzled Geordie who was the master. Without saying a word he locked the Scotch away. The Geordie grunted, 'Can't accommodate you. I'll rig a shelter on the bridge and you can camp out. Done any stoking? No? Well, you can work some of your passage.'

On the morning tide we edged into the Ganges. Along the starboard bank bodies were being charred on the burning ghats, a form of cremation, practised in the open for all to view. It horrified me to see the feet and toes sticking out of the brushwood.

I do not remember much about the voyage except that I was accompanied by an American writer who had also hitched a ride, and having beaten me to it with his two bottles of Scotch, occupied the only spare cabin. As we began to roll in the Indian Ocean, the chief engineer led me below where I stoked as though my life depended on it. Shovelling mechanically, I had hurled three spades into the furnace when chiefie called it a day. 'Can't afford to lose any more shovels,' he muttered.

When we tied up in Singapore I went ashore and walked to the dockyard gates where Japanese soldiers stood guard. Had I arrived too early? I walked through unchallenged, learning afterwards that until British troops arrived in any numbers the Japanese would keep order for us.

I asked the way to Raffles Hotel. Knowing Frank, he was as likely to be there as anywhere. Entering the foyer I encountered a mass of chattering women, mostly Eurasians, from the camps of Java and Sumatra, and pushed my way through to reception.

'Colonel Owen? Suite 23, and he's in.' Nobody heard my knock on the door. I opened it and encountered an astonishing scene. A wild party was in full swing. Towering above his guests, the Hereford Bull was wielding a Japanese officer's sword. 'Timely, young feller-me-lad. I'm just about to demonstrate how the Nips beheaded our chaps.'

Frank cleared a space and bid me kneel. '*Banzai*,' he yelled, and swept the blade inches from my face.

As the party in Suite 23 dissolved, Frank informed me we were temporarily dossing down at Raffles and instructed me to find a house and transport and, in the contemporary military argot, to 'get organized'.

At a total loss, I was musing outside the hotel when a young Chinese approached me respectfully and asked 'Need car? Need house?' I followed him to a looted Hudson tourer and he drove me to an empty villa standing amid banana trees in a large garden in Orange Grove Road, a salubrious *tuan besar*'s neighbourhood for local company chairmen and plantation bosses, off the top of Orchard Road.

Loy, villa head boy in peace and occupation, welcomed me. 'Japanese general gone. House yours.' I told him to hold possession for SEAC News-paper and returned to Raffles to collect our editor, Peter Eastwood, a Fleet Street chief sub-editor who was serving as a turbaned Sikh artillery captain when Frank discovered him in Burma.

Tan, our newly-acquired driver, returned us to Orange Grove Road to arrange with Loy to move in later that day. Loy volunteered to produce a dinner fit for a house warming. Strictly speaking we were under orders from the British Military Administration – a.k.a. the Black Market Administra-tion – to eat service rations and not to deprive the Singapore people of food. Loy would have none of this. Funded by the mess he was to feast us twice a day.

As we were leaving Loy, we almost collided with a jeep bearing a puce Indian Army brigadier who demanded what we were doing at *his* house. Peter informed him courteously that he was mistaken. The brig. remon-strated and Peter and I produced our trump card, a special pass from the Supremo proclaiming a priority which seemed to be second to none in South-East Asia. If a puce brigadier could pale, he did. 'Can't compete with that,' he spluttered through his gingery moustache, and drove off *jeldee, jeldee*.[1]

I was wondering what we would do for drink at our inaugural dinner when a Naval NAAFI wavy navy lieutenant wandered up the drive and introduced himself as a neighbour. Ted Fry, landlord in peacetime of a large

---

1 *Jeldee* was a word frequently used in the Indian Army during the Raj, meaning get on with it, quickly, quickly, as to a ricksha wallah, taking one to an urgent appointment.

and busy pub in Egham, had taken over a villa across the road. He supplied us immediately, mostly with Cyprus wine and brandy, some gin and several cases of canned beer. We promised his unit a good write up in our newspaper.

Having set all this up, I was relieved of some of my press duties to become part-time mess fixer, and with Loy's assistance launched into a menu repertoire which became the envy of guests from whom we sought favours, be they newsprint supplies or transport facilities.

Loy and I had devised a particularly appetising lunch, featuring roast sucking pig, when Peter panted into the mess. 'Clear the table. Cancel lunch and offer bully beef, ships' biscuits and water.' The brigadier commanding British Military Administration had invited himself to lunch and we were to demonstrate that we were complying with orders. The brig.'s face fell when confronted by our frugal table. 'I asked myself to lunch because I'd heard you had the best table in Singapore.' Peter's speech was quiet and strangulated at the best of times, as if a talent for tight subbing had infected his vocal chords. His eyes said it all: 'Resume normal service'. I scampered to the cookhouse at the bottom of the garden. Loy was unfazed. 'Lunch ready,' he smiled. He had anticipated this happy outcome.

We were in the brig.'s good books, and partly through his patronage I joined a Rajput captain (a British officer), a jemadar (an Indian army senior NCO) and two sepoys on an exploratory visit to Sarawak. An Australian Catalina flying-boat crew landed us on the Kuching River in Sarawak. The Catalina port and starboard blisters were excellent for observation and as we banked over the white rajah's capital I was eager to go ashore.

A path led from the river to the Astana Besar. It was lunchtime and the absence of life and noise reminded me that, until the Japanese changed all that, only mad dogs and Englishmen went out in the midday sun. The jemadar sahib shattered the silence, knocking with a vehemence that would have done justice to Black Rod seeking entrance to the Commons. There was no response.

The sepoys prised the doors open. As we entered I was confronted by a baronial style hall and a table stretching much of its length. Leather-crested chairs were placed as if for a meeting, and at the top of the table, still wearing his bush hat, sat a tall, lean colonel, every inch of six foot four. He rose as we approached and extended an enormous hand: 'Colonel England of the Australian Imperial Force and who the bloody 'ell are you?' We explained we were making a recce. 'Well, get this straight. Australia got here first.' The Rajput captain and I were invited to lunch and could see no gain in briefing the colonel that his claim was irrelevant. Sarawak was not a Crown colony.

After lunch Colonel England suggested we make ourselves useful by going up river to discover what the situation was in the area of the white rajah's summer palace. 'But watch it. There are a lot of Japs about and some may not know the war is over.' We embarked on a river boat and chugged for hours through the jungle until we reached the empty palace and set up our camp beds.

In the morning we came across a gaol and were admitted to the office of the governor. He was an imposing Sikh who asked if the war was really over. After satisfying him that this was so, he asked what he should do with his prisoners – civil offenders whose crimes, it seemed, ranged from murder to theft.

The Sikh produced a ledger bearing the names and crimes of the inmates. The Rajput took me aside. He whispered: 'We'll never get another opportunity like this.' Calling me to attention he declared, 'In the name of His Majesty King George VI, I declare an amnesty. Release the prisoners.' We entered something to this effect in a ledger and, as I remember, we signed it.

When I returned to Singapore I received an invitation from Supremo to drinks in a cruiser lying off the island. Peter and I spruced ourselves up and as we stepped off the gangway we saluted as required. Although I was wearing the green and gold badges of a correspondent I gave a naval salute.

Supremo, who never missed a detail, was aware of my naval origins and informed me jovially that it was my last salute. In the morning I would be a civilian. He had decided to launch an afternoon paper entitled *The Singapore Free Press*. Eastwood would be editor, and I, aged 21, assistant editor, 'since there is nobody else'.

As Supremo was to remind me, and whoever happened to be in the circle at parties in the years that followed, I questioned the validity of such an immediate demobilisation. Mountbatten issued a mock reprimand: 'Bishop,' he said, 'do you know who I am?'

'Supremo sir.' The future viceroy stiffened. 'Very well Bishop; I am Supremo, and that, Bishop, means I can do anything.' The story as he told it always ended, 'So here you have the only man in South-East Asia Command who ever questioned my authority'. It was an anecdote worth stoking for.

EDWARD BISHOP

Hold-Up on the Kabul River

The road from Kabul to Peshawar was always dramatic. It led down from the plateau at 6,000 feet, through the Kabul river gorge across the Jalalabad plain and over the Khyber pass. Every fortnight the embassy lorry, a legendary Leyland, would make this journey: in winter by day and in summer by night. One of us from the small British staff of the Embassy would travel with it as an unofficial King's Messenger carrying the confidential mail.

By chance, one June I came back to Kabul from Peshawar not in the Leyland but in a new embassy car with a Pakistani driver called Amirullah. We carried with us two sealed Foreign Office confidential mail bags. Leaving Peshawar in the morning, we had worked our way across the sun-baked Jalalabad plain and by early afternoon were half way up the Kabul river gorge. Rounding a bend, we saw ahead a rough wall of stones laid across the road. It seemed to indicate a diversion. But, as we reached it, armed men, shouting in Pushtu and brandishing rifles and pistols, sprang out from behind nearby rocks. They were a wild lot, unkempt, raggedly clothed, narrow-eyed, hard-faced frontier outlaws.

Surrounding the car, they pulled us out and prodded us up the bed of a stream which ran across the road the other side of the stones. Amirullah and I told them in Pushtu and Persian that we were foreign guests who were carrying government mail. But what did they care? One of them stripped a scarf from my neck and used it to bind Amirullah's hands behind his back. For what seemed an eternity, we believed they would shoot us, throw our bodies in the river and push the car in after us. But, in fact, they herded us farther up the stream bed and made us sit under the guard of a ruffian with a pistol. The others busied themselves with looting our suitcases and opening the mail bags. Coming across packages sealed with red wax which they believed contained money, they ripped them open furiously and, finding none, threw them aside with curses.

We then heard the sound of a vehicle coming down the road ahead of us. The bandits hid behind rocks as a lorry nosed round the corner. Many passengers were aloft, including two young soldiers. The bandits sprang out, one of the soldiers fired at them, they fired back. The other soldier jumped down to surrender. They killed him too. They then robbed the passengers of weapons, money and rings and herded them up the stream bed to join us. Amirullah and I breathed a sigh of relief. We were now surely too many for the bandits to shoot in cold blood.

During the next three hours a succession of lorries and jeeps fell into the ambush. Their Afghan passengers, who eventually numbered ninety-odd, were all robbed and then moved up the stream bed. As dusk was falling, the bandits wrapped their loot in turban cloths and loped off into the hills. We blessed our good fortune in surviving. Our material losses seemed of little significance.

We salvaged all we could from the debris by the roadside. The contents of the confidential bags comprised a number of smaller bags, some of which had not been touched, unlike the packages sealed in wax. Our car we found in running order, but most of the lorries had been immobilized and the telephone wires cut. We got back to the Embassy at three in the morning.

The next day I learnt the true weight of the confidential bag. The Ambassador was furious that his papers had been rifled; the Afghan government were humiliated that the hold-up had occurred on a main road and the Foreign Office demanded retribution. Fortunately, it transpired that nothing important in the bag had gone astray and it was accepted that our embassy car had been ambushed not by design but by chance. However, the Foreign Office instructed the Ambassador to make a formal protest. The next day an official announcement appeared in the press stating that:

On 3 June a party of twelve wicked persons, some of whom have taken refuge abroad because of their evil deeds, held up and robbed a number of lorries coming to Kabul. After hearing of this event, the authorities concerned captured some of these men and are pursuing the rest of them.

The twist came later. The Afghan government rejected the Embassy's protest. They stated that in many countries robberies took place which were beyond the control of government. The previous week, the Afghan ambassador in London had been giving a dinner party at his residence in Prince's Gate when thieves had entered the house by an upper window and stolen his wife's jewellery valued at thousands of pounds.

HUGH CARLESS

Interviewing an Idol

Harold Nicolson's broadcasts, writings and book reviews in the *Observer* had been for many years a major influence on my literary and historical education, so when in November 1953 he came to Oxford to give the Chichele lectures on the history of diplomacy, I persuaded the news editor of *Isis* to send me to interview my hero. I was then in my first term at Oxford, and by an odd series of events had become film editor of *Isis*, the venerable weekly undergraduate magazine, and to it I occasionally contributed other pieces.

Sir Harold – recently knighted (but, we now know, with great reluctance) after the publication of his official biography of George V – was staying with John Sparrow, his friend the Warden of All Souls.

At the appointed hour, I rang the bell of the Warden's lodgings and the door was answered by Warden Sparrow himself. I was rather impressed, having expected the Warden of All Souls to have at least a servant, or even a butler.

'Here is the young man from *Isis*, Harold,' called Warden Sparrow and ushered me into the drawing room where sat the substantial and somewhat rumpled Harold Nicolson. This was the first time I had met an idol, and was unprepared to find that he was so much older than the genial, dapper figure familiar to me in photos in the *Observer* and the *Radio Times*. He was also balder and fatter and, as the interview developed, crosser.

I had prepared questions ranging across his many celebrated rôles in English life for which I much admired him – writer, broadcaster, diplomat, MP, biographer, novelist, historian – but as I went through them his replies showed a trace of irritation. Did I make a mistake in expressing admiration of *Some People*? Many years later his published diaries disclosed that, proud though he was of its fame, he was sometimes annoyed if it seemed to be the only work of his to be remembered. Perhaps I dwelt too much on his literary eminence; certainly that was the aspect most familiar to me. Had I unwittingly given too little attention to his ten years as an MP?

My final question was as to which of his many rôles he would most like to be remembered. 'As a politician, of course!' he replied crossly.

At the time, this was to me a most surprising answer, almost ludicrous in its self-delusion: I had assumed his ten years as an MP had been a comparative failure and in any case subordinate to his greater significance as a man of letters. I knew that he had been a supporter of Churchill against Chamberlain, but I was too young to know of his earlier political career as a follower of Mosley, and then of Ramsay Macdonald's National Labour. Of these events and much more (there are, for instance, frequent references to his clubs, particularly the Beefsteak and the Travellers), I learned when his incomparable diaries were published in the mid-sixties. As a chronicler of his times and a personal diarist he is almost on a par with Samuel Pepys, and it is these three volumes which are his masterpieces beyond all his many other books.

There is an irony here: as his diaries (together with those of Chips Channon) are the most important primary source for historians of English political life in the 1930s and the 1940s, his observations are going to be quoted and studied for generations to come, so perhaps after all Harold Nicolson will be remembered most as a politician.

MICHAEL ALLEN

Going Public

At the time this story opens, I had just forsaken the publishing world in order to devote more time to writing a history of Sotheby's, on which I had already been at work for some years. I had spent two weeks at Mentmore describing the memorable sale of the contents of the former Rothschild home for a number of journals.

As the Mentmore sale reached its end, my wife and I decided that we needed a brief holiday. We booked rooms in what seemed a wonderful country hotel in Oxfordshire and told our daughter Lucilla not to tell anyone where we were, unless it was a matter of life or death. While we were changing for dinner soon after our arrival, the telephone rang. It was Peregrine Pollen, deputy chairman of Sotheby's. 'How on earth did you find us?' I asked. 'We told our daughter not to tell anyone where we were unless it was a matter of life or death.' Peregrine explained that he thought his reason for phoning was just that; but he would not tell me what the reason was. He was insistent that I should attend a vital meeting at the offices of Slaughter & May, a famous firm of city solicitors in Basinghall Street, at 9 a.m. the following morning. I resolutely refused, but Peregrine is a persuasive fellow, and after some three quarters of an hour on the phone, I reluctantly agreed, still in ignorance of what it was all about.

Next morning, instead of the hopeful long lie-in, we had to get up at the crack of dawn. Patricia dropped me at Slaughter & May's offices and I was ushered into a large meeting room. Sitting round a circular table were Peregrine Pollen and Peter Spira, the latter having not long before joined Sotheby's as finance director, and eight or more other men in serious suits who were completely unknown to me. Peregrine explained that the meeting had been called to find out from me the bones of Sotheby's history. So began the most amazing cross-examination in which I was asked to talk about Samuel Baker, George Leigh, the three members of the Sotheby family, John Wilkinson, the Hodges – father and son, Barlow, Hobson and

Warre, and Vere Pilkington: the offices they occupied; the sales they had held; the staff they had employed. Frankly, I was astonished how much I knew. I had had no inkling about this inquisition; I had no notes or reference books on hand of any kind. But all these shadows from Sotheby's past had become familiar friends and I enjoyed talking about them. After three hours, I asked for a break and I was told in a kindly manner to get some fresh air, and to come back in half an hour.

When I returned I asked for an explanation. In fact, I seem to remember saying that I was not prepared to go on unless it was explained to me what this was all about. After a lengthy insistence upon secrecy, I was told that it was planned to turn Sotheby's into a public company, and the long cross-examination about the firm's history had been to establish if I was capable of writing the necessary section of the relevant offer document. In view of the fact that Sotheby's had been established as long ago as 1744, the financiers felt that the history should be its most prominent part. After five years of Marshall, Morgan & Scott's climb to prominence (I had been managing director of this publishing group), which included a string of mergers and takeovers, this sort of corporate challenge was meat and drink to me. I had spent endless agonizing periods in the offices of Clifford Turner (now Clifford Chance), our solicitors, drafting documents by impossible deadlines. It took me no time at all to agree to undertake the job.

There followed several weeks of mayhem. I became just as thoroughly involved with the financial implications as with detailing the historical facts. I was endlessly engaged in drafting meetings when I would be asked to think up alternative wordings. The question always was: should they be bland, definite, incisive, aggressive. All such variants were called for and they were well mixed in the final document.

This share offer was to be the first since the great Stock Exchange meltdown in February 1974 when the FT Index had plunged to 140 (as I write, it is over (6000) and a really wealthy Middle-Eastern oil potentate could have bought the bulk of Britain's industry without seriously feeling the pinch. But in the event we were pipped at the post: BP came in with a sudden share offer, and we had to put everything on hold until that was out of the way. When eventually the Sotheby share offer was announced, it was over-subscribed by twenty-seven times by the closing date. Our advisers were jubilant and I received a host of graceful compliments; not only that, but from Rothschild's – one of our three merchant bankers – the other two were Kleinwort & Benson and S G Warburg – a transparent, plastic cube containing a miniaturized offer document, as a keepsake. I had not been allowed to buy any shares, but it was generally agreed that the history had played an important role in attracting shareholders. The worst part of the job for me, which nobody had warned me about at the beginning, was that I had to produce written proof of evidence for every statement I had made in my six long pages of text: this alone had taken four weeks.

The question I then had to ask myself was: what was I going to charge Sotheby's for several months of incredibly hard work that had gone on at all hours and over weekends, and had put a stop to all my other activities. I consulted my accountant, the redoubtable Henry Brandes, who said: 'Whatever invoice you send them, it isn't high enough unless you feel embarrassed about submitting it!'. Clearly I interpreted him correctly, because Sotheby's were taken aback by the size of my bill. It was agreed they would pay eighty percent and suggested that I should prepare – that is, write and design – the layout and text of their first annual accounts as a public company, *and* if we won the prize for the best produced accounts of the year, they would triple the missing bit. I had no idea that there were 3,000 applicants for such a competition, but in any case we won.

Three years later, after the history of the firm was published, I joined Sotheby's management as Director of Overseas Operations.

FRANK HERRMANN

The Frogman's Watch

My father was a naval officer and in the war he served as Master of the Fleet (fleet navigator) to Admiral Cunningham. When my father died in 1968 he left me, among other personal items, a watch taken from one of the Italian frogmen who blew up two British battleships in Alexandria harbour in 1941.

Of course I knew all about this episode. I knew all my father's wartime stories and, besides, his account is given in Oliver Warner's biography of Cunningham. My father had been fetching a coat from his day-cabin when the blast threw him to the ground. He had shaken the scuttle-glass out of his hair and had returned to the bridge. Some time later the Admiral had noticed him and said, 'We had better go and clean up or we shall be late for Colours'. This seemed to my father as typical of Cunningham's style, that the daily Colours ceremony went on as normal despite the fact that the ship was in a state of pandemonium and was at a fifteen-degree list. The Admiral ordered my father to find out why one drummer was missing from the band.

There was an envoi to this story. My father had obtained – he never said how – a watch belonging to one of the frogmen (all six of whom survived though they were all captured). Ten years later, when he was Chief of Staff to the Mediterranean Fleet, he had attended a NATO function in Malta, where one of the other officers present was, according to my father, the former owner of the watch, now an Italian rear-admiral. After a few moments' hesitation, my father had gone up to this man, saluted smartly, and said, 'Sir, I have the honour to return to you the watch which you so kindly lent to me in 1941.' The admiral had been much amused by this but he had insisted on my father keeping the watch.

In the mid-1980s I was doing some research into renaissance galley warfare, and was engaged in a rather one-sided correspondence with a Professor Cesare Ciano of the University of Pisa. Ciano was also a naval officer and head of the history department at the naval academy at Livorno. However,

he was not one of the world's great letter-answerers, and it was more to
stimulate a reply than for any altruistic reason that I mentioned the existence of the watch, said I had a feeling that it should go to an appropriate
Italian naval museum, and asked the Professor's advice. This stratagem was
entirely successful. Ten days later an enormous letter arrived containing
everything I could possibly want to know about the construction, rigging,
manning, armament, organization and tactics of the galleys of the Medicean
Order of S. Stefano. However, the real thrust of the letter was clearly elsewhere: 'Admiral de La Penne is still alive. I have spoken to him and he
would be delighted to receive back his watch which will then be placed in
the museum of the naval academy. Please tell me when you are coming so
that we can finalize arrangements for the ceremony.' This was not quite
what I had in mind, and I waited before replying. In fact I waited too long,
and another letter arrived: 'Please give us your dates as the programme of
the naval academy has to be published well in advance. As a suggestion, the
Accademia dei Cavalieri di S. Stefano is planning a conference, to be held
in the order's former council chamber on 21–22 October, on the subject of
"Life aboard Galleys". I would be delighted if you could attend, and perhaps we might arrange the watch ceremony for the 19th. Please answer by
return.' Professor Ciano had found it as easy to hook me as I had found it
to hook him.

It was several moths after accepting this invitation that I woke up in the
middle of the night with a terrifying realization. The watch which my father
had left me was not a frogman's watch at all. Frogmen's watches had luminous dials and rubber casing. This was a conventional and undistinguished
wrist-watch with a 'Marvin' Swiss movement and a gunmetal case. The case
had, it was true, a number which looked somewhat military and which did
not have the broad arrow found on all British military issue. But it could not
be a frogman's watch. My father was, I recalled, a born raconteur, a spinner
of nautical yarns in the tradition of Ulysses and Sinbad the Sailor. And like
all raconteurs he much preferred an elegant story to an accurate one. Anyhow, how had he come by the watch? Perhaps he had himself been duped by
some vendor of marine memorabilia. The implications of this line of thought

were horrific. De La Penne would see at once that it was a fake. In front of a huge audience, Italy's leading naval hero would denounce me as a fraud. 'It is not my watch,' he would say, 'I have never seen it before in my life.'

After breakfast I took the watch to a nearby watch repairer. 'Waterproof? Lord bless you no, sir. Don't let any water get near it, that's my advice.' I cancelled my appointments for the day and, armed with a notebook and an Italian dictionary, set out for the library of the Imperial War Museum where I ordered every book which I could find dealing with the Alexandria action. The results were not encouraging. 'Here is Luigi on a practice dive,' wrote Valerio Borghese, 'note the rubber-encased watch which he is wearing.' One of the frogmen's reports stated, 'As I sat in the interrogation room, I waited for the sound of the explosion and could not take my eyes off the luminous dial of my big frogman's watch which lay on the interrogating officer's desk.' At lunchtime I staggered out to a pub and ordered myself a large double whisky.

The afternoon's research was a bit more positive. The frogmen's plan was to rendezvous with their mother-submarine, the *Scire*, a bit down the coast. This involved walking through Alexandria and, since they did not want to be shot as spies, they proposed to do it wearing their correct naval uniform, gambling that it would not be recognized. Therefore, I reasoned, they must have had in their submersibles (Italian: 'pig'; English: 'chariot') a waterproof container to hold their uniform, cap, shoes etc. And clearly they would need a watch for the rendezvous and were scarcely going to walk through the middle of Alexandria wearing a big rubber-encased timepiece with a luminous dial. Furthermore, I solved the problem of how the watch had come into my father's possession. The interrogating officer was the head of port intelligence, Colonel Humphrey Quill of the Royal Marines, an old friend of my family and my sister's godfather. Coincidentally, his hobby was horology, and he subsequently became Master of the Worshipful Company of Clockmakers, though I doubt if gunmetal 'Marvins' were quite his style.

I was now sure that the watch had indeed belonged to one of the frogmen. On the other hand it seemed very unlikely that it had belonged to de La Penne. The story of his part in the action at Alexandria was well known. His 'pig' had succeeded in getting through the net protecting the battleship

Valiant but had then ploughed into the harbour mud and, at the same time, his crewman had become ill and had been forced to surface. Undismayed, de La Penne had managed to detach the nose-cone containing the mine and, with superhuman strength, had manhandled it until it was under the hull. He had then set the time-fuse and, completely exhausted, had gone to the surface where he had been captured. Morgan, captain of the *Valiant*, a nice man, had sent him ashore for interrogation, but this order had been countermanded by Cunningham, a less nice man, who had sent him back aboard *Valiant* with orders that he should be confined below the waterline. Though now in danger of being killed by his own mine, de La Penne had waited until just before the time he had set on the fuse and had then advised Morgan to clear the ship. After the armistice Morgan, by then an admiral, had asked Prince Umberto for the honour of personally pinning on de La Penne the Italian order 'Pro Valorem'. It was an inspirational story, but the implication was that de La Penne's 'pig' and all its contents were still in the silt of Alexandria harbour.

A sensible person at this stage would have packed the watch neatly in a box and sent it to Ciano with a letter explaining the circumstances and apologizing for any misconception caused by my father's exaggeration or my own naïvety. However, I felt that I had left it a bit late. Also it was abundantly clear from Ciano's letters that it was not the watch which they wanted, it was the ceremony, the honouring of a famous event and its protagonist, the reconciliation of former enemies. If some Italian had come up with Field-Marshal Montgomery's beret I doubt if it would have got more than a thankyou letter from the museum director and perhaps a two-inch column in *The Desert Rat*; but in Italy they do things differently. So I delayed, and once again delay was fatal. My niece Anna (née Orsini) rang up in a state of great excitement: 'Auntie Annamaria from Pisa has been on the phone. Apparently the story of the watch has been in the newspapers. She says everyone is talking about it.' With leaden heart I booked a flight to Italy.

The leaden heart stayed with me for a week as I toured Tuscany. It was not lightened by the masterpieces of the Renaissance, by the towers of San Gimignano, the ramparts of Volterra, by the taste of wild boar and Vin

Santo, not even by the Ottoman pennants (taken at Lepanto and a hundred battles) now kept in the almost permanently closed church of S. Stefano in Pisa's Piazza dei Cavalieri.

It must be said that the Italian navy does its officers well. The residence of Rear-Admiral Ficcara, commandant of the Livorno Naval Academy, was elegantly sumptuous. Professor Ciano had collected me from the Hotel Gran Duca and had briefed me on the order of batting: 'We will have a press conference before the ceremony. Then we go in. Admiral Ficcara will make a speech of welcome. Then Admiral Strozzi will talk about the history of Italian irregular naval warfare. Then you make your speech which I will interpret. Then the presentation. Then Admiral de La Penne will reply.' 'Oh, for a couple of inches in *The Desert Rat*,' I thought to myself. Ficcara's greeting was equally disconcerting: 'Mr Brownrigg, you have made me many enemies. So many senior officers wanted to be present on this great occasion. But I said no, if we let all these people in, there will be no room for the cadets, ha, ha! So they will have to read about it in tomorrow's newspapers.'

In due course Admiral de La Penne was announced. He looked every centimetre the hero. The British had admired him greatly, and nothing in his appearance or behaviour led me to feel differently. Surely a man of such sterling qualities was not going to denounce me as a charlatan? These qualities did not, it must be conceded, include the gift of tongues. The admiral was almost as innocent of the English language as I was of Italian. But we smiled and chinked glasses, and then it was time to show him the watch. The moment of truth had arrived. I turned scarlet as I fumbled in my bag. De La Penne received the watch with an air of extreme puzzlement. He muttered something to Ficcara. There ensued an embarrassing silence which was broken by Ciano, ever the diplomat: 'Henry, have you noticed the painting over the fireplace? It is a galley battle by a local artist. I think it is Lepanto. Or perhaps it is Actium.' I stared at the picture as if it held the secret of life. Eventually I turned back to the admirals. De La Penne was smiling and, summoning up his entire reserves of English, he said, 'Mr Brownrigg, thank you. It is with so great emotion that I hold again my old watch.'

The press conference was not too bad. 'Was it your father's wish that the watch should be returned to Italy?' This is what my Latin teachers would have called a *nonne* question. Next we entered the auditorium for the ceremony. Five hundred cadets sprang to attention as one cadet. We settled on the rostrum. Admiral Strozzi spoke at great length, and the audience seemed as bored as I was. Then it was my turn. I had decided on two things: firstly, that my speech should be short and, secondly, that this was no moment for British understatement. Fortunately the events themselves made understatements unnecessary, and I was able to say with perfect sincerity that this was the most economical naval action of the war, with two battleship incapacitated by six men all of whom survived. It became the model for all the later Allied frogmen attacks, for instance the British attack on the *Tirpitz*. I also mentioned Cunningham's visit to the naval academy in 1934, when he was very impressed by the standard of tuition but thought that the discipline was excessively harsh. This of course got a laugh from the cadets. I finished by saying that this was an occasion which I would always remember. They little knew how sincerely I meant it.

Two days later we all foregathered for the conference on 'Life aboard Galleys'. With the exception of de La Penne all the same senior officers were present, as was the admiral commanding the huge naval base at La Spezia. The street was closed and the door guarded by the carabinieri. The red cross of the Order of St Stephen flew from every balcony. It was about as different from a British historical conference as could be imagined.

When it was all over, Ciano and I had a farewell drink. 'My only regret, Henry, is there has not been time to show you the shrine at Montallegro. It is very famous; there is a unique collection of 'ex votos'. Of course nowadays the church likes to play down this belief in personal miracles, but sailors are always very superstitious. You know that from your work on the Knights of St John.'

'Yes, of course. One has only to think of the Knights' excitement at possessing the hand of John the Baptist, one of nine hands of John the Baptist in different parts of Europe! But personally I do not worry too much about a relic's provenance. If it is venerated and performs miracles then it is authentic, at least subjectively. Come to think of it,' I added on impulse, 'it is

much the same in the case of Admiral de La Penne's watch, don't you think?'
I am not sure, but I believe that Professor Ciano winked at me.

HENRY BROWNRIGG

The Squeezing of King Farouk

February, 1942. I was on a course at the Officer Cadet Training Unit in the
centre of Cairo, learning to be an infantry officer. We occupied Kasr el Nil
barracks, a picturesque building dating from Turkish times, not far from the
Nile, and we were drawn from all sorts of Commonwealth units – British,
Australian, New Zealand, Rhodesian and so on. The course was a strenuous
one, lasting five months, and certain cadets found the 'spit-and-polish' side
irksome. There was an awkward incident when an Australian was returned
to his unit for indiscipline. He reappeared a day or two later with a note
from his divisional commander: 'I selected this soldier for a commission – it
is up to you to train him. Please do so!'

One evening we were suddenly called out on parade and issued with live
ammunition. We were told that we were going out 'on a job' in the town,
but we were given no idea of the object of the mission. At that stage of the
war, soldiers were not told much. We marched through the streets of Cairo
as far as the square opposite the Abdin Palace, the royal residence, where we
took up positions. A number of twenty-five-pounder guns and a searchlight
had arrived before us, and all civilians had been excluded from the area. We
were then informed why we had been brought there. The mission was a
political one, and pressure was going to be put on King Farouk to accept
the demands of the British Ambassador.

The political situation was briefly as follows. Egypt was full of British
troops trying, with varying success, to keep the German and Italian armies
from advancing on the Suez Canal. The front line at that time ran roughly
along the Libyan-Egyptian border, with a British contingent surrounded
farther west in Tobruk. Britain's presence in Egypt was authorized by the
Anglo-Egyptian Treaty of 1936, and the Egyptian people more or less

acquiesced. There was, however, a strong pro-Axis political group in Cairo, and King Farouk was known to sympathize with it. At the beginning of 1942 the current 'liberal' government of Sirry Pasha was losing ground in the parliament, and the pro-Axis group was preparing to take over power, with Farouk's support. Sir Miles Lampson, the British Ambassador, knew what was in the air and decided to forestall a coup by a daring move. He made contact with the veteran Nahas Pasha, who was head of the once anti-British Wafd party, and he promised to bring him to power by forcing Farouk to choose him as Prime Minister. It was an offer that the ageing, but still ambitious Nahas could not refuse, and he agreed to form a government that was favourable to Britain. All that remained to be done was to 'squeeze' Farouk.

This was the reason why there was an impressive array of soldiery in Abdin Square. We were waiting for Sir Miles Lampson to call on the King and force him to accept Nahas Pasha. After an hour's wait, we saw a Rolls-Royce, followed by a staff car, draw up outside the palace. A group of people emerged from the cars and entered the building. There was tension in the air as we waited for the result, and we imagined what was going on inside. We wondered if we were about to storm the palace. Some forty minutes later the group emerged from the gate and drove silently into the night. We then marched quietly back to barracks.

Farouk had signed the document put before him appointing Nahas Prime Minister, but there was no mention of the event in the press next morning.

ANTHONY FORSTER

A Broken Dock, a Wrecked Ship and a Lucky Break

Having qualified as a dental surgeon during the early days of the first blitz on London, I remained at the London Hospital in the East End for the next six months as house surgeon. I joined the Navy in May 1941. I had a spell in shore-based jobs and eventually went to sea.

From 1943 to 1944, I was dental officer aboard HMS *Valiant*, with a crew of about 1600. We had done some considerable sea time and had been harassing the Japs for several months and were due a refit. At the beginning of the war, there had been a large floating dock in Singapore harbour, but as that was now in enemy hands it was decided by the powers-that-be that a similar dock should be sent out to Trincomalee harbour in Ceylon (now, of course, Sri Lanka), and this had been done with much expense and expertise. We watched the dock being assembled and, when it was ready, firstly a submarine was put in and refitted, then a merchant ship, then, I believe, a destroyer and a light cruiser. It was with much excitement and interest that HMS *Valiant*, a battleship, was slowly moved into the dock, officially handed over to the captain of the dock, and the slow pumping-out of sections started. I was taken over to the hospital ship *Vasna* to dine with their dental officer – a very pleasant evening.

Afterwards, my host and I were waiting on the upper deck for the *Valiant*'s picket boat to come over to collect me. We could see the dock all lit up, the big battleship very high, almost out of the water in the dock, and we watched my boat leave the dockside. When she was about halfway across, there was the most terrific thud and all the lights on the dock went out. I suggested to my host that the Vice-Admiral was having some special exercise, but when I got into the boat the midshipman in charge told me that the dock had broken. I told him not to be such a scaremonger and to get back to the dock. When we came alongside, it was obvious that there was something very wrong. He then asked me if I was 'abandoning ship in the first picket boat'. So, in full naval tradition, as I thought, I clambered back on board this great ship, which was by this time listing quite considerably.

When the officer of the watch saw me – there was all hell let loose on board – he said, 'you must be the biggest bloody fool, the ship has every likelihood of capsizing'. Fortunately for everyone, we were tied up to a water boat and those hawsers kept us steady long enough to open up the tanks of the dock and get us more or less seaborne again. This took several hours; as usual in these emergencies, everyone was cool and efficient and there was no panic. I learned afterwards that when the dock was delivered, instructions were given that certain ships could cause a weight distribution problem – the *Valiant* being one because she had been given extra armour at the beginning of the war, adding to her overweight, which was concentrated over a comparatively short length. Someone had not bothered to read the instruction manual! *Valiant* was very heavily damaged, two of her three propellers were useless and her bows were buckled. As the days wore on, this latter problem meant that all refrigerated stores (meat in particular) went rotten: the smell was overpowering in the heat of the tropics.

The wreck of the dock remained in Trincomalee for several years. Japanese propaganda made considerable capital out of all this by saying that they had no need to attack the Royal Navy: we sank our own ships.

As a result of the accident, and much to my disappointment, I was told that I would not be going home. Instead, I was appointed to a naval transit camp called HS Mayina, twelve miles out of Colombo on the Kandy road. I was extremely displeased.

At Mayina, however, the commanding officer was kind and most understanding of my feelings and, after a few days, he decided that I had not had any leave for about two years and suggested that I take some. This proved to be one of the most fortunate breaks, certainly of the war, and possibly of my life.

The camp's medical officer, who was something of a studious type (which I certainly am not) was very interested in Singhalese history and archaeology. He wanted a companion to go round the buried jungle cities in the interior of the island. Even in those days, I had no pretensions to be a pioneer (I had never liked the idea of joining the Boy Scouts) but I was thrilled to get away from the Navy and do something different.

We left Colombo and got naval transport going northwards to Negombo. Here we hitched a lift on government transport to Anuradhapura, which in the fifteenth and sixteenth centuries was the capital of an extensive Singhalese empire. It had been deserted for several hundred years and the jungle had taken over. There were scores of temples with their *dagobas* and enormous lakes. These man-made lakes were called 'tanks' and were part of an irrigation system. In fact, they had been the cause of the downfall of the community as they were responsible for the breeding of mosquitoes, which transmitted malaria.

From the lakes we went on to Mihintale, legendary land of the Buddha, where there is a large indentation on the side of the hill, supposedly formed by Buddha's foot. The really amazing place in that area is Sygiria, an enormous mushroom-type mass of rock rising several hundred feet out of the jungle. On the rock face below the summit are some of the most famous rock paintings, which are breathtaking. We managed to get to the top going up the flimsiest of wire and rope ladders and walkways. The view from the top was grander than one can imagine.

On the plateau were ancient ruins of a large city which had been defended against attackers for some considerable time (which reminded me of the Jewish defenders of Masada). That night we went for accommodation at the government rest house, where at first a very surly and off-putting rest house keeper tried to dissuade us from staying. However, my doctor friend knew enough about the regulations to deal with that; we even got an extremely good curry although, as rice was in very short supply, we ate chapattis.

The following day we again managed to find some government transport to the next of the most famous jungle cities, Polonnaruwa. Not quite as old as Anuradhapura and Sygiria, but the buildings were not as ruined. There were buddhas of every type seated, standing, lying down, and fertility altars including a very large stone phallus. Again we stayed in the rest house, but this time it was very well run with a keeper who looked after us.

Our next destination was Batticaloa, which is on the east coast some miles south of Trincomalee. We were given a lift to the nearest railway station for a journey that would take us to a station just north of the town. We left the train there and had to walk across a paddy field to the main road where we found ourselves in a very small village. We also found ourselves the focus of considerable attention: apparently two young naval officers were something of a rarity. We tried to explain that we wanted to get to the town, which we realized was still several miles away. It was very, very hot and we were both very, very thirsty. Although nobody either spoke or seemed to understand English, we managed to convey that we needed a drink. Fortunately for us, our request for water was either misunderstood or just ignored. Suddenly a lad was nipping up the nearest coconut palm and throwing down the fruit: two or three swift cuts and the outside thick covering was stripped off, a hole was punctured in the nut and it was presented to me. By gestures we were told to drink and we had the coolest and most refreshing drink I have ever had.

Soon after that, a bus appeared. It seemed as if the entire village surrounded the vehicle and we were courteously escorted on board. In about twenty minutes we were in Batticaloa. To our surprise we found a quite small and almost deserted little town, although it is (or was) the administrative centre of the Eastern Province. We made our way to the *kuchari* (town hall) where we found, it appeared, the entire staff asleep or at any rate dozing. I had been advised by a very Victorian aunt that it was essential, as a newly-qualified professional man, that I should have visiting cards printed. This I had had done (very cheaply). Oddly enough, they were often very useful, and this was the classic occasion. I left a visiting card for the Government Agent, the local senior administrator. We were told to return about an hour later, and when we got back to the offices a messenger was waiting to take us to the GA's residence.

Here we met the most charming and delightful man, a Mr Coomeraswamy, a Tamil. He apologized that he could not put us up for the night, but he had already arranged for us to stay in the rest house. In the meantime we were given afternoon tea in the old colonial fashion. We were also given a guided tour of the town and around, including a visit to a Muslim village (the Tamils are Hindu and the Singhalese Buddhists). He gave us a very good dinner and we were taken to the rest house by the *apu* (a sort of major domo). The next morning the *apu* appeared after we had breakfasted very well, and escorted us to the bus in which we were given front seats for a half-day's journey going south to Badulla. Our journey was not very comfortable: the bus was one of those old-fashioned (even in those days) open types with a canvas hood. When Buddhist priests are travelling on buses, it was the custom for them to be given front seats. Unfortunately for us, there were three of these gentlemen who, because of our being under the care of the GA, had to sit in the row behind. They made their displeasure quite patent: at every slowing down or bump we felt the tips of the inevitable umbrellas in the small of our backs!

We had decided that from Badulla we would go by train up to Bandarawela, which was one of the typical hill stations. We were going to indulge ourselves and stay in a real hotel. This we did. We found transport the next day going south to the famous Dehiluma waterfalls and on to Wellaweya on the southern plain. The rest house there was very run down, but the keeper's wife (?) made a great effort and the place was well cleaned up for us. The next morning we were put on a government vehicle going south to the coast. We had been invited to stay at Hambantota with the Assistant GA, a European. He and his wife lived in the *kuchari*. Our trip was very pleasant, but we were mystified by the frequent road blocks. The GA explained later that it was his idea to try to stop the black marketing of rice, which was very much in short supply and rationed.

At Hambantota we lived the old colonial routine: servants, swimming from the beach, bathrooms, clean towels, playing bridge in the evening after a most civilized dinner and so on. The GA had been in touch with his opposite number in Galle (on the south-western tip of the island). A fairly senior RAF officer was driving back to Colombo after a short leave. We were driven along the coast to Galle and introduced to the officer. We were slightly concerned at his manner, which was casual in the extreme – he hardly spoke to us. We left this lovely old Dutch/Portuguese fortified medieval town in a cloud of dust. Our RAF officer put his foot down on the accelerator and as far as I can remember did not take it off again until we arrived in Colombo some two or three hours later. He drove like Jehu, and God help any villagers who were on the road. Miraculously we did not have an accident. We decided that our 'friend' was drunk.

So much for our kind of 'hitch-hike' round the jungle cities of ancient Ceylon – my sole experience of such a way of travelling.

PETER MACKENZIE-YOUNG

Magic Man of the Himalayas

Like most people, I have always tied to combine business with pleasure on my travels. I cherish one such journey across the Himalayas twelve years ago in which some particularly grim business was followed by an outing of unforgettable pleasure. My business was with the Mujihadeen fighting the Red Army in Afghanistan. They had collected, from the bodies of Russian,soldiers, the most damning evidence so far seen of how low Red Army morale was, and how doomed the whole Soviet operation seemed to be. The evidence was held in scores of letters written home by the dead men which they had not dared to send by field post for fear of censorship. Instead, they were holding them to give to comrades heading back to Russia on leave.

The bundle of letters was duly handed to me. The picture they painted was nightmarish – of soldiers committing suicide, for example, by swallowing the anti-freeze liquid in their vehicle radiators rather than face another day's campaigning against such savage opponents in a savage landscape. Not surprisingly, I now felt the need for some light relief before returning to Islamabad for a flight home. The instruments were at hand, for I had hopefully packed, even for a sombre journey such as this, my travelling fly rod, in case there was any chance of a day's fishing in the snow-fed streams of northern Pakistan.

This proved easier to procure than the letters and I soon found myself being driven up a rock-strewn mountain road – far beyond the lovely Swat valley, where an unpronounceable torrent surged down from the peaks. As

I was travelling with the personal blessing of the then ruler of Pakistan, President Zia ul-Haq, I had with me, apart from our driver, a conducting officer and the manager of the government rest centre where I would be spending the night.

That was not all. By the time we jolted to a stop at the riverside rendez-vous, we were joined by other local notables including a bearded figure who appeared to be the community's official angler. He was holding two rods which caused me instant alarm – not just because they were little better than long wooden poles but; because, dangling at the end of each line (no tapered cast or any such frivolity) was a large metal spinner. Apart from any poaching, if these waters were being officially cleaned out by devices like that, what chance had the artificial fly?

There was one further cause for anxiety. Children were appearing from nowhere as they have a habit of doing in seemingly empty deserts, moun-tains, woods and plains all over the globe. There was soon a ring of little brown faces gathered on the bank to witness this great event of a white stranger fishing. What the stranger did next aroused their excitement to fe-ver pitch. I politely declined the offer of a long pole with its devilish appendage and drew from my canvas bag my Sigma Supra collapsible car-bon-fibre rod (grotesquely called 'Shakespeare'). When unzipped from its plastic shell it is a stumpy affair weighing a bare three ounces and only some eighteen inches long. But after each of the telescoped sections has been ex-tended it becomes a reasonably efficient trout rod nearly seven feet in length.

It was not, however, at a trout rod that the children were gazing – there had been gasps and further widening of the brown eyes as each section had been pulled out, seemingly from the body of its fellow. This, for them, was no longer a case of the white sahib returning to the waters of the Raj which his forefathers had stocked long ago. A necromancer, no less, had come amongst them, who would conjure fish up out of the deep with this magic wand of his. The white sahib grew even more anxious as the chattering died away into deep silence.

The pre-selected spot for his conjuring trick was an elbow of the bank where the green-grey water ran more quietly than out on the gushing mid-stream. But the current here was still too swift for the dry-flies of our English chalk-streams (half a dozen patterns of which always travel with me). I made up a duo of wet flies last used on our Highland rivers or the streams of the Austrian alps – a Bloody Butcher with a Peter Ross on the dropper. (More looks of astonishment: was this magician actually ordering insects to obey him?)

Then, before the casting, some fervent prayers for results: to the shades of Isaak Walton; of my venerable Piscatorial Society (founded the year before Queen Victoria came to the throne); of anyone else I could think of – though I am ashamed to say, I forget St Peter himself. Between us, we simply couldn't let this particular audience down.

The first two casts produced nothing, but I felt only the faintest twitch of puzzlement behind me. The children probably assumed that the magician was only waving his wand, not using it. It would now be for real. So, mercifully, it was.

I had noticed, at the far end of the elbow, a quiet eddy where any sensible trout who had survived these lures would be resting. As the cast dragged for the very first time across that spot there came again that sensation which never ceases to thrill, however many hundreds of times you have felt it – sudden contact with a hidden creature, who lives in another element. A lively trout I judged to be about a pound in weight had taken the tail fly fair and square. A few minutes later and he was in the official angler's net, which was almost as long as his pole. A few more casts and his younger brother had joined him on the bank. There was a buzz of delight all around me.

But somehow this had to be brought to all end. I felt myself – to put it mildly – unqualified to enact a Himalayan version of the loaves and fishes. Moreover, I just *knew* that there were no more trout in that river elbow. Presenting the catch to the boys, I asked them in return to bring me some tea. They scampered away to the nearby row of huts where they lived. When they came back with the jug, my Sigma Supra had disappeared inside itself. All was packed away; the performance was over. I took my leave, after distributing the few boiled sweets I carried in my pocket.

So Pakistan became the twenty-second country in the world where it had been my fortune to catch trout. There was, however, a small price to pay. It must have been the untreated milk they had poured into that offering of tea. I needed a lot of Immodium to get me though the next twenty-four hours at the guest house.

GORDON BROOK-SHEPHERD

Volcanoes

I suppose I shouldn't have been all that surprised when, shortly before noon one Philippine morning, and somewhere about a mile and a half up on the side of a volcano, both of my guides upped sticks, announced they were quitting, and ran away.

It was getting pretty frigid this close to the summit of Mt Mayon, and like most Filipinos the guides – one of whom confessed to having gone on a bender the night before, drinking-locally-made gin until dawn – were quite unused to cold. Besides, both men were soaked to the skin, the gales were plainly terrifying them, the black cliffs were rain-slick and extremely vertiginous, and the volcano was just then starting to emit ominous (but as it happens, quite routine) puffs of sulphurous gas.

So when Elmer, the previous night's party animal, cried out to me, 'Sir, we are both dying here!', began shivering and chattering his teeth uncontrollably with what looked like gin-induced hypothermia, and started to scamper back down the mountainside, I was dismayed – but I was not altogether astonished. No sticking power, I muttered darkly, along with one or two other choice imprecations, and then turned back up towards the top, teeth set into what really was a most inconvenient, unexpected and damnably cold gale.

Mt Mayon is said to be the most perfectly conical volcano in creation, a classic of its kind, a type specimen of the volcanic art. It has a base that is a flawless circle, 80 miles around, and from which it rises with a spare and unwavering elegance to a point that stands eight thousand feet above the sea. The angle of repose of its andesite ledges is a gem of geologic symmetry. A good map will show its contours as a series of perfect concentric circles, like a spider's web, a dartboard, an archer's boss.

From afar the sight is unforgettable, especially if the weather is fine, the tropical sky a deep clear blue. Dark green jungles cloak the volcano's lower slopes; temperate forests, grasses and bamboos in a range of paler shades limn its upper reaches; black and smoking rocks, streaked yellow with sulphur, are then riveted onto its final few hundred feet. The mountain towers over the surrounding rice paddies and corn fields and the grazing caribou, and mariners who sail across the Pacific into the Gulf of Albay say they can see its peak from a hundred miles and more. Mayon is a landmark, a source of much pride to the villagers and townspeople above whom it towers; and though it steams fitfully, and has an unfinished look to it in consequence, it remains, in fair weather or foul, breathtaking in its simple perfection.

Yet Mt Mayon – its name comes from the Bicol dialect-word for *beautiful* – is also terribly dangerous. Not because it is difficult to climb, though its cliffs and water-slicked rocks can injure badly those who are foolish enough to try: but because it has the irritating habit of exploding, prodigiously and without warning. It last did so in 1993: and more than seventy farmers tending their tomato plants inside a deep ravine known as the Bonga Gully were killed.

My guide said he had been on the mountain that day, trying in vain to lead three Germans and an Israeli to the top. He shuddered theatrically at the memory. 'All four of them got away, by running,' he warned me, the day before our own climb. 'But then I saw other men, the farmers, who were caught in a hot wind. They were *roasted* dead, like chickens on a spit. They had no chance. The hot wind can go faster than any man, you know. It is quite silent. It just races down and *cooks* people. They were' – and I swear at this point he seemed to lick his lips – '*done to a crisp.*'

All of the world's landscape is, ultimately, the product of geology. That much is almost too obvious to state. The type of rocks, their ages, the way each sits in relation to its heights – all of these simple facts determine as absolutes the shape of the land, what crops and foliage grow on it, what creatures live on it, and exactly how. Geology, like mathematics, is one of the core realities of the universe, its laws underlying all that we do and are.

What is a little less apparent, though, is that the earth's surface comes in two essential forms.

There is first the landscape that has been created by old geology, where the forces of creation are long dead, where the landforms are the product of events that happened in the very distant past, and where no new events seem likely. And then, second, there is the scenery that comes from new geology, landscape that shows that the planet is still in the throes of creation, where the geology is still alive and at work, where the earth can still be seen to be flexing its muscles.

By muscles, one means of course essentially two things – earthquakes, and volcanoes. The two almost casually destructive means by which the earth demonstrates its ultimate mastery over everything that lives upon it.

There are 1,300 potentially active volcanoes in the world. A glance at a good map will show that most of them, by far, are ranged around the long edge of Pacific Ocean. And while not all of these volcanoes have yet been explored and analyzed and classified in detail, and while there is still no foolproof way of telling which of them is going to erupt, how impressively, and when, a simple axiom holds good: that while around the edge of the Pacific there is such scenery and grandeur as to make the heart stop, all of this beauty and magnificence conceals a terrible and, what's worse, a quite unpredictable danger.

For where live geology reigns, dreadful things can happen. Japan's Mt Fuji, for example, is inexpressibly lovely – but the forces that made it so also devastated the nearby city of Kobe three years ago. San Francisco charms everyone who visits – and yet what made all the pretty hills is the selfsame geology that wrecked the city in 1906, and will do so again in due course. And the perfect symmetry of Mt Mayon lulls onlookers into forgetting that the lava flows and gas streams that made it so perfectly symmetrical can roast a man to death in ten seconds flat. Man dies in places like this because, once in a while, the earth chooses to remind us that it is still very much alive.

And in the main, the world appears to come most dramatically alive where the geology is newest, where the volcanoes and quakes are most numerous – around the long and ragged edge of the Pacific Ocean.

More specifically still: all of the world's truly great volcanoes exist and have long existed, and most of the true seismic and tectonic spectaculars take place and have taken place in Asia. The most stupendous of seismic events are not merely a phenomenon of the entire Pacific Rim, are not evenly sited along the so-called Ring of Fire. They are concentrated on the Rim's western side, on its Asian arc. They lie along the chain of island-states that begin with Sumatra in the tropical Indonesian west, pass via the seismically active islands of the Philippines (where there are 21 big active volcanoes) and end in Hokkaido in the frigid Japanese north.

More than anywhere else on earth, these five thousand miles of islands are where beauty and the beast most dramatically coexist – where one may see the most breathtaking scenery, and at the same time enjoy, suffer or derive vicarious pleasure from risking that something – and who knows what? who knows when? – may happen. One may see the loveliest and most symmetrical volcanoes in the world there – and at the same time risk, as Elmer's German and Israeli partners risked, the possibility of being bombarded by hot boulders, being swept into a newly torn crevasses, being licked by gusts of flame, drowned in lava, or sucked up by some terrible pyroclastic wind, roasted and *done to a crisp*.

Yet these days none of this seems to be much of a deterrent. Quite the reverse, in fact. As ever more travellers continue to weary, as they say they do, of the more conventional destinations, so volcanoes, at least in Asia, appear to be nudging their way into becoming some new kind of travel business. And there is also a new mood developing towards this kind of mountain, a new appreciation that has spawned a rash of books that argue that volcanoes are ultimately benevolent, giving us fertile soils and moisture, and doing far more good than their destructive, fearsome reputation deserves. Volcanoes are hero-mountains, goes the new thinking; they should not be shunned, so much as they should become the subjects of pilgrimage and reverence.

It is not an entirely new phenomenon. People have long been fascinated, if wary. You could always find a boatman to row you out to clamber up the remains of the great volcano of Krakatoa, in Java (though a visitor was killed there two years ago); or you could hire a strong young boy to take to you up Mt Kinabalu, on Borneo. There have always been men like Elmer, fit and wiry-legged fellows who hung out at the local bars near the big exploding hills, ever-available to anyone who wanted to come and climb.

But now the scale of the business and the personalities involved have changed. A new band of entrepreneurs appear to be springing up, enthusiasts who believe that volcanoes can offer the kind of challenge and spectacle that will lure even the most jaded of westerners will reivigorate both the body and the spirit.

A former US Air Force maintenance man by the name of Rusty Kitchin is one of this new breed – a man who is currently betting that today's travellers are made of stern enough stuff to be beguiled by all the combination of beauty and danger. He believes that there are enough sensible and thoughtful new adventurers who will figure that the risk of personal catastrophe is measurably small, and a risk that will in any case be well offset by the experience of seeing one of these great mountains first hand.

So he has settled in the Philippines, and is among the first to open a small guiding company – leading people to the top of what is perhaps Asia's most notoriously dangerous volcano: Mt Pinatubo.

When I arrived in the Philippines I had been planning simply to try to reach the top of Mt Mayon – it is the sort of breathtakingly beautiful peak that, once seen (as in a small black-and-white snapshot in Volume 6 of the *Britannica*) quite simply demands to be climbed. But for reasons I shall explain I had long also held a good reason for wanting to climb Mt Pinatubo too. So when I saw Rusty's advertisement in a Manila magazine, it seemed a fair idea, as I wasn't in a great hurry, to try his mountain as an appetizer. I tracked him down in the lobby of Swagman Hotel in that fleabite of a town called Angeles City, handed over a small fee for his services and for those of a couple of porters, and at dawn the next day, we set off.

'We're off to see the belly of the beast,' he said jauntily, as we swung onto a track leading up the lower slopes. 'Six hours, and you'll be able to have a swim in it.'

It had been seven years since I had last seen the mountain. I was then on the island of Cebu, in the central Philippines, and had been quite hopelessly marooned. Not that my plight won me much sympathy: the sun was shining, the sea was blue, the sand was soft, coconuts were plentiful and it is said that Cebuanas, who play sweet music on their locally-made guitars, are the most beautiful women in creation. None of this much mattered: I couldn't get away as all the planes were grounded and all the airports closed, because the hitherto little-regarded volcano of Mt Pinatubo had suddenly, and unexpectedly erupted – the first time for six centuries.

For a while Pinatubo became the most notorious volcano on earth. The images of its eruption remain – of great towering clouds of ash and smoke, fifteen miles high, billowing noiseless and fatal above the rice paddies of Luzon. Of villages smothered in tons of thick grey mud. Of jet fighters from America parked uselessly at Clark Air Base, their engines clogged with dust. And indeed the air base has long since closed: the runways stand empty now, deserted relics of both a long cold war and that short hot summer of 1991.

Mt Pinatubo had a thousand feet blown off its summit back then, as if a crude giant had sheared it off with egg-scissors. Huge flows of mud and ash and hot water known as lahars had cascaded down the flanks of the range, and had spread unchecked for dozens of miles. Scores of villages were submerged, for ever; hundreds died; a whole landscape was changed and ruined.

We walked first across the strange moonscape of one of these lahar flows, now frozen into peaks of compressed ash, chalk-white and edged with new grass. The cliffs are a hundred feet high, and razor-edged. The flow forms a huge impenetrable maze that only Rusty and his local Filipino guides know how to navigate: I felt that if by ill-fortune I was stranded here, I'd never get out. Only the course of an old river, the O'Donnell, suggests an entryway: we trudged up it, backing and weaving past immense towers of ash, for hours.

Then we came into a region of more substantial rock, hard and dark and volcanic, not the compressed dust of before. We were on the flanks of the mountain proper, clambering through the ancestral country-rock. We kept on climbing up a long canyon, passing half a mile high, an occasional cooling breeze swept down from the summit. There were clouds swirling across the tops, and once in a while a shower, and when the view improved we could see a rainbow over the buildings of the air base below.

We passed a sweet spring, then another of hot sour water that steamed and left a crust of chemicals along its bank. There was a small grove of trees, a patch of blue flowers, and then the canyon closed in – but only for a while, because suddenly the vista opened up and we found ourselves standing on the lip of the crater lake itself – a lake so new it appears on no map, nor has a name. Once this had been a thousand feet higher, the dome of the mountaintop: but it had been blown off, like a hat in a gale, and the lake is what remains in its place.

We clambered cautiously down a sheer cliff-face towards a dark sand beach, and stepped gingerly into the water. It was hot – not scalding, but like a pleasant bath. It was rich with chemicals, too, and had a faint but luminous green tinge. We swam in it: the solutes buoy one up, like the Dead Sea. My skin turned a strange colour for a while, but seemed to come to no obvious harm.

Some days before, two of Rusty's porters had obligingly lugged an in-flatable canoe up the track, and within moments I was out on the lake on it, paddling furiously for the far side. I wanted to go where I could see a sort of suture-line, with clouds of steam venting from the shore. As I paddled closer to it the water became hotter and hotter, until it was far too hot to touch, and the canoe started to melt, and sag in an alarmingly rubbery way. Close to the steam vents which now roared deafeningly the water was actually boiling, and the little craft bucked and tossed as though it was in a kettle. Small gobbets of sulphur were spat into the air, and before long the bow glistened with bright yellow crystals.

And then there came a deafening crack from up ahead, and a massive slab of black cliff dislodged itself, as though the mountain had shrugged its shoul-der: a vast rain of rock plunged into the lake, frothing the surface, and setting the canoe rocking even more alarmingly. Moreover the heat was now mak-ing the boat sag more dangerously, and my seat was uncomfortable and scalding, and what with the noise and the choking air, it seemed prudent to paddle away, and back to cooler, quieter, calmer waters.

Probably bottomless, a visiting geologist said of the lake. *One of the en-trances to hell*, said Rusty, more poetically. He and his porters insisted over lunch (cheeseburgers, grilled on a campfire, and a bottle or two of still-cold

San Miguel) they'll make a business out of bringing travellers to this most extraordinary of sights. 'You feel like one in a million up here,' he said. 'I mean, whoever else comes up to see a green and boiling lake, to paddle through a mess of steam jets, to watch a whole side of a cliff crash down a thousand feet?'

But that, I said, is just the problem. The volcano hissing and crumbling and steaming away in the background has to be one of the most powerful reminders of the old caution that Man Proposes, but God Disposes. 'Sure,' said Rusty, ever the optimist. 'But so long as He carries on disposing nicely, we'll be okay. I have faith in Him, you know. You have to, sitting under a volcano.'

The next day, after taking a perfunctory side trip to what is said to be the world's smallest volcano, the island-in-a-lake-in-an-island-in-a-lake complex known as Mt Taal (and where a spectacular hydrovolcanic eruption in 1965 killed three hundred) I flew on down to Legazpi City, in southern Luzon, to make my long-awaited attempt on Mayon. I had been there three times before in the previous decade: twice we started too late to complete the climb in a day, once we were beaten back by bad weather. This, I reckoned, was my last chance.

The pilot took a long and lazy descent around the mountain, spiralling down from the summit over the slopes where we would be struggling the next day. The evening was still and clear with not a cloud in sight: the great mountain cast a five mile shadow over the rice fields, and at the top coughed yellow smoke gently from what seemed from this height a small, untidy throat, like a hungry fledgling's. As we landed the mountain turned purple in the twilight, and a small shower of sparks danced at the summit, reminding us that it was very much alive. It was then that Elmer told me of the bodies he had seen and of his terrified charges, running ahead of the pyroclastic gales.

We rose at four, and drove through pitch darkness to the hut where we collected up our porters – two men who emerged blinking and sleepy, smoking hand-rolled cigarettes, and they hefted our bags onto their backs. Like the extremely hung-over Elmer, they wore plastic thongs on their feet; they had on ragged shorts and tee-shirts. It was cold just before dawn, and I felt

I needed my Patagonia fleece.

The guidebooks insist it takes almost eleven hours to make the summit – two and a half to Camp One, four to Camp Two, a further four to the final ridge. But we must have been a great deal fitter than the average guidebook reader, since it was still half-dark by the time we emerged from the jungles at the first camp: we had taken no more than ninety minutes.

But what we saw ahead was dismaying: an anvil-shaped mass of cloud was scudding out of the east, blotting out the rising sun, and, worst of all, spreading itself like a skirt over the lower slopes of the mountain. The gullies and ravines ahead began to fill up with a thick mist, and from time to time gusts of wind blew patters of rain down – cooling us after our hearty pre-breakfast walk, which was nice enough – but ominous.

We stopped for ten minutes, ate mangoes and chunks of bread from a new loaf, and drank noisily from a stream. Then we set off again, up one of the great radial gullies that reach down from the summit – a mile-long pathway of cliffs and river-smoothed andesite that sloped upwards at an ever-increasing angle.

It was murder to climb – slippery, steep, wet, deceptively long. Once in a while the guides took us into the forest, clapping their hands vigorously to keep away snakes: on the whole, however, it was just a constant slog upwards, wet, bruising, wearying.

We made Camp Two after a further two hours – we were well ahead of the plan, having taken a total of three hours and thirty minutes to achieve what the book insisted would take six. I was hot – my fleece went into the rucksack – and I drank gallons of water while talking to the one inhabitant of the Camp, a young dentist from Manila who was climbing with her boyfriend. 'But I kept falling and crying,' she said. 'In the end he left me behind. He ought to be up there.' She jerked her hand up towards a grey mass of cloud, from where I could hear the ominous sounds of a rising gale. The guides were looking shifty, I thought, and not at all happy.

The going above Camp Two became steadily worse and worse – ever more cliffs, ever more steep gullies, rocks made ever more slippery by the rains. And then the smell of sulphur started to pervade everything, and there were strange yellow-rimmed cliffs which, if you peered over, seemed the edge of a giant nothingness. 'Crater.' said Elmer, helpfully, and I kept well away from the side.

He was shivering, I noticed. And then he asked me to take the bag. It was getting too heavy. It was then that he told me about the party the night before.

To his credit, he and his men soldiered on for another half hour, up another three hundred feet. We passed the dentist's boyfriend, and his companion, a young man from Belgium, both on their way down, the look of failure about them. 'Too windy up there,' one shouted. 'Too dangerous. And we felt movement. A rocking, a bucking in the ground. As if it was going to explode.'

I gulped, but trudged on. By the time we reached the part where the slope became truly steep, where the ground became friable and broken, the wind was howling and knocking us flat each time we emerged from behind a sheltering wall of rock By the time we were at the point where the book said 'it is most advisable to be roped together', the remaining guides had clearly had enough. They conferred in whispered Tagalog and then turned away.

'What's happening?' I cried into the gale. 'Sir, we are dying here!' shouted Elmer. He was soaked and shivering, and looked terribly frightened. 'Eruption?' I shouted. 'No sir,' he replied. 'Just too dangerous. We wait below. You go on.'

And so we did, painfully, one handhold after another, one foot after another, hiding below the cliff edge every few moments for shelter. And slowly like a great grey tombstone, so the summit ridge eventually appeared out of the gloom, and we found our way to its centre, keeping well away from the edges and from a certain unpleasant death in that sulphur-edged crater.

A gust blew me, staggering, to the very lip, and I had a momentary feeling of vertigo, staring down into the glowing heart of the volcano. But I recovered, and, with the fumes now half choking me, and the gale buffeting me, I found myself eventually at the narrowest point of the ridge, a precarious and tiny black boulder from where all the rock faces and surfaces at long last pointed down.

It was eleven thirty in the morning. To reach the summit, at 7,943 feet, had taken five and three quarter hours. There was no view, nothing of which to take a photograph, no reason at all to linger. So we simply shook hands, turned back the way we came and, slipping and sliding and falling until were bruised and cut and bleeding, arrived back at the top Camp at two.

The guides were both there, hiding in a cave. Scared stiff, but not dead. Scared of my reaction, I suspect, and of the thought that I might not pay them. Elmer had taken my Patagonia jacket from my bag. He was also smoking a joint. He looked happier.

We shook hands. 'Congratulations,' he said. 'You were much too fast. But you did it. You climbed Mayon. Not many can say so.'

Then there came a rumbling from above, and a strange shaking deep in the ground, as though some giant was stirring in his sleep, turning over, grunting, acting restless. It was time to head down, I thought. We marched off, as fast as it was responsible to do. The sun came out. We were off the lower slopes by five, and then taking a cold San Miguel at the Trinidad Hotel in Legazpi by the time that twilight fell, and turned to dark.

Next morning the air was clear and still once more, and the mountain gleamed in the morning sun. There was not a cloud in sight – and other than a slight wisp of yellowish smoke drifting from the very summit, no indication that the mountain was anything other than it looked – serene, perfect, beautiful. The hotel receptionist, waiting for my credit card to clear, said she expected it would erupt again next year. 'But you really never can tell.' she said. 'That's what makes living in the Philippines so interesting .

SIMON WINCHESTER

Berlin: East and West 1973–75

After Rome, East Berlin was a shock. I knew something about the other East European countries, having visited them and dealt at the Foreign and Commonwealth Office with their affairs before going to Italy. But East Germany was always handled by the Department responsible for the Federal Republic. It is true that it had dawned on me that, with my background and a knowledge of German, I might be regarded as a candidate to be our first *chargé d'affaires* in East Berlin. I had put this thought aside, thinking that I could rely on the FCO to reject any such logical idea. And, unwisely as it turned out, I had taken the trouble to emphasize in London that I was happy in Rome and did not want to move. Whether or not as a result of that rash act, within weeks of returning to Rome from holiday, I was put on notice to go to Berlin to establish our Embassy to the German Democratic Republic.

My wife and I set off for East Berlin in a rather aged Ford car whose reliability was doubtful but which did not in the event let us down. It was the tail end of the winter of 1973 and we travelled by way of Hamburg. There was a cold and penetrating drizzle which did nothing to improve the atmosphere of that time of year.

The first sign of the realities in East Berlin was our arrival, soon after leaving Hamburg, at the border between the two Germanies which we were to cross at Horst. We drove between a series of high barbed wire fences until we were stopped in front of a large pair of armoured gates. Here we were told to get out of the car and sent into a heavily guarded waiting room, empty except for two soldiers and a member of the Volkspolizei (People's Police). The three of these watched us from a distance, as though we were a new and unwelcome species of the human race. Our passports were taken and we settled down to wait. So far the GDR had lived up to its reputation. The elaborate frontier system with its implications for the fate of any attempt by the inhabitants of East Germany to escape or visit the West without authority was in line with all our preliminary briefing. The same was true of the attitude of the officials.

At last, after about an hour and a half, our passports were returned, we were escorted back to our car, which had no doubt been thoroughly examined, and given instructions about driving through the frontier post before we reached the road for Berlin. It was quite clear that the officials knew exactly who we were; we were not asked any questions about the purpose of our journey. The barricades with their dim lighting together with the atmosphere of disapproval and the filthy weather created a feeling of gloom, not to say foreboding, though everything was done with what seemed to be correct and conscientious attention to detail.

We drove on through dimly lit villages and on generally poor quality, often cobbled, roads, our morale a few points lower than when we set off. We reached Berlin some two hours later in the dark. There we were very pleased to find Jimmy Reeve, the Commercial Counsellor who had gone ahead and who showed us into the Unter den Linden Hotel where we were to spend a couple of months until our house in south Berlin (Karlshorst) was ready.

I have described something of our impressions on the way to Berlin to show the contrast between the prosperous and open Federal Republic and the Communist regime next door whose conduct often seemed to demonstrate nervousness and a lack of self assurance. The East Germans had so far only dealt with diplomatic representatives of neutral countries, most of them Arabs. They had been largely isolated from the West, except for carefully controlled contacts allowed under the Four Power agreement to members of German families split by the division of Germany after the Second World War. Even their German language had evolved differently from that of the West Germans. The latter had taken over a good number of English, French and other western words and expressions. The East Germans spoke a language which could be described as old fashioned or classical, with a very few words borrowed from Russian or Slav sources.

This, then, was the world in which we found ourselves. As representatives of one of the Four Powers occupying Berlin we had no difficulty in moving between the eastern and western sectors, though we had to observe rules dictated by the fact that the Russians and East Germans were in control of the check points.

I spent a few days finding my way around Berlin and viewing the premises allocated to us for the offices of our Embassy. These were located on two floors above a dress shop opposite the massive Russian Embassy on the Unter den Linden. I was then given an appointment to call at the Foreign Ministry on a gentleman described as a Deputy Foreign Minister. Against the background which I have described I did not expect much from my first interview with a senior East German. It was immediately clear that, whatever his title, he was no more than a senior bureaucrat. His relief at being able to talk German to me was almost tangible. After I had handed over the official confirmation that I was acting as *chargé d'affaires* pending the arrival of an Ambassador, we had some relatively relaxed conversation and I asked him about the problems facing the GDR. He replied that he preferred not to answer this directly but to tell me a short story.

There was, he said, a citizen of the GDR walking in the woods near Berlin who came upon two dwarfs. He asked the first of these who they were and got the answer 'Snow White and the seven dwarfs'. He asked where the others were and was told 'shortage of personnel'. It was explained to me that this was a major problem causing the East Germans to import labour from other Warsaw Pact countries.

This interview, with an East German bureaucrat whom I had never met before, seemed to suggest that I was quite wrong about the calibre of officials at this level and to promise useful discussions in the future. There was also a hint of a lurking, if heavy, sense of humour. The circumstances of the arrival of our pointer dog (Toby) who had waited in Rome until we had settled in a house seemed to confirm the latter.

Toby flew into Tempelhof Airport in West Berlin. There were virtually no formalities and we soon drove back to the checkpoint, Toby's nose protruding from the back window of the car. The normal procedure at checkpoints, worked out to prevent any unwitting violation of the Western Powers' position was for us to keep our windows shut and show through them the cards with which the British Military Government had issued us as representatives of one of the Four Powers. On this occasion there was a small difference. A large gorilla of a man (an East German policeman) who had become familiar with our frequent crossings waved us down and came across to Toby's window. He looked into the car and, with a broad grin, said '*Wo ist sein Pass?*' In the same spirit we said '*Er hat's vergessen*'. Laughing, the guard waved us on. So Toby arrived in East Berlin with no documents, and lived there for nearly two years without any. There was never any difficulty over his subsequent journeys through the checkpoint.

There are other episodes which demonstrate something of the apparently contradictory atmosphere. Perhaps our visit *en famille* to the border with Czechoslovakia where the Tatra mountains provide an opportunity for ski-ing is a good example. We made the arrangements through an East German member of the Embassy staff who had been allocated to us and was generally regarded as having 'special' duties. All went smoothly, We were accommodated in a hostel which we gathered was used by Trade Union parties when on holiday. No food beyond breakfast was provided so on arrival we went out to a restaurant. This was packed, though places were somehow found for us and we were watched with apparent fascination by the other diners.

About half way through the meal a bottle of wine which we had not ordered arrived at our table. The waiter indicated a gentleman on the other side of the room as the donor and shortly afterwards he came across. He explained that he had sent the wine to welcome us and immediately asked who we were and why we had come to this area. He expressed no concern when we explained that we were British representatives from the newly established British Embassy. The reaction was to invite us to spend our next visit in his house. He was only the first. We ended with plenty of invitations and bottles. The problem was to decide whether those concerned were genuinely pleased to see us or whether they had some less attractive motive. Our judgement at the time was that they were genuine. We assumed that the strict rules preventing unauthorized contact between individuals and foreigners, of which we subsequently obtained a copy, had not yet reached this area. They did not know about the prescribed penalties for breaking these rules. We were after all the first Westerners they had seen since the Second World War.

Some of our hopes for a dialogue came true, but conversations were always carefully defined and limited, When we tried to entertain East German officials whom we had met we could never be sure who would actually come if the invitation was accepted. They clearly saw attending a western party as a duty to be carried out on a rota, though another motive was presumably to prevent the development of a close relationship. And there was always the depressing presence of the Wall along which, accompanied by the smell and dust of brown coal, a local product widely used for heating, I drove every day to the Embassy.

There was also what sometimes felt like an unspoken threat. At this time the East Germans' short-term aim was to secure full and visible recognition. They wanted our Ambassador to come as a senior representative of one of the Four Powers. His presence, and that of the Americans and French would be seen as bolstering the success of the GDR as an independent state. This despite the fact that GDR ministers were summoned to his Embassy by my Soviet colleague rather than his calling at the Foreign Ministry; and the presence of some half a million Russian troops stationed near the West German frontier with their headquarters close to our house in Karlshorst.

As the chargé d'affaires I was seen as the obstacle to the arrival of the Ambassador. The tactic they employed was minor intimidation or irritation. It was disconcerting to find that what could be interpreted as my 'misdemeanours' were reported to the Foreign Office by the East German Embassy in London. Once I bumped a car which stopped suddenly; more seriously I and other western representatives failed to stand up quickly enough when Willi Stoph, the Prime Minister, came into a gathering to celebrate the anniversary of the GDR. There were other trivial incidents. The Foreign Office loyally supported me but East German motives were clear.

There were no signs of poverty in East Germany. The people were well fed and clothed, even if their diet was boring and the clothes pretty uniform. And essentials could be acquired, though not always regularly, from the local equivalent of a supermarket. But equally there were few if any signs of enthusiasm for the way of life. We met the parents of a teenager who had been made ill by being compelled to train beyond her ability in order to swim for the GDR. Our neighbours opposite queued for hours to buy us cherries to greet our arrival in our newly reconstructed house, because, as they put it, we should otherwise miss the only opportunity of such luxury. And they told us, when we grew to know them better, that there was widespread pilfering from factories of materials and tools for maintaining houses and machinery. It took upwards of two years' salary to buy a car such as the outdated Trabant which spewed out pollution in the form of black smoke from its exhaust. In any case you had to put your name down for a car three years before you stood a chance of acquiring one.

Behind it all stood the Wall built in 1961 to stem the flow to the West of trained and qualified men and women. There were a number of occasions during our time when such would-be emigrants were shot trying to get through the minefields and over the Wall to West Berlin.

Indeed we were brought up against this aspect of life when late one night there was a knock on our door. Outside stood a young couple, the woman holding a baby of a few months. Very quietly they gestured towards the inside of the house. This was the dilemma which I had hoped never to encounter. It was a very dark and cold night and I did not feel able to turn them away. On the other hand I knew that the penalties if we were caught harbouring East Germans trying to escape to the West would be disastrous for them and very serious indeed for us. I was also conscious that at least some of the rooms in the house were bugged. If we spoke in normal tones we ran a good chance of being overheard by the East German authorities.

In the event they explained in whispers that they were indeed hoping to cross the Wall and someone had indicated our house as containing foreign diplomats and therefore safe. They needed somewhere to rest for the night. They would be gone at crack of dawn and no-one need know that they had stayed with us.

What should we do? We took a quick decision. They stayed and had disappeared when we got up next morning. We subsequently heard that they had somehow managed to get away. We heard no more but, after that experience, it was hard to take an objective view of the German Democratic Republic.

PEREGRINE RHODES

A Colonial Relic

In the early 1980s, I was about to travel with a colleague from London to Tokyo when I read in *The Times* that the Raffles Hotel in Singapore was to be demolished by its Chinese owners to make way for a nice modern building. At that time there were no direct flights to Tokyo and the custom was to divide the long journey with a stop-over, usually in Hong Kong. It seemed important to see the Imperial relic before it was too late, so Peter and I switched flights so as to stop for twenty-four hours in Singapore.

Our arrival at Changi Airport alerted us immediately to the modernization of the city-state: a huge modern terminal, far too big for the volume of passengers at that time. On the journey into town we noticed few reminders of its historic rôle as a bastion of the British Empire; the handsome high rises along tree-lined boulevards could easily have passed for San Diego, California.

However, Raffles Hotel had not yet changed – long low timber buildings, painted white and surrounded by grass and palm trees. Many of the rooms and suites bore the names of celebrated writers who had stayed there – Maugham, Coward and Conrad, for example. My room was about the size and shape of a ballroom with only one modern improvement, a small and noisy air-conditioning unit set into a distant window and making little difference to the hot and humid air.

Peter and I met at the Long Bar to sample the Singapore gin sling on the very spot where it was invented. The bar was indeed long and, apart from us, empty. We thought we should see something of Chinatown, then as much under threat as the Raffles itself, and rather unwisely chose to travel thither by bicycle rickshaw, not the ideal vehicle for a six-lane highway in the rush-hour. After an alarming journey, we arrived at what remained of Chinatown, just in time it seemed. Even at 8 p.m. on a Saturday evening, the demolition continued. In another couple of days there would be nothing left.

Back at Raffles, we settled into the vast dining room as the only customers.

In steamy heat we surveyed menus of impressive size and stiffness, and read with growing amazement a roll-call of the classic dishes of Imperial Britain: Mulligatawny Soup, Brown Windsor Soup, Mock Turtle, Lancashire Hotpot, Irish Stew, Steak and Kidney Pudding, Boiled Beef and Carrots, Roly Poly Pudding, Spotted Dick, Rice Pudding and Apple Turnover, followed by Welsh Rarebit. We were aghast.

What we did not know was that Raffles Hotel was traditionally the last stop for an English rubber planter on his way up country, or the first stop some months or even years later on his way home to England. Ideally the planter would be played by Joss Acland, with dialogue by Somerset Maugham.

'Ahem.' Our Chinese waiter thought we were taking too long over our choice. Indeed we were, as we could find nothing appropriate to the tropical heat.

'Have you no local specialities?' I ventured.

'Certainly not,' was the proud reply.

At least there was one corner of Singapore which had remained forever England.

MICHAEL ALLEN

The Yangtse Incident

I joined the Royal Navy from Eton in 1944 and after midshipman's time and training courses I was appointed in 1948 Acting Sub-Lieutenant of HMS *Concord* on the China station. Within a few months of my joining, the 'Yangtse Incident', as it came to be known, took place.

The frigate, HMS *Amethyst*, while on passage up the Yangtse river on a routine visit to Nanking, was fired on by guns of the Chinese Peoples' Liberation Army on 20 April 1949, and driven ashore, despite the fact that prior clearance had been granted. There was extensive damage to the ship and heavy casualties, including the commanding officer who subsequently died of his wounds; his place was taken by Lieutenant Commander J S Kerans, the Assistant Naval Attaché from Nanking. Gallant attempts at rescue by HMS *Consort* (destroyer) and then by HMS London (cruiser) and HMS *Black Swan* (frigate) incurred further casualties and damage, but were unsuccessful. HMS *Amethyst* was in effect impounded with about half her original ship's company by the Communists, who refused to grant her safe passage down river without an admission of blame – which was, of course, untrue and unacceptable. So Kerans, after many vicissitudes and seeing no other way out of this impasse and concerned, *inter alia*, about his dwindling supplies of food and fuel, decided to break out on the night of 30 July.

HMS *Concord* was acting as a guard ship on station near the Yangtse Kiang light vessel at the mouth of the river, the limit of territorial waters. We were hoping that HMS *Amethyst* might have tried to escape during typhoon Gloria a few days earlier, but this was not to be.

However, on the evening of 30 July, the petty officer telegraphist asked me to come down to the wireless office as he had a high priority signal in 'officers only' cipher. It was in fact notification that Kerans would attempt to break out that night. For a very brief period I was the only person on board who knew this but, of course, I immediately informed my captain who sent for the first lieutenant and engineer officer. We weighed anchor, darkened ship and went to action stations, and the captain informed the ship's company. We were instructed to go up river to aid the *Amethyst* as needed and, if necessary, return the fire of the Woosun forts – which in the event proved unnecessary. However, as we proceeded up river at about eighteen knots, I personally did not have much time to worry about all this, being involved with my navigational duties with somewhat inadequate Chinese charts, constantly shifting sandbanks and many buoys unlit and several actually missing. Needless to say, the echo-sounder was kept working continuously.

Meanwhile, *Amethyst*, with Communist river-lights rigged (green over red), slipped her cable soon after 2200 and followed a fortuitously passing merchant ship down river, but she increased to full speed and passed her about a quarter of an hour later, at the same time making smoke and weaving to confuse the flares and firing from the shore. The merchant ship, *Kiang Ling Liberation*, was fired on by the Communists and ran aground. Just before 0300 Kerans signalled 'one hundred up' – less than fifty more miles to go. We did not know that she had rammed a junk and had a brush with a patrol boat and been fired on from the shore.

Concord was waiting off Woosun and in due course picked her up on radar and then visually as dawn broke: it was one of the most moving moments of my life. We tried to steam past her and cheer but the shallow waters precluded this; then we tried to go alongside her but the swell was too great. So we took her to a nearby island anchorage and supplied her with fuel and food, etc, and a steaming party of a watch-keeping officer and several key ratings. That evening we started to lead her 'home' to Hong Kong but, to our disgust, our senior officer, Captain D8 in HMS *Cossack*, arrived from Japan and took over, instructing us to fuel at sea and return to station off the Yangtse entrance.

Three things remain in my mind of that momentous night. First, I shall always remember *Amethyst*'s triumphant signal:

'HAVE REJOINED THE FLEET SOUTH OF WOOSUNG. NO DAMAGE OR CASUALTIES. GOD SAVE THE KING.'

Second, the engineer officer, who was in fact only a few years older than me but as a middle rank Lieutenant(E) seemed vastly senior to an Acting Sub-Lieutenant, came up to the bridge to see *Amethyst* for himself and said to me, 'I reckon you earned your second stripe last night, Sub'. The moral surely is that the odd word of praise or encouragement may mean so much more that the speaker imagines – and its effects last much longer.

Third, I received later a letter from an old lady who was an 'arty' friend of my father's (and not a bit 'military') saying, 'I sometimes despair for our country but my pride and confidence in the Royal Navy never falters'. In fact the *Amethyst* was flooded by messages of congratulation: I saw most of them while we acted as W/T guard because she had only one exhausted telegraphist on board. I think, just as the troops returning from the Falklands were overwhelmed by the ecstatic reception they received at Portsmouth, the *Amethyst* had hardly been aware of how the eyes of the world were on her.

JOHN COTTESLOE

The Seven deadly Sins

One evening in the Club a group of people having coffee and port after dinner were discussing what were the seven deadly sins and, as so often, one of them eluded the party. Half an hour later, Monsignor Gilbey came out and as he passed the group he said quietly, 'Pride: you always forget the sin which is closest to you', and then he moved on.

PETER WORDIE

Prince for a Day

It was a time when people-power challenged Communist rule; new political parties sprang up overnight; symbols were being replaced or torn down; the pre-war flag reflown; Orthodox churches filled with worshippers; cities and street names changed; and, for the first time since the Cold War began, Bulgaria suddenly opened itself up to the outside world for all to see.

As an undergraduate studying Bulgarian history, politics and language at the School of Slavonic and East European Studies, it was these dramatic changes in the Balkans that led me to invite the country's exiled King to come to London and address a large group of London University lecturers and students. King Simeon II, who had ruled under a regency from 1943 until a rigged referendum abolished the popular monarchy in 1946, had had his first interview broadcast on prime time television throughout Bulgaria, and overnight the interest in him and Bulgaria's royal past soared.

The university gathering was a great success and the King clearly demonstrated that forty-four years in exile had not dampened his interest in the country he once ruled over and calls home. His astute diplomatic and political skills, as well as his charm and down-to-earth qualities, were clearly displayed and it was obvious to me why he was making such an impact back home.

Some weeks later, the British Council arranged for me to spend one month in Bulgaria: the only exchange student in recent times to be given permission from the Bulgarian authorities to attend its principal university in Sofia.

When I arrived in August 1990, the streets throughout the capital, Sofia, were full of demonstrators demanding their civil liberties, the release of opposition figures, the return of the monarchy and an end to Communist tyranny which they believed had placed over ten million people in hardship, fear and without any say in their future.

I had been to Bulgaria earlier in the year, when eastern Europe's longest-serving dictator, Todor Zhivkov, was still ruling over the country, after his fellow rulers in East Germany, Czechoslovakia and Hungary had been toppled from power. It was a country where I was followed constantly; the deserted streets heavily guarded; churches still classed as museums; the economy in ruins; and where it was impossible to talk to a local without official clearance.

Yet within the short period of my absence from the country, Bulgaria had come alive and a political consciousness had been created. The once-powerful Communist Party was seriously weakened, Zhivkov was on trial and, for the first time in forty-five years, the previously shy and inwardly-looking Bulgarians had taken to the streets demanding real change.

It was not long before I had met many of the opposition figures King Simeon had earlier talked about in London and suggested I meet. I was invited to attend the memorial service that was taking place on the occasion of the forty-seventh anniversary of the death of King Simeon's father, Boris III, who had ruled from 1918 until his mysterious death in August 1943.

On the day of the memorial service, I met up with a number of opposition figures at the Sheraton Hotel in Lenin Square. They told me that *Duma*, the main Communist Party newspaper, had stated that the younger son of the King, Prince Kyril, was in Sofia, having flown from his Kensington home to attend the event. I knew this was false, as the King had made it clear in London that no member of the Royal Family would travel for the foreseeable future to Bulgaria until such time as the political situation had stabilized. But Sofia was awash with rumours of one sort or another and within hours the people on the streets accepted it as fact.

To my utter dismay, they also informed me that many people believed me to be the Prince as they had seen me with various political and religious leaders over the past few days, and that others had seen me arrive from London. I called the King immediately and asked what I should do. He told me he was well aware of the confusion and had issued a statement to correct the misinformation, but since rumours were circulating that Prince Kyril had been arrested by the Communists, I should attend the memorial service, as mayhem would follow if no 'Prince' turned up.

The hotel quickly organized security for me and, as I entered the crowded Lenin Square through the tradesman entrance, thousands surged forward to greet me. Security arrangements were quickly overrun, and people of all ages reached out with tears in their eyes to shake my hand, kiss me, take photographs or just join in the impromptu street party.

Many of the people had read the newspaper reports and had travelled from throughout the country to give their first 'royal visitor' a truly memorable welcome. They threw flowers at me, asked for autographs, thrust gifts of bread, icons and knitwear into my hands. Before I had even reached the steps of the church, I had lost six of my blazer buttons, a camera and my sunglasses – taken, no doubt, as souvenirs or trodden under foot in the frenzy!

Inside the ancient Church of the Holy Sabbath, where in 1925 there had been a failed assassination attempt to blow up King Boris and his cabinet, I was given a prominent position between the welcoming bishops and priests robed in magnificent gold tunics and burning incense. The ceremony was very moving with a full choir and hundreds of prayers said for the late King.

But one hour into the service, it was interrupted as impatient crowds jostled the clergy and poured in with shouts of 'Long live the King' and 'Down with Communism'. The service came to an abrupt end when the bishop shouted through a loud hailer for calm. Clearly distressed, he informed the crowds that they were in a church and not on a political rally and that Prince Kyril was not in Bulgaria, and that the gentleman in front of him was only a friend of the Royal Family studying Bulgarian at London University.

The crowds were having none of it and, whether it was their Prince or a friend of the Royal Family, I was carried out on their shoulders regardless, to immense cheers. The thousands outside soon turned into demonstrators and, accompanied by many opposition figures who could not even get into the church, we walked, flowers in hand, the short distance through the square towards the Communist Party headquarters.

There were more rumours circulating that the authorities had ordered another clamp-down and that the huge red star on top of the building was to be lit up in defiance of the people below. As we entered the 9 September Square (date of the Communist uprising in 1944 and the scene for the annual military parade), I realized that in comparison to the thousands who had marched from the church, we were a drop in the ocean to the hundreds of thousands who had already gathered and filled every inch of the surrounding area.

I pushed my way through the crowds and entered streets which had been totally out of bounds to the general public and heavily guarded by Communist troops only hours earlier. The Georgi Dimitrov mausoleum, where the embalmed body of Bulgaria's first Communist ruler lay, was over-run with people of all ages gleefully burning the Communist flag, youthfully graffiting its walls with pro-democracy slogans and vehemently demanding the removal of the detested corpse which, every year, each Bulgarian was expected to file by with reverence.

Directly opposite the mausoleum, at the former Royal Palace, a vigil was being held by more robed Orthodox priests and royalists. Incense and can-dles in hand, they lit up the outside of the Palace and filled the air with a sweet aroma that seemed to attract many of the demonstrators waving plac-ards with posters of the Royal Family, including several of Prince Kyril. None of them thought of checking the Prince's portrait alongside my own!

There were other demonstrators in the square: some ridiculously demand-ing that Bulgaria become the 51st state of the United States; the Green Party sensibly urging the closure of the dangerous nuclear plant in the north of the country; reformed Communists urging to no avail the end of the one-party state; and independent trades union leaders demanding their unpaid salaries and rights in the work place.

A large group of Bulgarian Muslims, Korans in hand, were also venting their anger at the Bulgarianization programme the Communists had implemented two years earlier, forcing them to change their names to Bulgarian ones. In a short period of time, it resulted in hundreds of thousands of otherwise loyal Bulgarians fleeing into neighbouring Turkey.

It was like a market place of political, ethnic and religious ideas and yet, despite their diversity, they had all come together to make their statement and demand that Bulgaria follow the same route as their brothers elsewhere in eastern and central Europe.

As the day drew to a close, the red star was illuminated on the party building, despite calls from the opposition that this would be very provocative. Immediately, people both young and old, with real anger in their eyes, surged forward and broke through the police lines and into the doors where once only the highest Communist officials could enter. Within minutes, thousands of documents, party cards and files were being thrown out of the windows, along with furniture and typewriters. Portraits of current and past Communist leaders and Central Committee members were brought out onto the square and thrown on the numerous bonfires that had been hastily assembled by the crowds.

Within an hour, demonstrators could clearly be seen on the roof chiselling off the huge hammer and sickle engraved in stone and they finally managed to cut the power to the offending red star. The falling masonry was met with huge cheers from the crowds below as events quickly developed into mini-revolution. With the Communist Party headquarters in ruins, the mob simultaneously burst into the offices of the State Council, the Bulgarian State Bank, the Council of Ministers and the Central Committee building. Petrified armed police enforcements arrived, but they could not control the revolutionaries. Many deserted their posts, ripping off the stars from their drab uniforms, and some even joined the crowds, to the demonstrators' delight.

It was not long until all the political leaders gathered on the rickety iron balcony of the former Royal Palace to address the riotous people below. It was on this very same balcony in 1937 that King Boris and Queen Giovanna had appeared to receive the applause of their subjects on the occasion of Prince Simeon's birth, and it was not lost on the crowd that power had suddenly moved the one hundred metres across the square, from the cold stone mausoleum to the Palace.

I was asked by the leader of the Democratic Trade Union to join them. In an ante-chamber off the balcony area, I came face to face with the political leaders of the past and future Bulgaria. The Communist Vice-President and the defence minister of the People's Republic were visibly shaken by events outside. They realized their time was up. The main opposition leader from the Union of Democratic Forces was preparing his celebratory speech; the leader of the Bulgarian Muslims was praying on the floor for his good fortune; and for many others present it was a time of great joy and expectation. However, they all agreed that, for the sake of the country, the crowds should be addressed, and one by one the leaders went out onto the balcony, to plead with the crowds to stop rioting.

It was a game of Russian roulette – the revolutionaries reacted by stoning, cheering or booing each speaker. As the crowds had ignored their pleas, the leaders asked me to address them but I immediately refused, knowing my Bulgarian was at best basic and that I did not want to be at the mercy of the crowds.

The egg-soaked Vice-President and the main opposition leader told me that someone had to speak for the King and, due to the day's events and recent media coverage, it was essential that I change my mind. Not being able to call the King for advice, I had to make up my own mind, and quickly.

Pushed into accepting this dangerous invitation, I nervously approached the balcony edge and the microphone, and witnessed an amazing sight. The heat from the burning Communist Party building was so intense that the flames lit up the entire square and the million-and-a-half people contained within it. Worryingly, I noticed that the flames had spread onto neighbouring buildings, some of which were only metres from the very palace in which I found myself.

Taking a deep breath, I announced in broken Bulgarian that I had a message from the King. Immediately the crowds calmed down and listened intently. I announced that Prince Kyril was not in Bulgaria, had not been arrested and that I was a mere student of Bulgarian from London University. The crowds roared 'God save King Simeon' over and over again, but then I went on to report what the King had told me earlier in the day, that the situation had got out of control, that the King understood their concerns but peaceful demonstrations were the only answer, and that the riots had to stop. Immediately, the cheering crowds turned hostile and I, too, had to dive for cover.

This truly historic day is remembered throughout Bulgaria as the day the Communist authorities were finally forced to listen to the people. It was the moment when the Communist Party realized they had no mandate from the people and had no option but to step aside. The day also proved to King Simeon that, despite forty-four years of exile, his Saxe-Coburg-Gotha dynasty still had great public support and that the issue of the monarchy was back on the political agenda.

Shortly afterwards, the Communist authorities hurriedly announced the end of the one-party system, the calling of a Grand National Assembly to decide Bulgaria's political future and a referendum on the restoration of the monarchy.

The referendum was subsequently delayed, but it is expected to take place in the very near future when, after his long stay in Madrid, the King returns to Bulgaria once and for all as either the country's constitutional monarch or as a loyal citizen of the new Republic. As for Prince Kyril, he remains in London, but was recently appointed as the chief economic adviser to the current President of the Republic.

ANTHONY BAILEY

A Slow Change of Continents

We had planned to meet in Salonica at seven in the evening at the old Mediterranean Palace Hotel. Joan and I had flown up from the Peloponnese and Xan and Magouche Fielding were motoring all the way from Andalusia. We were punctual at our tryst but, embraces over, discovered that our hotel had been pulled down several years ago. Bound for a late-September journey in

Asia Minor, we drove across eastern Macedonia and Thrace next day, halted just over the Turkish border at Adrianople and in Constantinople found rooms at the rather run-down Pera Palace.

Round the corner soared the British embassy. Designed by a follower of Sir Charles Barry, the architect of the Houses of Parliament and the Travellers Club, it celebrates the long and brilliant incumbency of Sir Stratford Canning[1], but since the flight of the Turkish capital to Anatolia, the Great Elchi's palace harbours only the consulate. Impelled by a secret longing, I hastened there next morning.

Information about the Hellespont and how to swim across it was what I was after. (I had first sailed through it when I was nineteen, steeped in Lord Byron's poems; and I had secretly resolved to have a shot at it if I ever got the chance. Perhaps this was it.) I struck lucky, for the vice-consul dug out some recent notes left there by Mr Peter Naylor of Hull, who must be a very strong swimmer, thinking nothing of ten-kilometre swims that last four hours; he had tackled the Bosphorus the previous May, and fainted from the cold, but he managed the Hellespont with ease in September, taking only forty-five minutes. The distance, he reckoned, was about three miles, and the current, roughly, 2 m.p.h.: 'It always flows east to west, so swim with it!' His starting point lay in a military zone, which ruled out the classical and shorter Sestos-to-Abydos crossing, so he found a local fisherman who dropped him by boat just offshore.

I noted all this down, and we set off next day.

After Bithynia, a bit of Phrygia, the Maeander valley, Aphrodisia, Iona, Lydia, Sardis, Myra, Ephesus, Smyrna and Troy, we reached Çanakkale on the eastern shore of the Hellespont – it is the 'Channak' of the Gallipoli campaign and settled into the Anafartalar Hotel. Mr Naylor's fisherman was called Ahmed Kaptan; I hunted for him in all the coffee-shops of the town, but heard that he had sailed off to Imbros to fish. However, Mr Sevki Suda, part-manager of the hotel and a keen deep-sea fisherman, kindly promised to find a boat next day and to accompany us as well. It was important to

1 Lord Stratford de Redcliffe (1786–1881))

make the attempt between nine and ten in the morning, or, in the evening, between four and five, as there is a strong current; about midday, the wind stirs up tiresome waves. We settled on the following afternoon.

But after breakfast, Sevki Suda was in the hall, full of infectious eagerness, saying, 'Now's the time!', so I dashed upstairs for Joan. A little motor-boat, with a glassed-in cabin, belonging to a friend of Sevki, was waiting at the quay. We climbed in and headed upstream – north-east, that is – sticking tight to the Asian shore as far as Nata Feneri. The headland was fortified with embrasures, earthworks and communicating flights of steps, and '18–3–1915' was picked out in huge white lettering across the hillside. (It is the date of the sinking of HMS *Irresistible*. Downstream, we learnt, the Channak waters were full of ships that went down while trying to force the straits.) Dry land being out of bounds here, we stopped just far enough out to avoid running aground.

It was exactly 9 a.m. when I dived in. The boat veered west and I set off after it while Joan and Sevki shouted encouragement from the stern.

The distance to the European shore – 'the Thracian Chersonese' – looked far away and very forbidding, but the going was quite easy at first: lighthouses and minarets, the forts and the towers, changed places with heartening speed and the current didn't seem very strong. Soon a long Russian tanker with *Bogomiloff*, or something like it, painted dismissively across her bows in Cyrillic characters, loomed from the north and passed very close: she left a strong wash which kept lifting me up and dropping me down again. Then came a tanker from Tunis with, I think, *Gooriah* across her stern in Arabic. She was followed by the *Dâmbovitza* from Constanza: and from then on there were always a ship or two passing, most of them tankers and sometimes several at a time. Our boatman stuck a red flag with a crescent in the stern and had another ready to flourish when we looked like being run down.

Nearly half-way across, the current grew stronger and the water was suddenly choppy, ruffled, and much harder to get through. Joan and Sevki kept urging: 'Ten minutes fast now and you'll be there!' But I could see by the speed of the changing scenery how quick the current was running. Straight ahead, the flank of the Hill of Kilitbahir was picked out, in the same primeval *sgraffito* technique as the White Horse at Uffington, with the tall figure of a Turkish soldier on guard over a sacred flame. The giant lines of verse beside him became more legible with every stroke:

> '*Dur yolcu!*', they ran. '*Bilmeden gelip bastığın,*
> *Bu toprak, bir devrin battığı yerdir*' [1]

On the Aegean side, just beyond the watershed, lay Gaba Tepe, the site of Anzac Beach in 1915.

Swimming sidestroke, I began to notice a strange hissing and fluctuating sound under my left ear. It was very sinister, like an echo in a vast dark room underneath. It suggested the grinding of enormous masses of pebbles and silt many fathoms down. The surface current flows south-west from the Sea of Marmara but, close to either bank, deep under this, two dark and mysterious currents stream out of the Aegean to the north-east, and I thought that the noise, brought about by the narrowing of the Dardanelles, might be the shock of rival alluvia in never-ending collision. (I mentioned this a few days later to Mr Nuri Birgi, the Turkish Ambassador in London for many years, in his splendid wooden palace on the Bosphorus, and he laughed and said, 'Don't you believe it: they're Russian submarines, I often hear them out here at Scutari. They are supposed to surface, but they don't – or only one in every thirty or forty.')

So here I was, floundering across the wake of the Argo, a mile north of Xerxes' and Alexander's bridges of boats, only a few leagues from Troy and about a mile south of the point where Leander, Mr Ekenhead and Lord Byron swam across; but too concerned with the current to think about them in more than fitful snatches. The giant inscription had coiled upstream and

---

1   '*Eğil de kulak ver, bu sessiz yığın,*' it goes on.
     '*Bir vatan kalbinin attığı yerdir.*'
     'Stop, O passer-by! This earth you tread on unawares
     'Is where an age sank.
     'Bow and listen, this quiet mound
     'Is where the heart of a nation beats.'
From a poem by Necmettin Halil Onan

off-stage. This was the narrowest and deepest stretch of the whole channel and the vast castle of Kilid Bahr, with its great cylindrical bastions, its flutter of crescent-flags and its two mosques – one with the tall tapering cone of its minaret painted green – were rushing up from the south.

Joan told me later that Sevki was disappointed that I didn't shoot through the stiff midstream current at a lightning crawl; instead, I was advancing at a stately mid-Victorian clergyman's rate. Seeing our prospective landfalls retreating north one after the other, he asked her how old I was; when she said 'sixty-nine', he looked surprised, nodded with a fatalistic sigh that was half a groan, then backed her up with encouraging cries: *was I all right? I* was, though rather tired. I felt Joan might be sitting on her hands to avoid wringing them, and churned on. The Asian shore had faded into the distance, yet Europe still looked distressingly far; but, straight ahead, a row of bathing-huts slid by, quite clear in every detail, followed by a shuttered and derelict-looking hotel; then, quite suddenly, there was nothing at all except a hill-side, some pine trees and a dry torrent-bed.

Abruptly and bewilderingly, the coast was in full retreat. The channel was widening fast and I had alarming visions of being carried down the Hellespont and out into the Aegean between Cape Helles and Kum Kale. Describing this reach, the chart says – at least I think it does: it is rather indistinct – 'current 4 knots at times'; and, all at once, there was a strong and discernible drift upstream. (The abrupt emergence of this deep-flowing and furtive northeast current is shown on the chart by little arrows like air-gun darts all pointing upstream.)

I tried swimming on my back but, with the contradictory behaviour of the water, the steamers' wash and, I suppose, by now, the noon-tide waves, I couldn't see where I was going, so thrashed on as before, very tired, and in a sort of trance. Suddenly the boat slowed and Joan shouted 'You've done it!'; I dropped my legs; my toes touched pebbles; and soon, a couple of hundred yards from a wooded headland and a row of poplars along a valley, I was stumbling into Europe among shingle and boulders slippery with green weed.

Splashing back into the water and hauled on board, I drank some tea brewed by the fisherman, then swallowed a slug of whisky brought by Joan.

It was a joyful moment, and we headed full-tilt for Çanakkale and Asia, where Xan and Magouche were waiting with champagne: they had been following our course with field-glasses from a balcony, like Zeus and Hera on Tenedos.

I had reached the other side at 11.55, after swimming two hours and fifty-five minutes: I'm still not quite sure of the distance, but I think it was about three miles, perhaps more. Sevki said the poplar-clump was called Havuzlar – 'pools' – and it is marked on the Admiralty chart as Avuzlar. But, going by the rather blurred photocopy of the mid-nineteenth-century Admiralty chart in the British Archaeological School in Athens, it may perhaps have been a mile farther south, at the mouth of a stream called Suandere – which must be the same as Soğandere (the Turkish ğ with a diacritic on top is hardly pronounced at all).

Thank heavens, the sea had been warm. I was cold to touch when I got back on board, but didn't feel it. The attempt would have been no good in the evening: at my pace, dark would have overtaken us; and the next day turned out cold, windy and overcast with an angry ruffle a-midstream. The Hellespont is much warmer than the Bosphorus, which flows, after all, straight out of the Black Sea, where the Danube, the Dniestr, the Dniepr, the Donetz and the Don pour into it from the west and the north; but these frigid Euxine waters are warmed by their torpid sojourn in the Sea of Marmara before they dash south-west through the narrows and into the Mediterranean.

Everyone agreed that our day had been the last chance this year.[1] Too tired to eat anything, we slept like the dead, then sent for tea and toast and some wonderful Asia Minor Welsh rabbit came up as well.

My limbs having turned to stone, I slunk off in a taxi to a nearby hammam and lay dissolving on the marble slabs, watching the daylight fade beyond the colander-perforations in the cupola. Meanwhile, a burly masseur was slowly taking my body to pieces and then assembling it again by trampling up and down my spine like a processional elephant in a durbar. Outside,

1 1984

dusk was falling. Light as air now, I settled in a coffee-shop at the end of the lane and ordered a narghilé. Remains of the sunset still touched the mackerel-sky, and well-being seemed to drop from it as I sat smoking and looking at the reflected lights twinkling and moving about in the straits.

A prayer had been answered. A cheerful feast and several bottles of Doluçar and Kavaklidere – our companions all across Asia Minor – lay ahead; I knew that I was only the last in a long line of copy-cats; but I felt sure that I had beaten all records for slowness and length of immersion; certain, too, that this was a wreath no future swimmer was likely to snatch at. Serenity was complete.

PATRICK LEIGH FERMOR

A Question too Far

Some fifty years ago as a young solicitor I was appearing before a South Coast Bench, defending a motorist charged with careless driving. On a dark and stormy night he had knocked over a lady cyclist. He had told the police that he did not see her.

The young woman appeared in court, stood in the witness box and gave her evidence soberly and factually and it was then my turn to cross-examine.

It so happened that she was wearing a long black coat which covered her almost from neck to toe and so I said to her, 'Were you wearing that coat on the night of the accident?' and she said, 'Yes'.

Had I sat down then, I might have done my client some good. Instead, I went on and in my best Perry Mason manner, stabbing the air with a bony finger, 'Aha,' I said, 'perhaps that is why my client did not see you?'; to which she replied. 'No, the coat was white then. I have since had it dyed.'

The courtroom fell about laughing. The chairman of the Bench, a retired Brigadier, commiserated with me and they went on to convict my client.

Many obvious forensic morals can be drawn from this story.

MAURICE FOOKS

The Crocodile Princess

Just over twenty miles up the Mekong river from the town of Kratié, at a jungle village called Sambaur, there is a tomb of importance in the beliefs of the Cambodians. In it repose the ashes of the Princess Nucheat Khatr Vorpheak, who met a tragic death in 1834 while still of tender age. Bathing in the waters of the Tonle Sap near the then royal capital of Oudong, she disappeared. Some months later, her body, somehow preserved from decay, was discovered inside a crocodile killed many miles away in Mekong river at Sambaur. The beast had evidently swallowed the child whole, and carried the body undigested for miles down the Tonle Sap to Phnom Penh, where the river flows into the Mekong, and then upstream beyond Kratié, a journey of around one hundred and ninety miles.

The Princess was duly cremated, as was and is the custom, and a stupa, or conical funerary tower erected in her memory and over her ashes at Sambaur. She was high-born and beautiful, of royal descent; she had died while still immature and hence, as the Cambodians see these matters, unmarked by sin; the recovery of her remains seemed little short of miraculous. These qualities, taken together, indicated the special favour in which she stood with the *Tevodas*, the mysterious divinities which presided over and protected the Kingdom of Cambodia. It was not long before the spirit of the dead Princess made contact with the living through the person of a *Hora*, or medium, at the royal court.

Through a succession of clairvoyant astrologers, the Princess came to assert a benign influence on a succession of kings and rulers. The most potent of all the human spirits of the realm, her special care was said to be the national survival and prosperity and – in that light – the conduct of Cambodian foreign affairs. Princess Vorpheak was credited with having tendered sage advice throughout the trials and indeed near-extinction which threatened the country in the nineteenth century; while, in more recent times, she had predicted the success of the 'Royal Crusade' – the campaign against the French Protectorate conducted by the King of Cambodia which was to

179

result in the grant of independence by the French in 1953.

I was enchanted by the legend of the Princess when I first heard it on taking charge in Phnom Penh in 1964, and fondly thought of her whenever I made a major move in my relations with the Cambodian government. What would she think and how would she advise? Would she look with favour on my efforts, such as they were, to patch up old quarrels and indirectly help Cambodia in her struggle for peace and survival? I never knew the answer to these questions. Her presence was not widely spoken of. Few foreigners knew of her existence. No diplomats went to Sambaur. But I did decide, in September 1966, within a few weeks of the conclusion of my three-year mission to Cambodia, to visit her tomb. It was the season of heavy rains and dark grey clouds. I set out with a couple of scholarly Australian friends across flooded rice fields, along muddy river banks and through foetid dark jungle, on an arduous seventy-two hour round trip.

Close to sundown, we came to a halt where the laterite track disappeared under flood water. Here, we took a boat: a long pirogue with an outboard motor, plying as a sort of Green Line bus between riparian villages. Stopping here and there on our way, we slid up the Mekong, finally coming to a halt at Sambaur. Disembarked, we wandered along soggy paths between the wood-framed, rush-walled houses. Few people were about in the late afternoon: one or two dark-skinned peasants loped by, wheeling bicycles; some Chinese shopkeepers stared blankly from their dark interiors; a group of children scampered along; dogs barked. I exchanged some Cambodian with those who would listen, but received only baffled smiles. Eventually, we came into an open space where a rather dilapidated and apparently deserted monastery stood in the clear grey light. A large wooden building, the temple itself, stood in the middle of the square, surrounded by lesser buildings of leaf and straw where the monks no doubt lived when they were at home – we could see newly-washed yellow robes laid out to dry. To one side, stood the stupa of Princess Nucheat Khatr Vorpheak.

I chose not to approach the stupa at once, but walked into the temple and stood at one end, looking down the length of the dim nave to the figures of the Buddha which stood elevated on their thrones at that end. To them I mentally addressed my message, explaining why I had come. I have always felt at peace with the Buddha, in his simple Cambodian effigy: serene, but deeply human. I felt so at that moment, in that empty and decaying temple, in that remote retreat from the world of my origin.

I then plucked up courage to walk towards the stupa. A tall conical structure, it stood, in a clearing apart, on a stone terrace of its own. Although restored in 1956, the tomb was already showing the erosion that time brings so speedily in its wake in tropical countries. The mosquitoes sang in my ears as I approached and the heat seemed the more stifling for there being no sun. Behind the stupa stood the dark green of the jungle and the khaki of the hutments. Above the stupa's needle point, house-high in the air, the thick oily grey clouds sat overhead, heavy with more rain. A slight drizzle began to fall.

My mind felt blank, despite a quickening of the pulse. Perhaps I was screening it from self-conscious and superstitious melodrama or, worse still, from disappointment and bathos. But as I looked up from the foot of the stupa, I felt suddenly quite sad; it was not a distinguished edifice, being patched up here and there with cement, and covered by patches of light green moss; and I was struck by an emptiness, as of the tomb of Christ on the day of His ascension. Then something happened. My foot slipped on the wet steps of the terrace. I took this for the accident it was and walked a step or two nearer. After I had looked about me for a few minutes more, my foot slipped again. I could see that the stones beneath my foot were wet with rain. And I knew that the rubber soles of the comfortable jungle boots on my feet were worn smooth with long service. Yet I had been standing still when I slipped. Slipping and sliding a third time, I apprehensively backed down off the terrace, walked some distance away from the stupa and turned squarely to face it, like an Anglican looking at the altar at matins in a Shropshire, Norman parish church.

My mind then cleared. I felt rebuffed and resentful. Without either bogus reverence or Caucasian condescension, but certainly with an edge of reproach, I laid my thoughts calmly and consecutively before the Princess Vorpheak, as if I had been speaking aloud.

I said that I was a foreigner who did not know the Khmer customs, who had lived for only three years in Kampuchea, and who would shortly leave for a destination at the further end of the earth [Paris], never to return to Sambaur. But I had come as a friend of the country and its people, and as one who respected the legend of the Princess. This legend was the property of Khmers and not of the British, and it was not for me to believe it or to disbelieve it. It was true that in the mental world in which I lived and had been brought up, I found it hard to see how a child long since dead could be active in the affairs of the living. Yet my civilization laid no claim to all knowledge and to all wisdom and my personal over-scepticism could well be mistaken or, perhaps more probably, misplaced. In electing to visit the stupa, therefore, I had chosen to accept the legend as it stood; and I had had the presumption to offer the Princess, although I was an alien, some portion of the gratitude and respect which was unquestionably her due from all Cambodians.

The Princess, if she existed, and could receive my thoughts, would know with what a heavy heart I had first come to Phnom Penh and how initially critical and ill at ease I had felt there. The British Embassy's Chancery had been sacked by a government-directed mob; the Ambassador had been withdrawn and embassy dependants evacuated. Sent up from a comfortable and interesting job in Singapore, to take charge of the remnant, I had found that my attachés and I were in Coventry – Cambodians, apart from servants and language tutors, and Cambodian ministers and senior officials in the security of their offices, had been forbidden contact with us. My French had been initially rusty, my Cambodian limited, acquired only after a prodigious white-hot effort. So, my mission to Phnom Penh had not been of my choosing, and was no bed of roses. The responsibility which I then shared with the Foreign Secretary and his advisors in London was no mean thing for a young diplomat at the outset of his thirties: the attempt, through the Anglo-Russian co-chairmanship of the Geneva Conference on Indo-China, to win international recognition and respect for the neutrality and territorial integrity of Cambodia, and to count her out of the Vietnam war.

Her Highness would know that I had laboured to understand and to help. I had been grateful for whatever benevolence the Princess might have felt towards these efforts and I hoped that she would share my satisfaction that at least something had been done. I knew that there were tight limits to the effective action which my successors, as I myself, could take to advance the interests which it was the Princess' charge, under the *Tevodas*, to protect: the survival and happiness of the Khmer nation. But I asked her to be prepared to judge us fairly and generously, and to give us the credit of good intentions. Also I invited her, if she felt so disposed, to help the men who should come after me.

For a brief moment, I had the impression of contact, of a message not merely sent but received. Then the emptiness came back and the everyday worlds once more took me in hand. I walked up to the stupa again – this time without slipping – and tried to decipher the inscription in squiggly Cambodian lettering on the base. My friends approached from the monastery and we exchanged one or two commonplace remarks. I bent over my camera and took some photographs. The we strolled back to the riverside, in search of our boat. After a few minutes, the pilot took us away for half an hour upstream to deliver a passenger and a bundle or two on the last of his rounds. We smoked and gazed at the setting sun. Then the pirogue cast off for the last time and, turning into midstream, ran swiftly south with the current. It was dusk when we passed by Sambaur, silent in the shadow of the trees, one or two huts a-glimmer with lanterns. I stood on the roof of the cabin searching the skyline. Briefly, I glimpsed what I was looking for – the top of the stupa standing out in ghostly grey contrast to the black jungle beyond. Once again, the veil briefly lifted. This time, a wave of gentle emotion seemed to reach me from across the water. I felt that the Princess was sending me on my way with a message. For what I was, as such I had been accepted: a friend of Cambodia, within that wider discipline which made me before all else the servant of another country, the subject of another Crown.

LESLIE FIELDING

Hardly Shikar

My only meeting with him started well, but ended badly. I fear he found me incurably frivolous, while I thought he lacked humour.

We were fellow-guests of mutual friends, for dinner. When I arrived, he was already there, advising our hostess (an unlikely huntress) on how to shoot a crocodile: 'Don't depend on a brain-shot. Even a fully-grown adult has a brain no larger than a walnut.'

As the evening wore on, I gathered that his lifelong passion – it sounded like an obsession – was big game. As a young man forty years ago, he had hunted in East Africa. In old age, he retained a nostalgic enthusiasm for the sport. He was a consultant to a prominent field sports magazine for which he wrote about the 'golden age' of big game. He was also a member of the Shikar Club.

I told him that forty years ago I had been the District Commissioner in Moyale, a wild and remote Northern Frontier district in Kenya. This stimulated him: he had heard of Moyale, a semi-desert area with no shortage – in those days – of wild animals.

He said our meeting was 'very timely'. He was planning a series of articles for his magazine, on 'Adventures after Big Game in Africa', as enjoyed by 'amateurs' like me – as distinct from game wardens, professional hunters and safari firms. He was sure my reminiscences would interest his readers. He hoped we could meet again shortly to discuss this.

I had a strong feeling of being run away with, so I tried to rein him in. I said that though Moyale had plenty of wild animals, I had neither hunted nor photographed them. The only big animal I had 'bagged' was a colleague's Alsatian: I had had to put it down because of a rabies scare, and evidence that it might have been bitten by a rabid dog. I had enticed the Alsatian to come to me by offering it a biscuit, and then shot it in the head with my revolver. 'A brain-shot', I added.

After a pained silence, he told me (as one might tell a child) that an

Alsatian, even a large and potentially mad one, was by no definition big game. Not like a lion.

'Ah, I had forgotten,' I said. 'I did bump off a lion, a dangerous brute that had taken to man-eating. But I didn't shoot it, I poisoned it.'

'*Poisoned* it?' he cried, lifting his voice two octaves. '*Why?*'

'Early one morning,' I explained, 'a delegation of my nomadic Boran tribesmen came to my office, to say that during the night they had had a brush with a notorious lion, of whom I had probably heard. (Indeed I had: it was a solitary old male, lame, with an unmistakable spoor, and a bad record of snatching cattle, and sometimes herdsmen.)'

I went on, 'This time, it had raided one of their encampments some ten miles away, killed a young cow, and dragged it a short distance into dense thorn-scrub. The Boran had made an uproar and chased the lion off its kill, but they were sure it would come back. They had no guns, only spears, and they looked to me to put an end to the menace.'

'But why poison it?' he asked.

'I hadn't a suitable weapon, though I could have borrowed one of the ancient Lee Enfield .303 rifles carried by my Tribal Police. But basically I didn't feel competent to take on a hungry man-eater. However, I owed it to my people to make an attempt, and I had a tin of strychnine powder in my office safe, for precisely this contingency.

'So I went at once by Land Rover to the encampment, and then, taking the tin of strychnine and a sharp knife, was led on hands and knees through the thorn scrub, to the dead cow. My Tribal Police orderly came with me; he made several deep incisions in the corpse, and I tipped some poison into each – a dodgy procedure since it was a breezy day and the powder extremely fine.

'Then we crawled back to the waiting Boran, and I warned them not to think of eating any of the meat themselves; and to burn the cow when the lion had finished with it – and to burn the lion too.'

'What an appalling story! Did it work?' he asked.

'Perfectly,' I said. Next day a group of Boran came to thank me, and to report that the lion had duly re-appeared, had begun to eat the bait, and had died noisily on the spot. They added that various scavengers had also died, including a hyena and a vulture or two. The Boran were much impressed by "the government's poison".

'A pity about the strychnine,' he said, 'even if it served a local purpose.'

'Which reminds me,' I said, 'I once shot a snake in a mosque, likewise by popular request.'

'Worse and worse,' he grumbled. So I told him the story, which (like everything I told him) was true. One day a deputation led by the senior mullah had come to my house, asking me to shoot a snake which had somehow got into the township mosque. They said it had taken up a conspicuous position on one of the low roof-beams, immediately above the congregation. Its intention was unclear, and it had not yet attacked anyone, but its presence was most disconcerting, and a serious distraction to the worshippers beneath. It was hard to say what kind of snake it was, but it was exceedingly large, and they would be grateful to be rid of it.

So I had taken a shotgun and a few cartridges, and accompanied them to the mosque. There I had loaded my gun, taken off my shoes and entered the empty building. In a whisper, the snake was pointed out to me, lying in an untidy tangle on a low beam, and stirring a little as if in response to our arrival. I thought I could just distinguish its head, and hoped it was not its tail. As I took aim, the mullah uttered in a low voice the customary invocation, *Bismi'llahi-rahmani-rahim*, and I fired. Being indoors, the noise was shattering; but no second shot was needed. The hapless snake, a ten or twelve foot python, after a brief convulsion, fell dead to the floor.

'All your stories,' said my interlocutor, 'are more like pest control than hunting. What did the "invocation" mean?'

'It was from the Qur'an,' I said. '"In the name of Allah, the Compassionate, the Merciful".'

'That may have put the snake right with the Almighty,' he replied. 'But not with a serious hunter. I mean snakes aren't game. Your stories won't do for my magazine. They are hardly Shikar.'

GEORGE WEBB

The Eruption of Villarrica

December 1971 in Santiago sprouted the usual number of Social Events. On this particular evening we were at a cocktail party and met the new naval attaché at the British Embassy and his wife and two teenage daughters: when we said we were going to the Lake District in the south for two weeks over Christmas and the New Year, they said they would like to come too as father was going to be away. We explained that we would be camping and that even in summer it could be very wet. Never mind, they said, it would be an adventure. Little did they know.

There were five of us, including our three teenage daughters, and three of them: seven women and one man crammed into two cars with piles of camping equipment and somewhat top-heavy roof-racks. The first day we drove to Temuco, stayed overnight in the company flat and continued on the next morning to Villarrica. There we pitched camp in a friend's garden a few yards from the lake. And it rained.

We drove round the lake. And it rained. We visited our friends, and it rained. We found some drying wood, managed to make a camp fire and went to bed. The next morning it took us an hour and half to get the fire hot enough to boil some eggs for breakfast – so it was brunch and the main course was Christmas cake. The rain was easing off.

We decided to drive up the volcano on a road to an hotel and ski resort. The last eruption had been about six years earlier and the volcano was reckoned to have a six-year cycle. Certainly large chunks of rock could be seen emerging from the summit from time to time.

On the way down, my youngest daughter asked what would happen if there was an eruption. Blandly I replied that lava normally flowed at about five miles an hour and in the car we would get away easily. Ignorance in this case was bliss. We sat in a restaurant watching the sparks fly and went to bed.

Soon after eleven, the attaché's wife woke me and invited me to look at something at the lake-side. The eruption had started and from the lake we had a magnificent view of the most extraordinary firework display. This was accompanied by a rushing roaring noise which we could not understand. We later found it was caused by melted ice. All the volcanoes in the south of Chile are of the chocolate-box variety with conical snow-caps. Thirty-metre deep ice and snow being melted by red-hot lava comes down at about forty miles an hour, a hundred yards wide and thirty to forty feet high. Our car would have been swept away, as were many roads and all the bridges

I went back to the tent, awoke my wife and told her the volcano was erupting. Her reply was unprintable. I then remembered being told that on a previous occasion the lake had risen several metres. It was time to pack up. The seven women woke and did a magnificent job in the dark, striking camp and loading the cars in an hour.

In the middle of this, the mayor arrived with a loudspeaker and said we must all assemble in the middle of the town for safety. We said we could go to Temuco but he told us all the roads were cut. So we parked in the town and continued to watch the eruption, taking it in turns to walk about or sit in the cars.

Then a man came out of his house to upbraid me for keeping seven ladies hanging about outside in the middle of the night. We must all come into his house for shelter and rest. He had a picture window through which we watched the volcano while the family fed us coffee and *pan de Pascua* – the Chileans call Christmas *Pascua* (Easter) and Easter *Semana Santa* (Holy Week). So this was their Christmas cake – a sort of rich currant loaf with nuts.

At about four o'clock we were put to bed in bunks, on the sofa, on the floor – anywhere – and slept for three or four hours, when we were woken for breakfast. What wonderful hospitality.

We got official permission to return to the lake-side. The water had risen only about three feet and our camp was safe. But the sight that met us was extraordinary. For fifty yards from the water's edge there was nothing but floating wood of all shapes and sizes. Brushwood, logs, branches, tree trunks and even bits of furniture. And there were local inhabitants piling it upon the shore to dry out and sell as firewood. We had no trouble collecting enough firewood to last the rest of our fortnight.

188

Having re-pitched camp, we drove round the lake. On the side nearest the volcano, all the bridges were down and we had to drive very carefully over what were virtually river beds. Supplies into the town had been cut off and the eruption took place the day before the normal weekly delivery. We went to the shops quickly to see what we could find.

What had been little streams were now river beds a hundred yards or more across. Boulders the size of large sofas were scattered about and the bushes had been stripped of all leaves by the swirling mass of sand, stones and water. The downstream twigs looked like sharpened pencils. The scenes were dramatic and the sun came out. The weather stayed fine for twelve days.

Mercifully there were very few people hurt. The waters rushing down the mountain in two mighty torrents had met and then sprung apart, thus coming down in wide arcs either side of the town. Had this clash not happened, a forty-foot wall of water would have swept the town away. The prompt action by the mayor had also got people out of the way of the water. His house, sadly, was one of a few that were buried in a flow of sludge and stones.

We resumed our camping and our camp fire. A big challenge was to keep the milk simmering for ten minutes without boiling over – this was to avoid brucellosis. We also made strawberry jam over the wood fire: in a fit of madness I had bought ten pounds of fruit from a small boy. Despite the taunts of the family and the acute shortages of the Allende period, exacerbated by the eruption, we found sugar, lemons and preserving jars. We looked like Macbeth's witches round the cauldron but we produced our best-ever, slightly smokey, strawberry jam – better than Tiptree's!

Communications with Santiago were badly interrupted. Our friends and colleagues divided into those who didn't know about the eruption and those who did and wondered if we had survived. We had, and the holiday was voted a great success: one more adventure to add to the family history.

ROBERT ELY

Man Overboard

My tale begins on a morning in Fleet Street. Well, not quite in the Street of Adventure, because Lord Kemsley ran his London and provincial newspaper empire a mile or two away in less congenial Grays Inn Road.

Ian Fleming, relaxed by several weeks at Goldeneye, his home in Jamaica, and wearing his all-weather office uniform – blue short-sleeved shirt and almost matching bow tie – was at his sunny best. Bouncy and ebullient – to borrow one of his favourite words – he waved me to a chair. 'Fancy a trip?'

The Foreign Manager of the *Sunday Times* and the Kemsley Group – James Bond had yet to surface from his imagination – said, 'Elizabeth is joining Philip in Malta as a Navy wife. Take a photographer.' Princess Elizabeth and Lieutenant Philip Mountbatten were not long married. Pictures were imperative; but so, of course, were words. After filing as a 'stringer' (retained freelance correspondent) from Singapore since the end of the war, Ian Fleming had recruited me for Mercury, the foreign news service he originated for Kemsley Newspapers, and obviously felt I was right for this particular assignment.

Air travel was still an adventure. The Vickers Viking's moustachioed crew had Bomber Command written all over them and the Viking was a civil variant of the Wellington bomber. Noisy maybe, but luxury compared with economy seating. I registered at the Phoenicia and relaxed, as Ian would have expected, over a martini.

Halfway through my second, I called the Villa Guadamangia where the princess had joined the prince's uncle, Admiral Mountbatten, commanding a cruiser squadron at Malta. The Admiral came to the phone. He remembered me as one of his 'SEAC boys' (*see page 115*) and I explained my mission.

'Supremo' as we knew him in South-East Asia Command, suggested I call Mabel Strickland, owner of *The Times of Malta* and get myself invited to tea at her villa next day. Mabel obliged and we met. 'Difficult,' the Admiral said, 'they are our guests and there's the question of royal rota and pooling pictures and all that. Drop into Captain Caruana's bar in Valletta High Street at eleven tomorrow morning. When you hear my wife whistling "Danny Boy" pop out and she'll have a message for you.'

On cue, I rested my Cisk Maltese beer. Swinging a wicker shopping basket, Lady Louis paused at the open bar entrance. She said, 'This time tomorrow at the villa. Bring your photographer.' We were received at the villa by a distinctly unsettled royal detective. Our visit, he complained, was 'highly irregular'. Leading us to French windows opening onto the garden, he conducted Sid Beadell, the Kemsley photographer – who could hardly believe his good fortune – to the 'happy couple'. I was told firmly to remain behind the French windows.

We had a scoop, but how were we to get our pictures to Kemsley House in London? Technology was rudimentary. Stories were cabled and photographic transmission facilities were rare. Then I remembered Mabel. She offered a deal. Sid could use the *Times of Malta* darkroom and recently-installed transmission equipment, in return for copyright-free use of his photographs.

Ian Fleming cabled, 'Chairman over the moon your ebullient coverage [yes, that 'e' word again] and exclusive pics. Take extended Med. holiday on us. Cabling £100 bonus.' Martinis flowed and the Navy offered me a passage to Port Said, on to Suez through the Canal and return.

At breakfast a day out of Malta I should perhaps have sensed that the eccentricities of my host, the captain of the frigate *Peacock*, ran deeper than his elaborate breakfast ritual. Silence reigned while Commander Nigel Eardley-Wilmot, a much-decorated destroyer captain, assembled back numbers of *The Times*, *The Spectator*, and the *New Statesman,* and a bible. Answering my unspoken question he said, '*Times* with cornflakes to keep up with the news, *Spectator* with the eggs for Tory views, *New Statesman* with toast to keep abreast of Labour, Bible for God's news.'

Breakfast was so prolonged that in no time pink gins were served, followed by lunch and brandies. When the cabin clock showed four the captain suggested I knock back my umpteenth brandy. 'Strip,' he ordered, 'and when I say "go" run up the starboard side of the fo'c's'le and jump overboard.'

As he said 'go' he added, 'I'm coming too'. In moments I was teetering high above the sea. My attempted dive resulted in a painful and winding belly-flop. Bobbing in the swell I was relieved to see the skipper. We swam together. He said, 'When they spot us, they'll lower the sea boat.'

Only later did I discover that our rescue depended on Baldechino, a sleepy Maltese steward. Soon after four o'clock, when Baldechino failed to find the captain with his customary cup of tea, he had the presence of mind to report to the bridge that the captain and his guest seemed to have disappeared. Anxious not to irritate the officer of the watch, the steward offered the captain's tea. 'If they are not here,' he said, peering out to sea, 'then perhaps they are out there.'

Fortunately, the officer of the watch was only too well acquainted with the commander's eccentricities He alerted the aft lookout, who reported 'two obstacles in the sea and well astern, sir'. That was us. 'Men overboard! Away sea boat's crew.' The order ricocheted around the ship rousing the duty boat's crew from a soporific post-daily tot make and mend.

After some thirty minutes, strong tattooed arms grabbed me from the deep. As we came alongside, the skipper seized a rope fall swinging from the sea boat's davits and monkeyed up it with the agility of a physical training instructor in a Pompey naval barracks' gym. I failed miserably and suffered the indignity of being hauled up with the sea boat.

It was a year or two before I felt the urge to return to sea.

EDWARD BISHOP

The Triumph of Santa Claus

On 23 December 1951 an effigy of Santa Claus was hung from the railings of Dijon Cathedral and then burnt in front of several hundred Sunday school children. An extreme and insensitive act perhaps, but the Catholic authorities were correct in their view that Santa Claus or Father Christmas is an essentially pagan figure who has insinuated himself at the heart of modern Christmas.

Fathers and uncles dress up as him; he's on Christmas cards; and for nearly a century he's been at his post in the Santa's Grotto or Castle of department stores. I first became aware of what an international figure he has become when, living in Hong Kong in the early eighties, I came across a Chinese Santa Claus and learned that in Tokyo a telephone call will summon a Japanese counterpart to your home. Even 'moral panic' over child-abuse has not dimmed the appeal of a stranger who cuddles little children on his knee and gives them sweets, and who climbs down chimneys in defiance of burglar alarms bringing gifts with a sinister 'Ho-ho-ho'. He presides over the modern, international and not very Christian Christmas. Who is he?

In his modern guise he's American or Anglo-American, but his passport declares him to be St Nicholas and to have originated in the Middle East, spent many years in Europe, and then emigrated to the United States. The flimsy Christian disguise can be easily exposed. The American Santa Claus does of course take his name and some of his characteristics from the Dutch incarnation of St Nicholas or Sinterklaas, for whom the children of Dutch immigrants to America would put out their shoes on St Nicholas's Eve, 5 December, a custom that became popular beyond the Dutch community and was transferred to Christmas Eve. So far, so good, and, so far, Christian; but does the jovial, pot-bellied and rubicund figure, who travels through the air on a sleigh drawn by reindeer and enters houses by the chimney, bear much resemblance to the ascetic saint on a white horse that was St Nicholas?

The main characteristics of the modern Santa Claus emerged almost complete in the 1820s from the pen of one man, Professor Clement Moore of New York State. His poem, *A Visit from Santa Claus*, was published anonymously in the *Troy Sentinel* in 1823 and immediately became wildly popular. Moore's creation of Santa Claus may well have drawn upon Washington Irving's *Knickerbocker History of New York* (1809) and upon an 1821 issue of *The Children's Friend*, which portrayed the visitor as travelling in a sleigh drawn by a reindeer, but it was Moore who made popular what has become the standard image of Santa Claus.

Moore described a Santa Claus who arrived on a sleigh drawn by a flying reindeer on Christmas Eve; came down the chimney with a sack of gifts; and filled the stockings of children. He was merry and red-faced:

He was chubby and plump, a right jolly old elf.
And I laughed when I saw him, in spite of myself.

This personification of the Christmas spirit was very different to St Nicholas and was, in fact, the embodiment of older, pre-Christian, traditions. Every European society has some legend or personification of Christmas, legends which were part of the southern European Saturnalia or the Yuletide of the north before they took on a superficial Christian coating. Within the English Christmas there had lingered a Father Christmas, Old Christmas, Sir Christmas or Captain Christmas, as he was variously known. This somewhat Saturnalian version of the spirit of festivity was often portrayed as an impish Lord of Misrule, holding a glass in his hand and holding sway over feasting and carousing, which involved a world turned upside down, a link with pagan midwinter feasts, where masters had waited upon servants and men dressed as women and women as men.

The new Santa Claus/Father Christmas of the nineteenth century was an amalgam of English, Dutch and German traditions. The custom of his bringing presents to children came from the Dutch tradition but Clement Moore drew upon the old Christmas of England for the jovial character and appearance of his creation. Indeed, if Santa Claus was part St Nicholas and part a Father Christmas descended from the Lord of Misrule, the latter characteristics were more pronounced. It is significant that Moore failed to mention the Nativity in his poem.

He reached back into the collective consciousness of the European mind and, perhaps, back as far as the early Asian impact on that mind. Anthropologists have suggested that Santa's airborne progress may be based on the levitational accomplishments of the shamans or holy men of north-eastern Siberia, who accomplished their feats after eating the fly agaric mushroom with its scarlet cap and white warts. The sleigh drawn by reindeer would fit in with this, as would the descent down chimneys, for the *yurts* of Siberian tribes were entered from the roof. Perhaps Santa Claus was in America before Columbus and was lodged in the culture of the far north where there were close links with Siberia. Perhaps he was not unknown in the northern islands of Japan before he appeared in Tokyo department stores.

But his historical and anthropological roots do not explain the success of the pagan Christmas visitor in dominating the major festival of the modern world. What made Moore's Santa Claus a fitting figure to preside over the new Anglo-American Christmas, which was so effectively refurbished in the nineteenth century that we now think of it as 'traditional', was his suitability for an urban, humanitarian, family-centred, child-indulging and largely secular civilization. There had been a special day for children in the Roman feast of Juvenilia, but the old English Christmas had been far from child-centred; the new Christmas, which spread from the Victorian middle classes, was about home, family and children. Unusual and conspicuous expenditure upon food and drink had always accompanied mid-winter festivities, while, among aristocracy and gentry, the custom of present-giving was well-established, but it was only in the nineteenth century that presents and shopping for them became an important part of Christmas. Santa Claus fitted into this festival very well and swept aside all rivals, such as the German Pelz-Nickel and Kriss Kringle (the Christkind). Those companions of the friendly spirit, the Dutch 'Black Peter' or the German Klausauf, who brought punishment to naughty children, had no future in an age which was becoming convinced of the innocence of children and even the prospect of Santa leaving only cinders for delinquents would soon disappear. In England, Santa Claus rapidly imposed his personality and customs upon Father Christmas and the names Father Christmas and Santa Claus became interchangeable, although English artists depicted him in a red habit with a hood, rather than the red suit and cap favoured in America. If Charles Dickens was the major designer of the modern Christmas, the credit for creating the odd figure who hosts it must go to Professor Clement Moore.

There was still, however, room for development, particularly as regards Santa Claus's physical appearance. The illustrator, Thomas Nast, fixed the appearance of this spirit of Christmas until well into the twentieth century. His earlier drawings for *Harper's Weekly*, which he began in 1863, show Santa as resembling Moore's 'jolly old elf' but in his later work he settled on a portrayal much closer to that which has become traditional: a large, jovial, white-bearded figure dressed in a red suit with a matching cap. It was not until the 1930s that the definitive American Santa Claus was completed in the work of Haddon H Sundblom in his many advertisements for Coca Cola. His creation, a Santa Claus described by Peter Hunt[1] as 'glow[ing]

1 Our very own Peter Hunt: *see pages 262 and 294* (The Editors).

with warmth and life, with a white beard billowing over a long red jacket lavishly trimmed with white fur, an enormous brass buckle fastening a broad leather belt round an ample belly and large, floppy leather boots', is one of the great images of the high age of American popular culture and remains standard today. It has almost pushed Father Christmas from British department stores, yet, like much else in the development of the modern Christmas, Sundblom's was something of an Anglo-American creation, for in establishing a red suit with white fur trimmings as the proper dress for Santa Claus, he drew upon the English Father Christmas's red habit with fur trimmings and transferred colour and texture, together with length of beard, to Nast's jump-suited figure.

The modern Santa Claus, like the modern Christmas itself, is infinitely exportable, because he is secular, sanitized and, almost, politically correct. A nasally-deprived or differently-advantaged reindeer, Rudolph, has joined the team, the pipe that was forever in the mouth of Thomas Nast's Santa had to go, and, instead of the hard-drinking Old Christmas, a Coca-Cola-swilling Santa presides over a children's festival. Those of us who are unreconstructed admirers of the Old Christmas like to feel, however, that, as with the mistletoe, the 'Ho-ho-ho' of the modern Santa Claus is an echo of the Lord of Misrule.

BILL PURDUE

Encounters with George Brown

In the course of a diplomatic career which began not very long after I was demobilized from the Army in 1946, apart from directly serving Anthony Eden and Harold Macmillan as a Private Secretary in the mid-fifties, I came into quite close contact with a number of British Foreign Secretaries. These included Ernie Bevin, Selwyn Lloyd, Lord Home, George Brown and Jim Callaghan.

With George Brown I had two amusing encounters, one while he was in office, the other much later, after we had both retired from public positions.

The first was in Bonn in 1966 when he came on an important official visit to the Federal Republic. On this occasion a plan was made for him to pay a formal visit to our embassy and the Ambassador (the late Sir Frank Roberts) and I, as his Head of Chancery, decided that it should be more than a matter of the Secretary of State looking in at one or two of the key departments and saying a few words to some of the pretty girls in the Registry. So we hired a large marquee to stand near the main building with benches inside to provide seating for all the UK-based staff (it was one of our largest embassies) and a few of the German staff who had worked for the embassy since the early days of the Federal Republic.

George Brown opened his speech by saying, 'Well, I gather you are the whole British staff of the Embassy'. Fearing that Mr Brown might follow that with some jocular but perhaps disparaging remark about Germany or the Germans, I rapped out, 'and some of our longest-serving German staff'. George said loudly, 'Who's making this speech, Stark?' I quickly replied, 'You are, Secretary of State'.

The second story dates from long after George Brown had ceased to be an active political figure and I had retired from diplomacy and become an industrialist. The date was in the late eighties, when I was still Chairman of the London branch of the huge Maersk (A.P. Moller) Shipping Company. In that capacity, I was asked one day if I would take one of the senior lady members of the parent company's headquarters in Copenhagen, who was then on a visit to London, to tea at the Ritz Hotel, which she had long wanted to see.

While we were starting tea at our little table, I saw entering the hotel by the revolving door from Piccadilly none other than George Brown. I told the lady that George was a former British Foreign Secretary and waved gently to him as he came along the corridor. He walked over to our table, got down on one knee at my feet and, with a smile towards the pretty lady, kissed my hand and said, 'That's how I used to have to treat ambassadors'. We laughed and he passed on after warmly shaking the hand he had just kissed.

ANDREW STARK

The Secret Saga of the Three Ms

This is a story where fiction is a stranger to fact. In the late 1970s my work at Sotheby's entailed the supervision of some thirty offices scattered all over Europe and beyond. Their task was to collect material that could either be sent to London for sale in our Bond Street auction rooms, or could be kept for occasional auction sales held in Zurich, Monte Carlo, Florence, Amsterdam or Munich. I learned very quickly that my principal role was to interpret what were considered perfectly normal British attitudes and expectations to other nations who more often than not regarded these as quite extraordinary; conversely, I had to make clear to our British management at weekly meetings that people who didn't think or behave as if they had been brought up in English public schools were perfectly competent and pleasant people for all that. My task was not made any easier by another fact which I quickly discovered, that the Dutch didn't like the Belgians; the Norwegians positively disliked the Swedes; that the Austrians hated being equated with the Germans, and so on.

I flew around week after week pouring oil on troubled waters and naturally began to take a particular interest in some of the countries which I had hardly known before. One was Norway. In my ignorance, I was astonished to find, for example, how important a maritime nation Norway was and what a long and fascinating tradition lay behind it. I met many people in shipping circles there – a good many were art collectors – and what little spare time I had I spent in the libraries of various shipping and maritime institutes, reading up the background, and asking questions when I had an opportunity for discussion with experts.

After one such trip to Oslo I received a letter from the director of one of the shipping research bodies where I had worked, who knew that I had written a great deal on the history of collecting. He asked that I should let him know when I would be returning as there was a family who very much wanted to meet me. As it happened, a trio of Munch lithographs had to be looked at and collected for sale in London, and I was soon back in Oslo.

My friend took me to a charming and elegant house, some thirty miles outside the capital, where I was introduced to the couple who owned it. Their name was a prominent one in the Norwegian maritime world. They seemed a little on edge but we chatted amiably and they asked what research work I had done for my various earlier books. It was a topic near and dear to my heart and time passed quickly. But I soon sensed that we were approaching the moment when the reason why I had been invited to their house would be revealed.

It turned out that there had recently been discovered in their family company's Bergen office, ten or twelve substantial cases of old papers and files that had been placed in the back of the huge basement safe and probably not looked at since long before the Second World War. On inspection, these turned out to relate to the early days of the firm, from the eighties and nineties of the previous century. The bulk of the early papers were almost entirely in English. This, apparently, was not surprising as my host's grandfather had been English. Would I be prepared – was the eventual question – to study the papers and to prepare a report on their contents, and perhaps a summary of what they contained. It was made clear to me at this stage that absolute discretion was essential. I explained that I was intrigued, but that it would not be easy for me to find time for such a project, except during periods of holidays. A long correspondence and many more meetings followed and eventually I found myself in Bergen for ten days, with a room to myself, a large desk, easy access to the papers and a charming lady who could translate any Norwegian document that I couldn't understand. This is the story that emerged.

Sometime in the eighties of the nineteenth century, a professor of humanistic studies at Durham University – let us call him 'M' – was given a book as a Christmas present, entitled *Norway and its Glaciers Visited in 1851*, by J. D. Forbes. M was a keen climber, was fascinated by the book and during his next summer vacation he took the steamer from Newcastle to Stavanger and began to explore Norway, following in Forbes' footsteps. It was the first of many such journeys. He seems to have had a marvellous ear for foreign languages, and as he became more and more familiar with the country, he began to speak Norwegian really well. As there were few people in Norway at that time who spoke any English, the fact that he could readily converse with the locals proved a great advantage.

Though M was a resolute and adventurous climber, he seems to have had a strong streak of caution in him. He always sought out the most experienced guides. His equipment was the best and most advanced that money could buy. But one year, on the Snohetta Massif – one of Norway's highest mountain ranges – he and his companions got caught in an unexpected storm followed by an appalling freak blizzard. He slipped and fell into a concealed crevasse while crossing a glacier. He broke a leg and an arm and sustained terrible injuries to his chest. Twenty-four hours exposure in the open air while help was being fetched did him no good at all. And by the time he was carried down to the nearest village, he was in a bad state.

He was nursed back to health in the house of one of the guides. At first he needed constant attention and the local doctor considered that it was too dangerous to move him the forty or fifty kilometres to the nearest hospital, but M had the constitution of an ox and soon began to recover. After the initial crisis, the worst thing that befell him was extreme boredom while nature was healing the fractures. Above all, he yearned for something to read. A local schoolteacher produced some English books. She spoke some English too and sat with him each day for a while. Marianna was, in fact, a student teacher on temporary secondment to the village in which M lay. History relates that she had very bright blue eyes, a chubby, cheerful face and long blonde hair done up in a chignon. Her father was a man of some substance in far-off Stordal. Although there was considerable disparity in their ages, she and M became extremely fond of each other. Indeed, M accepted an invitation to meet the girl's parents once he could hobble about.

The whole saga hinged on that first visit to Stordal. M found the change and bustle of a thriving maritime town entirely to his liking. He seems to have spent hours in the harbour observing the mass of boats coming and going out to sea. He got to know the fishermen and fish porters, the builders of ships and the pilots, as well as a huge range of other locals, and found their activities fascinating. Although his host was a much older man, there seems to have been an immediate degree of *rapport* between the two, which eventually turned into a lifelong friendship. Judging by the letters and note-books he had kept, M had an innate curiosity about how other people earned their living and the Norwegian – let us call him P – was only too delighted to have such a receptive audience and showed M every facet of the shipping and shipbuilding business.

In the year M and P met there were some 7,700 large Norwegian sailing ships on the high seas as well as more than three hundred of the relatively new-fangled coal burning steam ships. P himself owned nine great sailing ships and three of the infinitely more costly, but much faster, steam ships.

As his leg grew stronger, M clambered around these ships studying the holds, the cabins, the great variety of sails, the derricks and the way the men loaded and unloaded the cargoes, making himself familiar with navigational instruments and charts, and even learning how to tie unusual knots.

With his formidable intellect he soon began to make suggestions for im-provements, both in the methods of work and the equipment being used. At first P merely listened indulgently but when occasionally M's ideas were put into practice, they proved to be immediately effective. After three weeks in Stordal M was declared fit to travel home. By that time he and P's daughter, Marianna, had become engaged and the parting was a great wrench.

I must now accelerate the story.

M and Marianna married and continued to live in Durham. As P grew older he asked M to give up his academic career and to join him as a partner in the shipping enterprise. M and Marianna moved to Stordal. Their son was born there. By the turn of the century the one-time professor was in sole charge of the business, which prospered and grew mightily under his management. And in due course the son, MM, joined his father in running it. They were a formidable combination and much respected throughout Scandinavia. When the First World War broke out Norway remained neu-tral, but M's fleet carried endless cargoes for Britain and its Allies. Despite huge losses to German U-boats,[1] the fleet grew and grew. By late 1917 M was a tired old man, but a wise one. He realized that the war could not last

1 Norway lost 829 ships as a direct consequence of German naval action between August 1914 and December 1918; and somewhere in excess of sixty further ships by sabotage.

much longer and that such an enormous fleet as his would not be needed in peacetime.

He himself was lost at sea when he commanded a ship – a rare event – when it disappeared on its way to Britain. The son, MM, took over. Early in 1918 he was invited over to Durham for a memorial service for his father in the University. After many years of unceasing hustle he took time off for a few days cycling around the Northumbrian countryside, to ruminate and work out how he saw his own future.

Through an earlier chance meeting he had got to know Sir William Burrell, a great ship owner himself, who was already at that time building up the collection that eventually became the Burrell Museum in Pollok Park, outside Glasgow. It later transpired that Sir William had got to know M during his university career. On the night MM stayed with Sir William in his home, Hutton Castle, a third guest in the house turned out to be James Caird, later Sir James Caird, the begetter of the Maritime Museum in Greenwich. Caird had started a shipyard in Chepstow in 1916 to build standardized ships quickly. Despite early setbacks the enterprise was such a success that the government stepped in and bought it in 1917.

The two older men found themselves intrigued by the likeable, much younger, Norwegian: he was only twenty-three at the time but he seemed to have a much older head on his shoulders. They discussed the wartime problems of the shipping world for hours, well into the night, and after MM had explained that he had in the last few days evolved a plan in his mind for the large enterprise which had become unexpectedly his after his father's sudden death, they enquired tactfully whether he would outline it to them.

MM must have felt that this was a unique opportunity to test the reaction of two highly experienced captains of industry with precisely similar interests to his own. He explained that, in his view, the tide of war was turning, in fact, had already turned, in favour of the Allies. He thought that hostilities would last no longer than twelve or eighteen months. That afterwards there would be a great glut of shipping throughout the world. So he had decided that he would at once dispose of his own shipbuilding business, which at the time was at the height of a boom. Simultaneously, he would reduce the number of vessels in his fleet dramatically. Burrell and Caird –

MM noted in his diary of the time – looked at him open-mouthed with astonishment. He continued that when the war was over, he would buy foreign vessels to make good his fleet because these were likely to come onto the market at a knock-down price. Ultimately, when the world had settled down after the consequences of the conflict, instead of concentrating wholly on the traditional Norwegian tramp-shipping and dry freight carrying, he would move into the business of carrying mineral oil in freighters, a business he considered was bound to grow. This would probably necessitate a switch from coal-burning ships to ones driven by diesel. He was convinced that this was the mode of transport of the future. And, as a final thought, which again, according to his diary, he hardly dared utter to the two wise old men, he would probably build such vessels in German shipyards, because these would be clamouring for orders for a long time after an Allied victory.

To say that Burrell and Caird were deeply impressed would be an understatement. They had thought that they were unique in having similar views, which they would carry out shortly afterwards. In any case, that evening's discussion forged a close link of friendship between the three men.

Back in Norway MM carried out his plans to the letter. As was evident from the many files I studied, it all caused – as he had predicted to Caird and Burrell – enormous antagonism, but he remained undaunted. His business thrived when many others later went to the wall. He became extremely wealthy.

The remainder of the Bergen archive charted his subsequent progress as an entrepreneurial genius. His interests spread principally to the USA and to the Argentine and grew swiftly in two new directions: the production of chemicals and the ownership of newspapers. I was intrigued about the latter, but a study of MM's notebooks gave the answer over and over and over again: it was his obsession with secrecy; the determination to keep his name out of the press which he felt in the long term would always be damaging. If he owned prominent newspapers in the areas where he was most active, then he could at least be sure that he would never see his name in their pages.

He found particularly able lieutenants to help in running the businesses. This at last gave him time to build up the wonderful collection of paintings he had always craved.

The last four crates were entirely devoted to papers covering his dealings with art galleries, dealers, auction houses and museums. It was really only at that point that the reason why I had been asked to dip into this magic world came into its own.

It must be quite clear that I got completely hooked on the project. I spent more and more time in Bergen, sifting through and studying the papers. My pile of manuscript grew and grew. At least I had the sense to get the family's agreement that whatever I wrote for them should remain my copyright.

After a couple of years I finished at last what was, in essence, only a summary of the salient facts of the story of M and MM. I delivered the final typescript, which ran to nearly 200,000 words, to the family in Oslo. And waited, and waited. A silence of such prolonged duration was slow even by Norwegian standards. At last a letter arrived. Would I come over for another visit?

In retrospect one takes even life's most stunning knocks with a certain degree of equanimity and, after all, my work on this project was basically a hobby. The family said that they had considered my work most carefully. They had read it all several times. They had taken advice from many quarters. That I had extracted an endlessly fascinating saga from the Bergen archive. But even after all the time that had elapsed since the days of MM, they felt that father and son would not want the bare facts of their lives known as I had chronicled them, as their own papers revealed them. In particular, there was concern over making public MM's amazing collecting activities.

They were truly delighted to have the story in simple, readable form for the benefit of future generations of the family, they said, but straight publication was out. Absolutely impossible. MM's craving for obscurity and obfuscation lived on. The only possibility they would consider was to turn the whole thing into a novel, avoiding all reference to real names; rendering fact as fiction.

My reaction was immediate. There was far too much material for a novel; I could not face the thought of working through it all again to re-shape the story and, in any case, I was no novelist. I also felt uncertain that any publisher would take on such a project. It was saddening too that I could not share with a wider audience this fascinating chapter in the history of Norwegian shipping which my researches had revealed.

Thus a vast pile of manuscript of riveting fact may still be waiting to be turned into fiction in a bank vault in Oslo . . .

For obvious reasons, in order to keep my troth with the family, parts of this narrative have, in fact, been rendered in a fictional manner.

FRANK HERRMANN

A Romantic Interlude

Flying westward over the Pacific in November 1971, I was on the third leg of my first journey round the world. In those early days of jumbo jets, flights were often surprisingly empty. To stimulate trade the RTW ticket had been invented and for less that £1,000 one could fly first class Round The World with as many stops as one liked. After New York and Los Angeles I was on my way to visit EMI's partner company in Japan, Toshiba-EMI. In Los Angeles, my friend and colleague Brown Meggs, the chief of Capitol Records, had persuaded me not to fly direct to Tokyo but to make a twenty-four hour stopover in Hawaii, on the grounds that it would be a shame to miss that balmy, tropical isle, the thrills of surfing and the many other pleasures of the tropics. He booked a room for me in the Royal Hawaiian Hotel on Waikiki Beach and arranged for Roger, Capitol's representative in Hawaii, to meet me and make sure I enjoyed my stay.

We were flying in brilliant sunshine, indeed the whole trip since London had been uniformly sunny. Then I saw ahead and below a patch of thick cloud and asked the stewardess what it was.

'Hawaii,' she replied.

The 747 descended into the cloud and landed at Honolulu Airport in the rain. When I came out of customs and immigration, there was Roger removing a lei – the traditional flower garland – from a polythene sleeve.

'Aloha,' he said, and hung it round my neck. I was amused to see behind him a large slot machine which dispensed fresh leis for a couple of dollars each, a fine combination of Hawaiian hospitality and American efficiency.

'The car's outside,' said Roger, taking my bags and guiding me out and into the back seat of a waiting car.

'I hope you enjoy your stay,' he said from the sidewalk as he closed the door.

'Aren't you coming with me?' I asked.

'Sorry, I've a lot of things to do,' he said, 'but if there's anything you need, just call me.'

He waved goodbye and the car moved off into the rain. It had been no more than two minutes since we had met. I wondered if he knew that I did not have his 'phone number.

The approach to a famous place from the airport is often unimpressive, and so it was as we drove into Honolulu in the rain. The principal sight was the gasworks.

The Royal Hawaiian Hotel, however, was not a disappointment: a pleasant pink building, it stood virtually alone on Waikiki Beach. Nowadays there are resort hotels wall-to-wall round the long curve of the beach. But in 1971 I could from my veranda gaze right round the beach to the peak of Diamond Head in the distance and saw that it was completely empty both of buildings and people. So much the better. It was the off-season and no doubt the rain had deterred such few tourists as might be around.

However I was not deterred. In swimming trunks I descended to the beach which began immediately outside the ground floor french windows. In fact it began somewhat before that – there was a lot of sand on the carpet. Splendid.

I walked along the beach in the warm rain to hire a surfboard and was disconcerted to find that Hawaiian boards are huge and heavy. I had in recent years become a fanatical surfer on the Atlantic beaches of North Cornwall, but that was on the short light boards on which one lies prone and head-first, skimming for hundreds of yards on the run-in of the rollers over the flat sand. This is known as skin-surfing in the USA. But on Waikiki the surf is different and the only boards are almost the size of a rowing boat. I

206

hired one and looked round to find the waves. There did not seem to be any. The sea was flat. I then saw some two or three hundred yards out to sea some faint indications of surf so I sat on the board and paddled slowly out to sea – slowly because the board was heavy and the only paddles were my hands. When I got to them I found the waves to be barely one foot high and exceedingly gentle. I heaved the board around, got on and we bobbed gently towards the shore. When all momentum ceased I paddled back out and bobbed gently in again. The rain continued to fall. It was an absurd parody of real surfing; no doubt that was why no one else was around, but having little else to do I continued for a couple of hours until I was thoroughly weary.

Later, at what would have been sunset if it were not for the thick cloud, I sat at the beach bar, protected from the rain by the palm thatch and sipped a Planter's Punch. Magic. Then I sipped another and fell into conversation with a pretty blonde girl who seemed to be the only other customer. Over more Planter's Punch she told me her story. She was Danish and had come to the USA as an au pair. She was now married to a wealthy publisher who was much older than she was – there seemed to be a slight emphasis on this point – and he was on a business trip and would not arrive until the following day. We chatted with increasing amiability and more punch for an hour or so. The romance of the islands was stirring at last. We thought we would dine together and found we could do so right there at the bar.

Then I suddenly found I was falling asleep – indeed had already fallen asleep with my forehead on the bar. Time change, jet lag, the effort of surfing and four or five Planter's Punches all caught up with me at once. I tried in vain to stay awake. I just about managed to stand up and said to Inger, 'I know this is an odd thing to say, but I have to leave you now. If I don't get to my room I'll be unconscious on the floor in two minutes.'

I just made it to my room and fell fast asleep still dressed.

In the morning I awoke, breakfasted and took a taxi through the rain, past the gasworks, back to the airport to get the flight to Tokyo exactly twenty-four hours after arriving.

MICHAEL ALLEN

A Traveller's Tale of Trial and Tribulation in Taif [1]

OR

as-sabr min allah [2]

The aircraft was delayed and The Traveller did not arrive at Huwiya[3] until sunset. He decided to stay at the al-Massarah Continental for the night. At sunrise he saw the beautiful clouds so called for a taxi to take him to Taif. The concierge told him that the hotel could not call taxis, but he summoned a private car for the journey.

'How much for the journey?' asked The Traveller.

'Fifty *ryals*,'[4] was the reply.

'But I am only going to Taif.'

'I thought you were going to the airport.'

'I am, but first I wish to take photographs in Taif at the Prayer Ground.'

The Driver agreed to the journey. On the way The Traveller marvelled at the growth of al Qaim[5]. He asked the Driver where he was from, and the latter replied, 'Taif'.

The Traveller told the Driver to take him past Bustan Ma'ashi – '*busatin*'[6] insisted the Driver.

On reaching the Prayer Ground, the Traveller directed the Driver around the wall until they reached the side of the hill between the house of Prince Saud and Taif.

---

1 Taif: Saudi Arabia, 65 miles west of Mecca; onetime summer capital of the Hijaz. The author sent this account to his official Saudi sponsor.
2 *as-sabr min allah al 'ajalla min ash-shaitan:* Patience is from God, Haste from the Devil
3 the airport for Taif
4 £8 approx
5 once a few scattered houses, now a densely built-up suburb of Taif
6 once an outlying garden – '*gardens*' according to the Driver

'Wait here,' said the Traveller, 'I am going up the hill to take photographs of this place.'

When The Traveller descended, he found the Driver had gone. He assumed the Driver might have thought he would descend to the main road and so started off in that direction. Then he saw the Driver returning. As he took another photograph, an official jeep appeared behind the Driver's car. 'Get in,' said one of the men in the jeep.

'Good morning. Who are you?' said The Traveller.

'Get in,' was the reply.

The Traveller got in. Another jeep arrived with a police corporal. The latter spoke quietly with The Traveller's escort and then told him to proceed. The Traveller asked to be taken to the Chief of Police or the Security Headquarters. The escort said nothing. Asked his name, he offered it, and added that taking photographs was forbidden. The Traveller offered him his camera. He refused to take it.

'If photography is forbidden, why did the Driver not tell me?' asked The Traveller. 'Three days before the *'id* [7], the Army were camped here and the Duty Officer told me that I could not take photographs because preparations were being made for the King's *'id* visit, but that I could return afterwards.'

The Escort said nothing. They drove behind the late King Feisal's palace and through Qarwa to Mithna.[8]

'Ah,' said The Traveller, 'I remember that house being built over thirty years ago, it was the first modern house by these gardens.' The jeep turned into the courtyard of a house opposite to that remembered by The Traveller (once used by the American Military Mission and now by the Saudi Agricultural Bank).

The Driver entered a room marked *dhabit al khafr* [9] but motioned The Traveller to remain outside with his escort. He soon came out and demanded The Traveller's camera. The Traveller refused but offered it to his escort in the jeep, who took it and passed it over to the Driver.

7 the feast at the end of Ramadan, the Islamic month of fasting
8 southern suburbs of Taif
9 'Duty Officer'

'My passport is in my baggage in your car,' said the Traveller to the Driver, who disregarded him. To The Traveller, the sentry's modern carbine and another notice reading *ist'lamat fi khidmatak* [10] were the only signs that this was 1981 and not a generation ago.

It was now 7.20 a.m. Ten minutes later, three people in civilian dress came out of the Duty Officer's room where obviously they had been sleeping. One of them questioned The Traveller about why he had been taking photographs and asked for his passport. 'Let us speak in English,' said The Traveller. 'I cannot,' replied the Questioner. He, and his two companions, returned to the office but the Escort remained outside joined by another man, who first eyed The Traveller with suspicion but after a few minutes fetched him a chair. The sentry at the gate – the only person in uniform – suggested that The Traveller should rest in the shade.

At 7.45 a.m. a man said to be the Duty Officer emerged to speak to The Traveller, taking him across the courtyard into the guards' rest room. The Traveller explained his reasons for taking photographs of a place which had once been his home for five years.

'Wait,' said the Duty Officer, 'I have sent for the *mudir.*'

'How long? – I hope to leave Huwiya for Jedda at 9.20,' said The Traveller.

About 8.15, a dark-moustached man appeared who gave The Traveller an unfriendly look and told him not to stand by the Duty Officer's office. The new sentry motioned The Traveller to sit down and offered him a share of his breakfast delivered to him whilst still on duty!

At 8.30 the Questioner appeared together with the Driver.

'You said you were going to the airport and then went to Taif,' said the Questioner.

'No,' said the Traveller, 'the hotel might have said so, but I told the Driver exactly what I wanted.'

'True,' said the Driver.

'Photographs are forbidden,' said the Questioner, handing back The Traveller's camera. 'Did you take any pictures of military camps?'

'No,' said The Traveller, 'only seven or eight pictures of the area by the

10 'Information: at your service'

Prayer Ground – surely that is not forbidden? I have taken hundreds of pictures of the Kingdom.'

'Yes it is – and mosques and holy places must not be photographed.'

'I am sorry – keep the camera.'

'No – take it, we have not interfered with the film. The Driver was doing his duty. You can go.'

'How?'

'The Driver will take you.'

The Traveller bade farewell. On the way past the souk the Driver said, 'It was my duty to make a report – see, here it is', and he proceeded to tear up what appeared to have been the statement he had made. He then went on to point out places of interest as they drove through Taif. It was 8.40 but he assured The Traveller they would reach the airport by 9 a.m.

'Why did you not tell me not to take photographs?' asked The Traveller.

'I am a soldier,' said the Driver, 'since fourteen years. I must watch first.'

The Driver and The Traveller then spoke of officers and NCOs they knew. 'That is the new Army Transport Maintenance Depot,' said the Driver.

'I built the first ammunition depot at the back of that camp,' said The Traveller.

'I remember it,' said the Driver, who then proceeded to act as guide for the rest of the journey. They arrived at the airport at 9.05, two and a half hours after leaving the al-Massarah hotel, but the Driver said he would not charge The Traveller for waiting time.

Verily, patience is from God, but the Traveller is still wondering whether such knowledge that morning came from wisdom or just old age, and how a stranger would have fared in similar circumstances.

ST JOHN ARMITAGE

A Fishy Tale – but True

In the early 1960s the British Embassy in Brazil was still based in Rio de Janeiro. There was a small Beau Geste-type building in the outback of Brasilia, where the First Secretary kept monkeys in the courtyard, but all diplomatic business was conducted from Rio.

The most envied weekend recreation for us in Rio was to go to a little fishing village called Buzios, near Cabo Frio to the east of Rio. There was no bridge to Niteroi in those days, so it meant a lengthy initial journey by ferry. The road thereafter left a lot to the imagination. Once I had to wade waist-deep in flood water to find where it was.

Buzios was idyllic – a few fishermen's huts on a pure white beach. Its pleasures were nevertheless not totally unknown. Once while I was there Brigitte Bardot stayed in the next door hut owned by the Mouraviev-Apostols. It rather affected the tranquillity of the spot as the Brazilian Air Force saw it as their duty to fly helicopters over from time to time when she sunbathed. Clearly they had her security uppermost in their minds.

Fishing was one of the great joys. It was so easy to snorkel out in the morning and see a pair of eyes and antennae in a cleft of the rocks: with one shot of a harpoon one could pull out a sumptuous lobster to take back to cook fresh with a butter sauce and a bottle of vodka.

My best friend there was an Anglo-Brazilian called Peter Ribero dos Santos. He was marvellously fit. Only a few weeks before, he had been in-volved in an air crash in Rio harbour. He broke the aircraft window and swam with his son to safety. There were no other survivors.

One day Peter arranged a fishing trip in an old fourteen-foot boat with a grizzled local fisherman. Along with us came Alison Burnett, the daughter of the local Shell manager. There were just the four of us. We spent a lei-surely morning catching fish after fish effortlessly with spinner bait over the stern of the bat.

When we had all we could possibly eat – and the fisherman sell – we set off back to the village.

The sea was as flat as a tortilla when suddenly beside us the water erupted. A colossal manta ray appeared, slowly flapped its huge fins like wings as it flew above the water before disappearing below the surface. It must have been more than thirty feet across and had it landed on our boat would have sent us straight to the bottom. We were stunned into silence which was then broken by the sobbing of the fisherman. He told us we had just seen the Devil (*Diablo*) and when it appeared it meant that someone on the boat was going to die. As he was the oldest, he knew it would be him. We sailed mournfully back to his hut. He had fourteen children. He at once took to his hammock and, surrounded by his family, prepared for death.

This all took place on a Sunday. Three days later, I attended the funeral of my friend Peter Ribero dos Santos in Rio Cathedral. He had died from a rare form of leukaemia.

When I last heard of the old fisherman he was fit and well and counting his grandchildren.

JOHN MORGAN

Peking after the Picnic

In autumn 1997 I walked round the old Legation quarter and peered over the outer wall of our old compound, the wall on which long, long ago the inscription 'Lest we forget' used to commemorate the defence of the Legations against the Boxers. The stone gateway into the compound is still there and the swooping roofs of the No. 1 House still show above the coping of the wall. A block of flats has been built on what forty-five years ago was my garden. I could see no further; but gone clearly are those lawns and scarlet-pillared bungalows, the chapel, the two senior neo-Georgian houses; the range of flats at the back in the style of British India (scene of so many curry lunches), the trees where sparrows sought diplomatic asylum against the revolutionary campaign for their eradication.

Gone too is the old character of the city. The people are more prosperous and freer in how they dress and behave. They have paid a price which the young ones will ignore and their elders may think worth paying. Peking was still, in the mid-fifties, a huge walled city, the biggest I suppose in the world. The gates of the city, the arches across the avenues, the dozen or so ancient temples, and above all the Forbidden City dominated the grey *hutungs*, a myriad of lanes threaded between one-storey courtyards. Through their near-circular moon gates one glimpsed a tree, plenty of washing, pots and pans, grinning infants with holes cut for convenience in the seat of their trousers. Camels, their feet muffled in sacking, were allowed to bring coal in from the hills after dark. During the same hours the night soil was carted to the market gardens outside the walls, until (it was reported) Attlee protested against this practice on good sanitary grounds during his visit in 1954.

Many of us fell in love with this city, more mediaeval than modern, in a way difficult now even for the most devoted businessman, as he sojourns in his glittering hotel, navigates the traffic jams and, through the grey industrial haze, surveys mile after mile of Communist architecture. Our work was odd rather than arduous. We were only half-recognized as a diplomatic mission, and ordinary diplomatic work was scarce. But I had, though completely untrained, to hold up to the light and examine for tuberculosis the X-rays of White Russian refugees and then decide whether to grant them an entry permit to Australia. I had to counsel unenthusiastically some of the forlorn American deserters from the Korean war, for example when one of them got into trouble with the authorities for kissing a girl in the park. Twice a year, on May Day and on the first of October, we stood amazed hour after hour, a puny group of spectators for a parade of half a million Chinese filing past their leaders. I have a black-and-white snap of Chairman Mao, high on the Gate of Heavenly Peace a tiny figure above his own huge portrait, saluting the crowd with his cap. According to the new ritual of the People's Republic, he presented himself first to the east, then walked to the western end of the long balcony, strong in the mandate of heaven as the half million shouted and sang in the square below him.

But our main pleasure lay in expeditions into the hills. There were no modern maps, so we had to rely on pre-war versions. These did not show the use to which the old temples and monasteries were being put. It was, moreover, far from clear where we were allowed to walk. The only way of finding out was to try. The peasants were glad to see us and, in those days, to chat to our Chinese-speakers. But soldiers and officials tended to be suspicious, to bar our way or to turn us back. I have a picture of Teddy Youde, later Governor of Hong Kong, sitting on a chair in a village square writing himself and the rest of us a pass. These were the days of bureaucratic innocence and respect for paper; once our identity was set down in writing, suspicion melted. The Western Hills were best in the spring, when cherry blossom lit the brown slopes; the valley of the Ming Tombs in autumn, when persimmons glowed orange in the trees as a bright afternoon sharpened towards hard frost, and we found our way back to the Land Rovers down the avenues of stone beasts.

These were for me happy, almost magical years. They came to an end in farce. I had negotiated arduously with all concerned a method of leaving China which no other Briton had attempted for decades – by train from Peking through Mongolia to connect with the Trans-Siberian Railway to Moscow. All was in order; the day of departure dawned. The diplomatic corps was small, and there was a pleasant custom that your friends gathered in person to see you off. There on the station platform were my British colleagues, the beautiful Swedish girls, Indians, Pakistanis, Indonesians – all those with whom I had sung carols, danced reels, walked, drank and gossiped for two years. I shook hands and kissed as appropriate. My luggage was in the train. All that was lacking was my passport. There was an argument going on down at the entrance to the platform between our administration clerk and a Chinese official. The trouble became clear later. My exit visa said that I was leaving (as was normal) by plane; but here I was attempting to leave the People's Republic by train. The implications of this wrong doing were clearly massive, and the official needed time to ponder them. Eventually he gave in, tossed the passport to our clerk, who sprinted up the platform and thrust it at me. But by then the train was moving, just too fast for me to jump on board. 'To the next station!' came the cry. So I ran down the line of gaping diplomats, and into the Land Rover. We reached the next station just in time to see the tail of the train disappearing towards the Great Wall and Mongolia.

A few days later, humiliated and frustrated, I finally left for Mongolia indeed, but by air. In those days people sometimes disappeared in the People's Republic, but never property. My suitcases had already been returned to me in perfect order, sealed with a label which, roughly translated, read 'These belong to the damned fool who tried to leave China by train.'

DOUGLAS HURD

150 Years of BBC Experience

We thought they were taking pity on us by giving us something nice and easy for once.

Our masters in the BBC's TV Centre at Wood Lane asked me for some pretty pictures and a reasonably good story to go out as a curtain-raiser to one of the regular meetings of the Farm Ministers in Brussels. Their task, as ever, was to try to keep farm subsidies within bounds at a time when the UK was a big paymaster just after joining, and was about to become the biggest. This was the mid-seventies and before Mrs Thatcher became Prime Minister and began demanding 'our money back'.

I dreamt up a splendid expedition to the beautiful region just near Orléans and within easy reach of Paris. An additional attraction was that we had been invited by the local farmers to have lunch with them.

It all went beautifully. The sun shone, the camera (it was still the time when we worked with colour film) worked without jamming, and the camera crew they'd sent from London to join me were old friends of mine. Both of them, cameraman and soundman, had immense experience as well as being able to handle the language.

Our hosts first took us to a huge building where the apple harvest had been carefully stored. The trouble was that the apples had flooded the market and were un-saleable at any price. Of course, the Common Agricultural Policy had an answer: money was available to smooth out marketing problems like this. Subsidies were forthcoming to denature the product so that they could not be fraudulently introduced into the market at some future time.

The process of denaturing was simple in the extreme. Huge high-sided trucks were loaded with apples and driven under a kind of bridge. Men with large cans sprinkled them liberally with a mixture of molasses and water and that was that. It made good pictures, but we wanted more. We explained all this to our hosts during a lavish lunch, the kind they claimed to eat practically every day.

We hit on the idea of following the trucks to see where they went. It wasn't a long journey, only a few miles. We filmed them on the journey and as they turned into a huge field. Once there, the apples were simply dumped onto the ground in large mounds. Then appeared what seemed like all the cows in Christendom.

They eagerly gathered round the mounds and gratefully munched away at the bounty, growing fatter obviously and giving ever more milk and providing more beef. There was the rub. Milk was also a big problem with the CAP. There was always too much of it and a great deal of the EC budget went on ways of storing the stuff or just buying it up and pouring it away. The milk lake and the beef mountain were terms of derision for the tabloids and of despair for the poor old bureaucrats who were only doing their best in Brussels.

All this made for a substantial two-and-a-half-minute film. We had nice pictures and a punch line about 'Here's the CAP in action, solving one problem for the fruit producers and making another one for the dairy farmers: the conundrum which the farm ministers will have to try to resolve at their meeting.'

We had also been well fed and watered by the locals and we planned a good evening out in Paris before going back to our various HQs, theirs in London, mine at the time in Bonn.

But we hadn't planned for the sudden whims of our masters in Wood Lane.

On return to the old Claridge's Hotel in the Champs Elysées, a favourite of mine since I was chucked out of the Crillon just because Richard Nixon was arriving on a visit, there was an urgent message to call the Desk in London.

We told them we had an excellent entry for the following day's bulletin and we were pulling out. Yes, they said, please do, but we want you to go somewhere else first. Beirut was burning. It was the start of real trouble there, one of the bouts of the civil war that eventually brought the Israelis into southern Lebanon and the Syrians into the capital itself.

Well, if the city was burning, we didn't really wish to go, especially at dead of night. As usual, the editor explained that we were the nearest people available at short notice to do this 'fireman's' job. It is well known in the trade that editors have the smallest scale maps possible. I've always believed they organize assignments by looking at their world globe pencil sharpeners.

I did ask where the man was whose job it was to cover the Middle East and who actually lived in Beirut. The answer was that he was completely out of touch. He was with the Moroccan masses on their so-called Green March, reporting the attempted takeover of the former Spanish Sahara.

So there was nothing for it but to forego our planned dinner at La Coupole and take the last flight by Middle East Airlines (slogan: '75 percent of our flights are non-stop!') getting us to Beirut somewhere around midnight.

Fortunately another old friend came to the airport, despite the danger, just to guide us to the current hotel where the world press were gathered. For this trip it was the Mayflower. The old St George's Hotel on the waterfront, where we usually stayed, had been burned out the previous year.

Next morning, we were up early to report the mayhem. That task completed, we got the censor's stamp on the film bag and found a businessman to take it in his hand luggage to London that afternoon.

Both our films, the one from the peace of the French countryside near Orléans and our latest offering from the war-torn ghettoes of Beirut were well received. They told us by telex that they both went out on the same nine o'clock news bulletin. Congratulations were duly celebrated.

But as we were travelling around the next day doing a follow-up, my excellent cameraman tapped me on the shoulder and brought us all back to earth.

'Do you realize, Bob,' he said as the stray bullets whistled around us, 'that between the three of us there are more than 150 years of BBC experience in this car? Do you think they are trying to tell us something?'

ROBERT ELPHICK

A Seafaring Story

Within a few days of my sixteenth birthday I was on my way to Australia aboard an old coal-burning ship, at the start of the first of seven voyages to Australia and New Zealand as an indentured apprentice with Port Line, a subsidiary of Cunard. My parents, who had agreed that I could go to sea providing I matriculated, paid £50 to secure my indenture. The traditional terms were modified only by the insertion of a clause that the £50 would be refunded providing I was 'of good behaviour' for the full four years. Apprentices received food, accommodation and training. All of these were, in Port Line, of a very high standard indeed. The training included every aspect of seamanship and ship maintenance, in addition to navigation and teaching the passengers how to play deck golf.

Using the finest refrigerated cargo ships ever built, Port Line traded to Australia and New Zealand, either from Europe via South Africa or by way of Canada and the United States via the Panama Canal. It was observation of the carriage of cargoes around the world that awakened a fascination with international trade and economics that had persisted throughout my working life and led me to an early decision to study economics at university as soon as I was free to do so.

At the end of the four-year indenture, I passed the examinations to qualify as 'Second Mate of a foreign-going steamship'. In addition to the written tests in navigation, ship construction, marine engineering and cargo stowage, the examinations included an oral test, the requirements for which necessitated a word-perfect memory of all the then 32 Articles of the International Rules of the Road.

With a brand-new and impressively inscribed Board of Trade 'ticket', the next objective was to get to Australia as cheaply as possible; my purpose being to study economics at the University of Tasmania where my London University matriculation was readily recognized and where I had already met Margaret, my wife-to-be. The cheapest way to get to Australia was to work my passage aboard a 'delivery' voyage, but that required hanging about in London until an opportunity arose.

After spending two months as third mate of the *Baltrover*, on a voyage to Poland, I signed on as an able seaman on a small Dutch dredger being sent to work on a contract in the harbour of Newcastle, New South Wales. There were two other qualified second mates also working their passage as ABs. The rest of the crew were a motley bunch of disreputable-looking characters, all of whom appeared anxious to leave the United Kingdom for one reason or another. We left Rotterdam in November 1951 on a voyage that was to take 93 days.

The dredger was not designed for long sea voyages. The vessel, of about a thousand tons, was equipped with neither radar nor radio direction-finding equipment. The only radio on board was a Philips mantel radio intended to allow the captain to listen to weather reports: but as that radio soon broke down, the vessel from then on had contact with the outside world only when it reached port every four weeks or so.

What is more, the dredger did not have a real name. My last sight of Britain for seventeen years was of the Lizard Point signal station vainly trying to determine the vessel's name as we disappeared over the horizon. To their repeated question, 'What ship?' the Lizard Point signallers could make no sense of the morse code reply 'HAM 301' sent by the small vessel's Aldis lamp.

Apart from lacking communications and navigation equipment, the HAM 301 also lacked a refrigerator. A large wooden ice-box had been installed on an open deck below the bridge and at each port of call this was filled with ice and some fresh food. After that it was a diet of tinned food until the next port. For a four-week passage across the Indian Ocean the only fresh food, after the first few days, was a large white shark caught by towing a hook to which, as bait, was tied a white linen collar. No shark ever tasted better.

The first port of call was Lisbon, where the crew made the most of a few days while the captain discussed with the owners whether the safest route would be via Panama or the Suez Canal. Panama would take longer but would avoid the growing political disturbances surrounding the Suez Canal at the end of 1951. The final choice was to go via Suez, Aden, and Colombo.

By the time HAM 301 reached Port Said, the canal workers were on strike and the Royal Navy sent a boat to take our mooring lines. The situation ashore must have been desperate for foreigners at that time as the captain was persuaded to take on board a passenger. To entrust him to the HAM 301 and its ruffianly crew, the family of the young man, Greek traders, must have been extremely anxious to get him out of Egypt in a hurry. The crew were not at all happy that the passenger's presence brought the total number on board to an unlucky 13. The young man received rather heavy treatment from King Neptune when HAM 301 crossed the equator. As it was rumoured that he had a package of diamonds in his luggage, he was perhaps lucky to arrive in Australia at all.

Christmas was spent in the Red Sea, where it was decided the HAM 301 might as well stop so that the whole crew could have a festive dinner together: after all, the vessel certainly was not going anywhere in a hurry. New Year's Eve was celebrated at anchor off Aden, where the security situation ashore was not that much better than in Port Said.

From Aden, bound for Colombo, it was very quickly discovered that the blunt nose of the dredger would make it impossible to progress against the seasonal north-easterly trade wind. The captain decided the only thing to do was to go south to the equator, away from the usual shipping routes, and then turn east to make for the Sunda Strait. Surabaya, not Colombo, was to be the next port of call. By the time we were passing the spectacular crater of Krakatoa, the supply of fresh water was very low. I remember taking off my shoes to climb down inside the water tank with a teacup to bail out the day's supply from what was left between the ribs of the tank's bottom.

In the years that followed, I have found it a sobering thought that if the dredger's engine had failed we would have drifted for a month, well away from the usual sea routes, before anyone began to wonder about the HAM 301 and where the vessel and its crew might be.

In early 1952, Surabaya was yet another port where there was serious concern for the safety of foreigners especially, in this case, if they were thought to be Dutch. It did not help in such places and in the political climate of the time, that the HAM 301 was both Dutch-owned and registered in South Africa. At an early stage, the captain had decided it might be discreet to fly the red ensign over the stern in the hope that no-one might notice the words 'Cape Town' engraved in large letters.

From Surabaya to Newcastle took a further four weeks, anchoring briefly off Thursday Island to ask for and to pick up a very surprised and somewhat apprehensive Barrier Reef pilot. By this time, if members of the crew were speaking to each other at all, it was almost solely for the purpose of threatening violence. Just as the voyage was nearing its end, the HAM 301 hit the worst and most dangerous weather of all. We spent nearly three frustrating and very uncomfortable days just south of Brisbane, within sight of the same lighthouse, with no alternative but to stem a southerly storm hoping that the fuel would last.

Signing off in Newcastle, the delivery crew were generously treated by the owners to one night in an hotel, before being cast adrift in Australia. I looked forward with pleasurable anticipation to my first fresh water bath in three months. But the standard of hotel chosen by the owners' agents was such that hot baths were discouraged through the simple procedure of removing all the bath plugs. My seaman's ingenuity was at least sufficient not to be defeated by such mean action. I wasted no time in plugging the drain with a well worn piece of underwear!

I arrived in Hobart, by flying boat from Sydney, at the beginning of March 1952 with nothing to my name but a five-pound note and a trunk full of second-hand clothing – and my Second Mate's ticket.

RICHARD TALLBOYS

The Capture of Asolo

In the last week of April 1945 the American and British troops in Italy fanned out over the Po valley, meeting with very little resistance. On 29 April the German forces in Italy surrendered.

During that time I was attached to the American 85th Division to report the progress of the advance to Army Group headquarters. Resistance was crumbling, and the Italian partisans were active everywhere. The divisional headquarters moved every day, and we found ourselves one evening at the town of Bassano. At the evening briefing I noticed on the map that there was a place called Asolo on our line of advance, the forward troops being well past it.

Next day, as there was time on my hands, I decided to go and have a look at Asolo because the family of a friend of mine, George Lawrence, used to rent a house there for holidays. He had suggested that, if I found myself in that part of Italy, I should go to see if it had survived. So I and a fellow officer took a jeep and motored along the main road to Treviso in perfect spring weather. Asolo is a pretty hill town situated a mile or so north of the main road. When it came in sight, we turned left and were advancing peacefully when suddenly round a corner we were faced by half a dozen German soldiers standing across the road. We stopped, cursing our stupidity at being captured in the last days of the war. But the soldiers, who were unarmed, remained rooted to the ground, and after a few seconds a little Italian, dripping with hand grenades, emerged from behind a tree and cried, 'Welcome, liberators!'. He then dismissed the soldiers and came to talk to us. He was the local doctor, and he told us that there had been partisan skirmishes in the area. 160 Germans had been captured, and a large gun. For the last day or two the Italian leaders had been regularly going down to the main road to plead with the advancing Americans, trying to persuade them to come up to Asolo – but of course they had insisted on pressing on towards Venice. The concern of the people of Asolo was to get rid of the captured Germans, who were assembled under guard in the local cinema. We never let on that we were there 'unofficially', and we did our best to look like liberators.

We then took the doctor on board and drove up into the town, where total silence reigned. There was no one about; everyone was indoors, behind closed shutters. In films, one sees cheering crowds, welcoming the 'liberators', but in fact the inhabitants often keep quiet, fearing a change of events.

The doctor led us up to the cinema and asked me if I would address a few words to the Germans. This request worried me as I couldn't think what to say. When we entered the cinema, we were faced with the extraordinary sight of an assembly of German soldiers sitting quietly on wooden benches like well-behaved schoolboys. As I mounted the stage, my guardian angel came to my rescue and gave me an idea. I told them that they were now prisoners of war, and that I had come to take them over and arrange for their evacuation to a base area, where they would be treated 'in accordance with the terms of the Geneva Convention'. There was audible relief at that moment, and even a little hand-clapping. The Italians had told them that unspeakable things might happen to them when the Allies arrived.

A tour of the village ensued, and I asked to see my friend's house. This was arranged and we found ourselves sitting in the drawing-room deciding what to do next. The problem was how to get the prisoners back to the base area. I had to contact 85th Division, and I asked the doctor for ideas. He simply replied, 'Telephone'. We were staggered at this suggestion as in a war area all civilian communications are usually out of action, but the advance had been so fast that the lines were intact. I believe I could have telephoned that day to Venice, which was still in German hands. So the lorries were summoned.

We then settled down for a cup of tea. We were a party of twelve or so, including an elderly English lady who had continued to live in Asolo throughout the war, generally unmolested. We told her how we had arrived in Asolo, and she told us that she had a nephew in the army in Italy, and she hoped he would come to see her. Twenty minutes later the nephew turned up – liberator no. 3! An hour after that, the American lorries arrived to collect the prisoners.

ANTHONY FORSTER

224

An Unlucky Encounter in Salazar's Portugal

Parede is a stop on the coastal railway between Lisbon and Cascais. Not much, if anything, is to be found about it in guidebooks because there is not much there apart from leafy streets of villas looking out towards the Atlantic and one or two restaurants. I did not see much of it the only time I have been there because it was late on a dark December evening and I was there for only about half an hour spent mostly riding about in the taxi that had brought me from Lisbon trying to find the house of a lawyer named Joachim Pires de Lima. It was consequently a place I might have quickly forgotten had mischance not made my visit something to be remembered, especially by Mário Soares, later to be Prime Minister and President of Portugal, who had sent me there to see Pires de Lima. In consequence of my visit, Soares was arrested four days later, held for two-and-a-half months in detention and then exiled to Portugal's equatorial island of São Tomé.

It happened in the days when Portugal was still a police state ruled by the dictator Dr António de Oliveira Salazar. Dissidents like the Socialist Mário Soares lived under constant surveillance by the Polícia Internacional e de Defesa do Estado, known as the PIDE, Salazar's secret police, and were periodically arrested and detained without charge or exiled to one of Portugal's overseas territories. Soares, a Lisbon lawyer representing political dissidents and the family of Salazar's opponent, General Humberto Delgado, murdered in 1965, was a focus of attention by the PIDE as a leader of opposition to the regime. He had been jailed eleven times for political activity by the time I met him in December 1967 but had not yet been exiled overseas. He later wrote in his memoirs: 'The Government was looking for any pretext to put me permanently out of action . . . They found what they wanted at the end of 1967.'

The strange events that led to my meeting with Dr Soares and his arrest and exile to São Tomé after my visit to Parede began with the arrival in

London at the offices of the *Sunday Telegraph*, for which I was then a reporter, of a letter from a freelance journalist in Lisbon. Soares was in no way connected with the letter or its contents but some of his colleagues in Lisbon's legal community, among them Pires de Lima, had become professionally involved as advocates in the sensational story it related. For reasons which were immediately apparent, the story had not been reported in Portugal's heavily censored press.

The letter reported that the 35-year-old regime of Dr Salazar was being threatened by a scandal linking prominent Portuguese, including at least one Minister, with teenaged call-girls in a Lisbon vice ring. Several men, it said, had been charged with corrupting the morals of minors and Lisbon was buzzing with rumours, emanating from the legal district, that the Minister of Justice, Dr João de Matos Antunes Varela, regarded as a potential successor to the 78-year-old dictator, had resigned from the Government because Salazar had suppressed a prosecution for fear of the consequences if the scandal became public knowledge. The letter said it would not be possible for the writer to do the story himself and suggested it might be worth a trip to Portugal by a staff reporter

It was a story no Sunday newspaper could ignore. Scandal is meat and drink to Sabbath journalism, and this was the real thing, not the hyped-up ersatz variety with which papers have so often to make do. It was also exclusive, because if word of it had reached any other journalist in Lisbon it had not appeared in any British newspaper. Within two hours of the letter's arrival on Tuesday, 5 December 1967, the decision had been taken, and I was on the 10.40 TAP Portuguese Airlines flight to Lisbon next morning with £50 in travellers cheques for my expenses.

Every visitor to Portugal in those days encountered the PIDE on arrival and departure because it conducted immigration controls. For most, the encounters resulted in no more than a stamp in the passport, but I feared that the word 'Journalist' in my own passport might prompt awkward questions about the reason for my visit. I decided to say that I had come for a holiday. Fortunately the only question I was asked was if I was carrying any firearms. Apparently satisfied by my reply that I was not, the officer stamped my passport with a 60-day visa below the letters PIDE.

The first thing to be done was to try to see Dr Antunes Varela, the Minister said to have resigned after thirteen years as Minister of Justice. The letter from Lisbon said he had returned to academic life as Professor of Civil Law at the University of Coimbra, where he had been assistant to a former holder of that post before joining the Salazar Government in 1954, so my immediate destination had to be the ancient university town 120 miles north of Lisbon. After buying a return rail ticket at the Santa Apolonia station beside the river Tagus, where I found there was not a train until the evening and reserved a seat on it, I took a taxi to the office of the journalist whose letter had brought me to Lisbon.

Tom Hendrik, as I shall call him, substituting a pseudonym for his real name, was a slightly mysterious figure in the Lisbon of the late 1960s. It was an odd place for a freelance journalist because rigid press censorship left little to report of interest to foreign papers apart from an occasional non-political story such as storms the previous week which had killed more than four hundred people and caused widespread havoc. Some suspected he might be working for a western Intelligence agency. He was reputed to have important contacts in both the regime and the PIDE. He left Portugal after the regime was overthrown by the military coup of 25 April 1974.

His office was on an upper floor of a building in a noisy square filled with traffic fronting the Cais do Sodré station, terminus of the line to Cascais. He was seated at his desk, a slim, spare young man, with light brown hair cropped close to his head and fair skin tanned by years in the South African sun before he came to Portugal. He looked surprised and not at all pleased when I walked in. He said at once that I should not have gone to his office and I must not go there again because it could be dangerous for him to be linked to the story. It became immediately apparent he was anxious I should leave.

I told him I had reserved a seat on the evening train to Coimbra where I would be spending the night at the Astoria Hotel and would be at the Tivoli Hotel in the Avenida da Liberdade, Lisbon, after my return from Coimbra next day. He said he would call at the Tivoli about 9.30 a.m. on Friday and asked me to wait in the lobby. He said he would then give me some names and phone numbers of people to contact. In the meantime, he suggested, I should ask my office in London to get the current issue of the French weekly magazine *Jeune Afrique* which he said he had heard contained something about the scandal. He stressed I should not try to contact him.

Within ten minutes I was back in the street, watching Lisbon's charmingly old-fashioned trams, which looked as if they had been built about 1910, chasing each other round the Praça Duque Terceira in front of the Cais do Sodré station. I felt not a little put out. I wondered if Hendrik was expecting a visitor and did not want his visitor to see me. It not occur to me that his office might be under surveillance by the PIDE.

The journey to Coimbra, normally two-and-a-half hours by rapido, was much longer than usual because of flooding caused by the previous week's storms. The flooded countryside could not be seen in the darkness but the train kept stopping. It was nearly midnight when I reached Coimbra and checked into the Astoria Hotel, a triangular-shaped building with faded 1920s decor in a small square beside the Mondego River below the town.

The university stands like a citadel on the hill-top of the old Moorish city, approached by cobbled streets and flights of steps rising steeply from the river. The route goes through an ancient arch, still known by its Arab name as the Gate al Medina, in the thick city wall. After an early breakfast in a small dining room which I shared with a boisterous group of Brazilian businessmen, I began the walk to the hill-top. Mass-tourism having not yet reached Coimbra, the cafés, handicraft shops and postcard displays now found along the route passing Coimbra's fortress-like Romanesque cathedral had not yet appeared. The streets and steps were empty except for local women in black dresses and shawls, some with baskets on their heads, but students in long black gowns came into view when, having reached the summit, I went through a gateway into the spacious courtyard of Coimbra's former royal palace in which the university, founded in 1192, had been located since 1537.

Locating Dr Varela turned out to be easier than I had expected. Some students directed me to his office, just a short walk from where I was standing. The university had given him a palatial suite in a building below a tall baroque clock tower at the end of a colonnaded walkway. This was approached by an imposing double stairway rising from the courtyard beneath a portico decorated with the Portuguese coat of arms and figures of Justice and Fortitude. The walkway passed the university's splendid ceremonial hall hung with portraits of Portugal's kings.

By a lucky chance the new Professor appeared to be in his office. The door was open, offering a partial view of its gracious interior and a tall window, and voices could be heard within. As I waited in an anteroom a young man came out. I introduced myself and said I was seeking an interview with the Professor. He went back into the office, leaving the door open, and I could see him talking to someone. He emerged moments later and said, 'Dr Varela asks you to excuse him as he is very busy.'

Retracing my steps down the cobbled streets and stairways, now presenting spectacular views of the rooftops, river and surrounding countryside, I did not feel I had had an altogether wasted journey. It would have been a coup to have secured an interview, but I had at least established that the former Minister had returned to academic life, thus confirming that he had resigned from the Government. Not then realizing that the university, which had provided many key members of the regime and where Salazar himself had once been a professor, was now a hot-bed of student unrest, like so many universities in Europe and the United States in the 1960s. I did not seek any comments from Dr Varela's students, fearing to risk upsetting the university authorities. Besides, though still early in the day, I had to telephone my office and suspected this might take a long time.

My suspicion turned out to be well founded. The rest of the morning was spent at a post and telephone office in the centre of a small square in front of the town's main police station trying to get through to London. Eventually I gave up and sent a telegram to George Evans, assistant editor (news), asking him to get the current issue of *Jeune Afrique*. The woman in charge of the telephones then called triumphantly 'Londres!' and directed me to a cubicle where I spoke to George. He seemed to be not too disappointed with my progress. He was pleased that I had confirmed the Minister's resignation.

Further waiting followed at the station because the Lisbon train had been delayed by flooding on its way from Oporto. Several passengers were in the compartment where I found a seat. A middle-aged man and woman seated opposite each other by the window were speaking to the others in Portuguese. Later, the woman produced a cake, cut it up and offered pieces to everyone including myself, saying something to me in Portuguese. I smiled and thanked her in English. 'Oh,' she said, laughing, You're English. We're English, too.'

We got into conversation. The man introduced himself as the manager of a Sandeman estate at Oporto. They asked if I was in Portugal on holiday or business. Thinking that both looked like *Daily Telegraph* readers and might be helpful, I said I was a reporter for the *Sunday Telegraph* and told them why I had been in Coimbra. I realized at once I had made a mistake. Their manner changed. The man asked why British newspapers were always attacking Portugal and if it was realized how much harm this was doing to Britain, and British business interests, among the Portuguese. He then launched into an attack on Harold Wilson and his Labour Government, then in office, speaking at length about how they were ruining the country. The rest of the journey was spent mostly in silence, looking out of the window at the flooded countryside, until darkness fell.

When I eventually reached the Tivoli Hotel, a notice in my bathroom warned me that the tap water was not safe to drink because of the flooding. There was also a telegram from George Evans saying he had asked the paper's Paris correspondent to get a copy of *Jeune Afrique*.

Next morning I waited for Hendrik, as requested, in the hotel's spacious lobby. Having noted his apparent anxiety not to be seen with me I placed myself in an armchair at the back of the lobby well away from the reception desk. Suddenly he was sitting in the armchair beside me as though he had just materialized, having apparently come from somewhere at the back of my chair. He declined my offer of tea or coffee, explaining that he couldn't stay long. After listening to my account of my visit to Coimbra, he said I should speak to Mário Soares because he would know about the scandal and would be willing to talk because he was a leader of opposition to the regime. He then gave me phone numbers for Soares and for some other lawyers he said could help. He wished me luck, and was gone.

Having now only the rest of Friday to stand up the story, it was time to seek help from 'diplomatic sources'. At the British Embassy in the Rua S Domingos à Lapa, there was some surprise that I had been sent to Lisbon for a story that locally-based correspondents had left severely alone. A diplomat said the Embassy, like others, had heard the rumours, but added, 'Lisbon is a city of rumour. Local people say that if you tell someone something at a café at one end of the Avenida da Liberdade [the city's mile-long main thoroughfare] you will hear the same story much elaborated in a bar at the other end twenty minutes later.' He warned me to watch my step and be discreet, saying: 'You're likely to stir up a hornet's nest if you're not careful. The Portuguese won't like what you are doing. The PIDE will be on to you, if they are not already.'

Having been given this warning, I did not return to the hotel but called the numbers Hendrik had given me from a coin-box at a public telephone office in the Avenida da Liberdade. The number for Soares turned out to be his residence where a woman said he was not at home and asked me to phone later. My calls to two or three other numbers also drew a blank, but my next call was answered by a young lawyer who agreed to see me. In the living room of his flat on an upper floor of a tower block on the way to the airport, he told me the background to Dr Varela's resignation, saying he was willing to talk because he was hostile to the Government and was offended by the way the affair had been handled.

The sequence of events had started in a small way with a minor matter, the prosecution of a young prostitute. Inquiries by the criminal police, under the authority of the Minister of Justice, had revealed that the girl was part of a vice ring including other teenaged call-girls, and the girls had named prominent men including bankers, aristocrats and at least one Minister, among their clients. Men named had been interviewed by police and had retained lawyers to represent them. No reference had been made to the men in court proceedings against the prostitute, but her testimony and that of other girls had been in the dossier given to the judge. The judge had sent the dossier to the Minister, and Dr Varela had decided it contained a *prima facie* case against the men named for corruption of minors. Dr Salazar had ordered the case to be dropped and the Minister had resigned in protest.

The story threw a bizarre light on the affair because, according to the lawyer's account, some of the girls had been introduced to prostitution by their mothers, who were taking part of their immoral earnings. The prosecution had arisen because one of the girls refused to pay her mother, and her mother went to the police out of spite.

The lawyer was not himself representing anyone in the case but said that, like other members of the Lisbon Bar, he knew about it from lawyers acting for some of the men. The affair had become widely known and talked about in Lisbon's legal community. He said an important industrialist had been arrested, and had been forced to resign his directorships after being held for two days by police and then released. Other men involved had so far been untouched by the scandal, but a Lisbon lawyer had been charged with obstructing police inquiries by inducing a witness to tell a false story.

After leaving the lawyer I returned to the telephone office in the Avenida da Liberdade and made another call to Soares. Worried he might prove elusive, I was glad when he answered. I told him I was a British journalist and asked if I could see him without saying what about. He told me to come to his office in the Baixa district near the Praça do Comércio at 7 p.m. He said there would be no one there apart from himself. He said he would leave the street door open and told me to come up to his rooms on the top floor.

As 7 p.m. approached I made my way on foot to the address Soares had given me. Walking in the darkness along the narrow and deserted street I listened for other footsteps, remembering the warning I had been given at the British Embassy about the secret police. Some distance ahead, on the other side of the street, a man was standing under a street lamp. As I drew near I found he was almost opposite Soares's address. The door had been left ajar. I pushed it open and slipped inside.

The interior of the building was in darkness unrelieved even by light from a window. As I moved cautiously forward trying to find the staircase I heard a noise above and, then a voice which said: 'I'm up here. Don't put on any lights.' As I went up the stairs and my eyes adjusted to the darkness, I could make out a dim figure standing on the landing at the top of the stairwell. When I reached the landing he led me into his office and closed the door. His first words were: 'Do you think you were followed here?' I said I didn't know. He asked if I had telephoned him from my hotel. I said I had rung him from a coin-box in the Avenida da Liberdade. He then took me to the window overlooking the street and indicated the man under the street lamp. 'You see that man,' he said, 'he's from the PIDE. There's always someone there. They are watching me all the time.'

The man under the lamp was wearing a raincoat and reading a newspaper. He was smoking a cigarette. There was no need for him to attempt to conceal his presence because the surveillance was overt and not clandestine. He was standing under the street lamp so that he could read his paper while noting the comings and goings of Soares and his visitors. He did not look up as we stood by the window looking down at him. It was like a scene in a film, but clearly part of everyday reality to Soares who lived with round-the-clock surveillance.

We sat amid the shadows created by the dim light from the street. I could see him only as a silhouette. I told him of the story which had been received by the *Sunday Telegraph* and of my attempt to see Dr Varela in Coimbra. He confirmed that the story was common knowledge among Lisbon lawyers and being openly talked about in legal circles. He said he had no idea whether or not the allegations in the police dossier were true. His concern was solely with the way the prosecution had been suppressed to protect important figures in the regime. He said 'If there was a public opinion and a free Press in Portugal, the affair would topple the Government.'

I asked what he could tell me of the identities of the men named in the dossier. He replied that I should see Dr Joaquim Pires de Lima, a barrister and opposition supporter, who had been retained by one of the girls in the alleged vice-ring and had read the dossier. He gave me his address in the village of Parede near the resort of Estoril and its neighbour Cascais where Pires de Lima had his office.

Picking up a taxi in the big square at the southern end of the Avenida da Liberdade, I was in Parede within half an hour after a fast journey on the auto estrada to Estoril and Cascais. The address Soares had given me was difficult to find. My taxi driver did not seem to know the place and there did not appear to be any street signs. We went from street to street and house to house asking for the residence of Joaquim Pires de Lima until at last we found what seemed to be his address, a house set back from the street in a garden.

I knew that something was wrong as soon as the door opened. Soares had led me to expect a young man. The man confronting me on the doorstep was in his fifties, but said he was Dr Joaquim Pires de Lima. He listened in silence as I introduced myself and explained why I had come to see him, telling him that Mário Soares had said he could help me. He then drew himself up and said with dignity, 'I can give you no information. I am an opponent of the régime, but I am not a traitor to my country.'

By this time he had been joined on the doorstep by a woman of about the same age, who I assumed was his wife. She at once launched into a blistering tirade against the *Sunday Telegraph* for trying to create a scandal in Portugal when there was nowhere in the world more depraved, in her view, than 1960s 'Swinging London'. She recited a sneering catalogue of what she apparently regarded as its most decadent features, spitting out each like an insult with a contemptuous curl of her lips: Carnaby Street! The Beatles! The mini-skirt!

On the way back to Lisbon I tried to fathom what had gone wrong, unable to understand how Soares could have been so mistaken about Pires de Lima. He had spoken of him as someone he knew well both as lawyer and opposition supporter, describing him as a widely respected advocate with a distinguished background as a nephew of Dr Fernando Pires de Lima, a former Professor of Civil Law at Coimbra University. It did not occur to me that the man I had just seen was not Joaquim Pires de Lima.

Next morning the phone rang in my room at the Tivoli Hotel as I was about to leave for the airport. It was Hendrik, ringing on the internal phone from the hotel lobby. He said he had had a call from the British Embassy advising him that I should leave Portugal as soon as possible. 'It seems you had an unfortunate meeting with someone last night,' he said drily. Too astonished to ask how he or the Embassy knew this, I told him about my meeting with Soares and of what had happened afterwards. He said I should get to the airport without delay and check in for my flight. He had gone by the time I got down to the lobby to pay my bill and get a taxi.

On the way to the airport, I concluded that Pires de Lima must have reported my visit to the PIDE. Not then aware that he was not who he had let me believe he was, I thought he must have told the PIDE to protect himself and also perhaps because his family, according to Soares, were friendly with Dr Salazar. It seemed that he must also have telephoned the

British Embassy and complained to the duty officer about my visit, and the duty officer, not knowing who I was and where I was staying, had telephoned Hendrik as a British journalist known to the Embassy on the chance that he might be able to contact me.

To my relief, there was no problem at immigration control after I checked in for the TAP Portuguese Airlines 9.40 a.m. London flight. The PIDE official placed an exit stamp in my passport and I went through to join other passengers in the departure lounge. Eventually the flight was called and passengers moved forward to the boarding gate. A young woman in the airline's uniform then came up to me and said: 'I am sorry there is a problem and we cannot take you on this flight'. Suddenly worried, I asked why. She looked apologetic. 'There has been a problem in the catering department and we don't have lunch for you,' she said. I laughed and said I didn't need lunch because I had just had a good breakfast and besides, it not being yet 10 a.m., it was a bit early for lunch. She smiled. 'Yes, but we serve lunch on this flight and IATA regulations require that we must have lunch for every passenger so I regret we cannot carry you.' I had a sudden inspiration. 'How do you know it's my lunch that you don't have?' I said. 'Does it have my name on it?' She frowned, unable to answer the question. 'This is absurd,' I said, deciding to try a bit of angry bluff and bluster. 'I must be on this flight. I'm a businessman. I have an appointment with an important client in London and must not be late.' She looked suddenly puzzled. 'You're a businessman?' she said, sounding surprised. 'Yes!' I said angrily. 'A businessman. I must be on this flight.' She frowned again. 'One moment,' she said and went to speak to a man in airline uniform. He looked at me and nodded. The young woman came back. 'Okay,' she said, 'you may board the flight.'

There had, of course, been no problem about lunch. Once the aircraft was over the Bay of Biscay, a mid-morning lunch was served to every passenger, including myself. It appeared that the airline must have been asked at the last minute to try to delay my departure to provide time for the PIDE to question me about what Soares had told me, now knowing from Pires de Lima that I had seen him, and had made an inept attempt to do so, but my activities had not been considered sufficiently serious to justify more heavy-handed action.

There were possibly regrets that firmer action had not been taken when my story appeared next day as second lead on the front page of the *Sunday Telegraph* under the heading: Vice Scandal Shakes Portuguese Cabinet. It reported that prominent Portuguese including at least one Minister had been named as clients by teenaged call-girls in a Lisbon vice ring and Dr Antunes Varela had resigned as Minister of Justice because Dr Salazar had stopped the men being prosecuted for corruption of minors. The story was attributed to 'reports rife among the legal and diplomatic communities in Lisbon' and information from anti-Salazar groups in Paris published in the French weekly *Jeune Afrique*, a copy of which, air-freighted from Paris, had awaited me at my office.

Dr Pires de Lima was named as a lawyer believed to know the full background of the affair and to have read the secret police dossier as counsel for one of the girls, and I quoted what he had said to me on the doorstep. I also quoted Dr Varela's response when I tried to see him at Coimbra. But no one else was named apart from Dr Salazar and Dr Pires de Lima's uncle. The remark by Dr Soares that the affair would topple the Government if Portugal had a free Press and public opinion was attributed anonymously to 'a leading anti-Salazar lawyer'.

The story brought a swift response from the Portuguese authorities, who at once concluded (entirely wrongly) that it had come from Soares. He was not only the chief immediate suspect but was linked to the story by what I had told Pires de Lima, believing him to be a friend and supporter of the opposition. There was also speculation in journalistic circles that Soares had leaked the story to the foreign Press, the Washington-based magazine of Amnesty International later reported.

Two days after my story appeared, Soares was arrested at his office where I had talked to him in the darkness the previous Friday evening, and was accused by the PIDE's second-in-command José Sachetti of damaging Portugal's good name by disseminating false news to foreigners. Soares recalled in his memoirs that Sachetti then said: 'And this time you've brought the Prime Minister into it personally' – a reference apparently to the report that Dr Salazar had personally suppressed the prosecution of prominent Portuguese accused of corrupting the morals of minors.

No reason was given publicly, then or later, for the arrest of Soares, but his wife Maria told international news agencies that it was because he had spoken to a reporter of the *Sunday Telegraph*. Her statement was reported in the *Daily Telegraph* with a paragraph by myself stating that the story had not come from Soares.

The arrest of Soares added immediate weight to the story by apparently confirming, as Soares put it, that the regime had something to hide. Two American correspondents, Roger Stone, from the Paris bureau of *Time-Life*, and Tad Szulc, Madrid correspondent of the *New York Times*, flew to Lisbon and were both refused entry. Stone was placed on an immediate return flight by the PIDE. Szulc was questioned by the PIDE at Lisbon airport for four hours before being put on a flight back to Madrid.

The banning of the two correspondents increased international interest in a story contrasting so piquantly with the image of moral rectitude projected by the Salazar regime. Highly-coloured and sensational accounts juxtaposing pictures of important Portuguese with photographs of scantily clad girls appeared in French, Italian and German news magazines. I learnt from one account that I had been tailed by the PIDE throughout my visit and had got out of Portugal just in time!

Soares remained in custody for two-and-a-half months until a writ of *habeas corpus* secured his release on 1 March 1968. After a holiday with his wife in the Algarve where they were watched and followed day and night by the PIDE, he was arrested again on 21 March, and told he was to be deported next day to São Tomé in the Gulf of Guinea to remain there under surveillance for an indefinite period. Several hundred supporters who went to Lisbon airport to see him off were attacked by the police with clubs when they cheered him and about a hundred people were injured, including Mrs Soares and the couple's 15-year-old daughter.

Soares feared he might pass years in the oppressive climate of São Tomé, a small island off the West African coast just north of the equator, and so he might have done had Salazar remained in power. But a stroke in September 1968 ended the dictator's 36-year rule and Prof Marcelo Caetano succeeded him as Prime Minister. Early in October, after six months in São Tomé, Soares returned home, his prestige much increased by his deportation. He then went into voluntary exile, living in Paris, where he completed his memoirs which he began writing in São Tomé, until the overthrow of the dictatorship by the military coup of 25 April 1974, brought him back to Portugal to become successively Foreign Minister, three times Prime Minister and eventually President of Portugal for 10 years from 1986.

I never saw Soares again after our meeting in the shadows, and it was not until his memoirs, *Portugal's Struggle for Liberty*, were published in 1975 that I learnt what had gone wrong at Parede from his own account of the episode and my part in it. The man I saw there was not Joaquim Pires de Lima, the lawyer and opposition supporter who had seen the secret police file, but his father, a senior Government official holding the post of Director-General of Political and Civil Administration. Both men, Soares wrote, lived in the same house and the father deliberately misled me by pretending to be his son, claiming to be an opposition supporter when he was in fact a pillar of the regime. 'Realizing,' Soares went on, 'what O'Brien meant to write and wishing to spare his son any unpleasantness, the elder man thought the easiest thing to do was to blame me for the whole "misunderstanding". And this I in turn realized very soon afterwards, when the PIDE interrogated me at their headquarters.'

A Portuguese journalist who rang to interview me for a piece about the events of 1967 when Soares became President of Portugal in 1986 had a slightly different explanation for the mischance. Father and son lived in separate houses in Parede, he said, but I went to the wrong house. Whichever way it was, I saw the wrong man.

Soares, of course, would still have headed the list of suspects whatever had or had not happened at Parede and would, in any case, have been linked to the story if I was followed to his office, but my meeting with Pires de Lima, senior, clinched the matter for the PIDE. Soares kindly did not criticize me in his memoirs for my unwitting part in his arrest and deportation. I can only assume he was unaware that father and son both lived at Parede because otherwise he would surely have warned me to be sure I spoke to the right man.

R BARRY O'BRIEN

A Raised Finger

We were living in Beirut in the early seventies: I was working with the UN, my wife Gloria was studying archaeology at the American University, and our daughter Rosemary was at the College Protestant acquiring an enviable French accent. French was much spoken, around the swimming pools, and in other sophisticated circles. Beirut was a lively, noisy, cosmopolitan city, growing rapidly, the shaded houses coming down in favour of glaring concrete blocks.

Damascus, 140 kms away over Mt Lebanon, made a pleasant change. Driving up the steep slopes of the mountain, we descended between hillsides covered in asphodels, and reached the city by way of water-meadows and a sluggish, green-brown stream. Damascus seemed to have retained the calm belonging to its origin as an oasis in the Syrian desert. There were boulevards, lined by old houses with courtyards, *iwans* opening onto them – large rooms without a fourth wall – and fountains. There were the Byzantine churches, the Azim Palace, and above all the magnificent Omaiyid Mosque, with its fantastic mosaics, scores of the faithful on their knees, bowing to the ground in silent prayer.

I had meetings to attend. Gloria would wander off into the crowded souks, and along the street called Straight. She would find hand-embroidered dresses, sold by the Bedouin in the streets, and Ming porcelain, Damascene brocades, antiquities ranging from Roman necklaces of glass beads to neolithic pottery. The city was an Aladdin's cave.

But no French! In Syria French was not spoken. We learned this as we drove about the country, across the agricultural plains, and visited the Crusader castles and other famous examples of mediaeval and Islamic architecture. We tried to speak to people in French, but they did not respond, though certainly the older ones knew the language. Arabic, through our driver, drew no response either. The régime did not approve of fraternization with Europeans.

Amongst the noteworthy places we visited was Hama; on our way to

239

Aleppo to stay with Krikor – 'Koko' – Mazioumian and his wife Sally, at the Baron Hotel, we intended to spend the night. Hama, famous for its water-wheels or *norias*, is perched on the banks of the Orontes. The water needed for its abundant gardens, and fine buildings, including another Azim Palace and Great Mosque, can only come out of the river below. Gigantic wheels, centuries old, lap up water in shallow troughs, which, on reaching the top, empty themselves into wooden conduits. The wheels, driven by the current, never cease to turn; and they give vent to creakings and groanings so loud that they can be heard well away from the town.

We had chosen a hotel in the main square, a rambling building, and we were led in silence to our room through a maze of dark passages. When we were rid of the porter, Gloria asked which of the two beds I would have; and knowing that she preferred to be near the window, I said the other one. While we were unpacking, and preparing to go out to dinner, she uttered a horrified cry; and there, bustling over my pillow, was a two-inch cockroach, looking quite at home. There were more advancing across the floor in the fading light. We hunted out the porter. Not in the least impressed, he indicated that he would attend to the matter. We had dinner in a garden restaurant, overlooking the river and a water-wheel. On our return to the hotel we found our room to be a miasma of pesticide. No creature could live through it, and we wondered about ourselves. I was kept awake for some time by the cries of the *norias*. When we awoke in the morning light we saw that the floor was covered by cockroaches, which exploded as we put our feet down. We did not have breakfast in our room.

Gloria went to Hama a second time, alone. I had had to return to Beirut from Damascus, with our driver. Diplomatic relations had recently been restored between Great Britain and Syria, and I left her in the care of our ambassador. She was going to Aleppo again, and there was a bus service between Damascus and Aleppo. Gloria was almost the first to board the bus, and while the driver stowed her luggage in the bowels of the vehicle, she sat down in the front seat, next to a Syrian woman. Gloria gave her the usual Arab greeting, but it elicited no more than a smile in response. The Syrian woman remained silent for the whole of the journey. The bus stopped for a while at Hama, and many of the passengers followed the driver into a café. Gloria, at a table by herself, ordered a cup of tea, and sat reading. After a time, impatient to continue the journey, she looked round the café, and noticed it seemed to be strangely empty. She went outside, into the street, and there was no bus. It had left, without a warning hoot from the driver; nor had anyone come to tell her it was going. She had been left by herself in Hama, without her luggage. In something of a panic, she looked up and down the street. Without Arabic, how could she hope that the few people she saw would be able to help her? Then, some way off, she saw a youngish man, dressed in a neat European suit. The appearance seemed miraculous. She approached him, addressed him in French, and he answered in the same language. He was a dentist, who had trained in France. She explained her predicament. After making some enquiries he told her that that was the last bus of the day, and the only way for her to reach Aleppo was by taxi. She begged him to telephone to Koko. The dentist, clearly nervous about being seen in the company of a comely lady from the West, remained with her until they could find a taxi. At length one appeared, rusted and dented, on its way to Aleppo, with three men in it. They made room for Gloria.

The taxi soon broke down. None of the tyres had treads, and one had burst. The driver carried no spare wheel. All got out, and waited on the roadside. There was plenty of traffic; it was growing dark, and there were carts and horses without lights, and cars and lorries, some with only one light, some with no light at all. The journey was likely to be hazardous. Eventually the driver was able to stop a taxi having a driver he knew, who was persuaded to lend his spare tyre. At last they arrived in Aleppo, and Gloria was able to telephone to Koko.

He came at once. As soon as he had had the telephone call from the dentist he had gone to the bus depot, and waited for the bus. On its arrival he asked the driver for Gloria's luggage. The driver denied that there was any luggage. He went further, and denied that Gloria had been on the bus at all. An altercation ensued, and Koko threatened the driver with the police. The Syrian woman had not yet left the bus, and was sitting silently in her place. Koko perceived her surreptitiously raise a finger, and point it towards the rack above her head. Lying there was Gloria's white woollen cardigan, indubitably European. The bus driver surrendered. When Koko picked Gloria up, her luggage was already in her room.

We did not go to Hama again. We never found the opportunity to express our gratitude to the dentist for his unusual services, or to the silent woman for her eloquence of gesture. Notwithstanding some features of great beauty, Hama had shown itself to be, as a stopping-place, unattractive – one can say Kafkaesque, remembering the cockroaches.

WILLIAM DALE

East meets West

As everyone knows, the traditional ethical code of Japan demands behaviour in which repayment of obligations and stark renunciation of personal considerations are a *sine qua non* for acceptance in whatever social group one belongs to. It might therefore be expected that a certain degree of Puritanism would have taken deep root. Yet physical pleasures are sought and valued providing they are kept in the right compartment and do not intrude on the serious business of life. This lesson in cultural differences was driven home to me one afternoon in Tokyo's Imperial Hotel in 1975 in June, the middle of Japan's wearisome rainy season.

It was teatime and, tired of the crowded Ginza streets, I had sought out the hotel's coffee-shop where I had found a seat at the bar counter, ordered coffee and chocolate pie and retreated from the world with a book. The practice in that coffee-shop was for the waitress to put the bill in a glass tumbler directly in front of the customer so I was surprised when some thirty minutes later a slim, elegant arm reached across me from the bar-seat to my right and took out my bill. The owner of the arm was a young and attractive woman, Japanese, smartly dressed in the western style, a string of pearls at her throat and slightly over made-up, I thought, but not so much as to spoil the overall effect. She had also ordered chocolate pie and coffee I noticed, as a whiff of some heady perfume drifted in my direction.

'Pardon me, I think that's your bill,' I said, pointing at her glass tumbler. 'Sorry, my mistake. My name is Yoshiko Sato and I am 23 years old. Who are you?' The boldness of this reply did not intrigue me for I assumed that this was some entrepreneurial initiative by an off-duty bar hostess. So I turned back to my book, wondering why the management of a hotel like the Imperial did not prevent this kind of thing. Perhaps they were not expecting it at teatime.

A little while later there was a slight nudge on my shoulder. 'What are you reading?' came from my right side. 'Listen, young lady, I am not interested. Please try elsewhere.' 'I am a student or I was a student,' came the answer, 'and I want to know you better.' 'And I would like to know why, if you are a student, you are trying to pick up a strange man in the Imperial Hotel coffee-shop. If you want to improve your English there are western women over there.'

'That is not what I want. You see I have graduated from university and am now engaged to be married. My parents were good enough to arrange this. Here is my card. My father is a doctor and we live in Osaka. We also have an apartment in Tokyo where my brother and I lived while we were studying. I am at present staying there for a few weeks before I return to Osaka to prepare for marriage. My brother is away so I am alone. I have discovered that my brother has a collection of blue movies and I have been showing myself them in recent days. Some of them concern western men and I am curious. My wedding will be next year but before I am married I would like to have a love affair with a western man to see what it's like. I am intelligent and have time and money. Please help me.'

She put all this to me in grave tones which could have come straight from a student of anthropology about to try out an experiment. I could see her situation clearly enough. She came from a conservative family and romance was never the mainspring of the traditional Japanese view of marriage where the emphasis was on procreation and the continuity of family life. 'Being in love' western style did not necessarily enter into things. And there was nothing wrong with erotic pleasure which had traditionally been viewed as a legitimate relaxation provided it did not become a major obsession and was kept separate from the more serious activities of life. I could not think poorly of Yoshiko, an apparently honest girl. She was showing commendable resourcefulness and discretion in choosing the Imperial as her hunting ground, for it was highly respectable and well removed from her usual neck of the woods.

It is said that in Japan it is the warm, languid days of the rainy season that inspire a person's thoughts to love and my sympathies with this young lady's predicament were complete. However I was a non-starter for her researches. Yet friendly assistance seemed appropriate so, after a chat over more coffee, I suggested that she might like to meet a European friend of mine whom I could recommend for his charm and reliability and whose company would surely meet her needs. I would be happy to act as go-between in the Japanese fashion. This I did but although they did meet, I had moved on and have never learnt the outcome. For myself, I have never been able to look at the more explicit of the Japanese erotic woodblock prints without remembering Yoshiko's single-minded innocence and her dalliance with her brother's blue films.

JOHN TOWNER

Untouched by Hand

One of my favourite memories goes back many years to the time when I had first started on my research into the spread of the Assassin or Ismaili state, based on their great castles.

I had been asked to extend the scope of my research from Persia to Afghanistan and Pakistan and to see if I could locate the tomb of Nasir-i-Khusraw, a very important figure in Ismaili history in the eleventh century. He is still justly regarded as one of Persia's greatest poets and was a distinguished philosopher and mystic. I knew that he was supposed to be buried in a valley near Fayzabad in Badakshan, which lies in the Hindu Kush, and after many false trails I found myself in the village of Yamgan near Jurm. It was a pretty village set in a lush green mountain valley and my little party were entertained by the village schoolmaster. He would willingly take us to Nasi-i-Khusraw's tomb, he said, but first he would like to pick my brains and ask me a few questions. After some enquiries about Europe and Britain, which I had been expecting, he suddenly became very serious and to my astonishment asked me what were my opinions of the philosophy of Descartes? Did I really think that you could prove the existence of God or Allah by reason alone?

The next day, we visited the tomb of the great pir, and our host then suggested we journey to the valley of Hunza and the neighbouring valleys in the north-western frontier area of Pakistan, where the inhabitants particularly revered the great philosopher-poet. I had heard much of the beauty of this valley from Hunzakuts whom I had met before. They were all highly intelligent people with a deep love of their mountain paradise. I had been told that the inhabitants lived to well over 100, sometimes 120, fortified by the mountain air and the local wine. I had heard of their Mir, who ruled justly and wisely. There were no police, no prisons in Hunza. Disputes were settled by the Mir in open court and his decisions were always respected.

Without hesitation we accepted the teacher's suggestion. In any case, we could not resist the lure of this Shangri-La and so we decided to travel back to Kabul, passing innumerable fields of opium poppies, and then made our way through the Khyber Pass to Rawalpindi. From Rawalpindi we flew in a Fokker Friendship plane, whose wings almost shaved the mountains sur-rounding the valleys beneath us, to Gilgit, an important military base during the Raj. In Gilgit we hired a Chinese jeep, as this was the only type of vehi-cle able to negotiate the treacherous bends of the old silk road. At times the road was so steep that a lad had to sit on the bonnet of the jeep to keep the front wheels on the ground. The silk road has now been replaced by the magnificent Karakoram highway, constructed by China and Pakistan in part-nership. Eventually we reached the capital of Hunza, Baltit, where the Mir and his family have lived in their ancestral castle for centuries.

We were invited to stay at the official guest house and soon received a formal printed invitation to dinner. Fortunately our clothes were just re-spectable enough for me to accept and we had the most delightful meal with the Mir and his somewhat eccentric wife, the Ranee, who smoke end-less cigars during the meal. Before we left, the Mir invited me to return the next day, when he would show me around the castle with all its treasures.

There was one particular portrait he wanted to show us, which he felt would give us great pleasure.

The following morning, we walked gingerly around the castle, as the floors and stairs were crumbling dangerously. Then the Mir showed us into a small gallery. He pointed to a somewhat faded portrait hanging precariously on the wall. 'There,' said the Mir, 'you didn't expect to see her here, did you?' No, we did not. The 'portrait' was a canvas advertisement dominated by the regal figure of Queen Victoria, dressed in blue, holding a fan, and wearing a miniature of the Prince Consort. Above her head in red letters were emblazoned the words MELLINS FOOD, and below her august presence we read:

FOR INFANTS AND INVALIDS

UNTOUCHED BY HAND

PETER WILLEY

A Flying Visit to the Ngorongoro Crater in the Serengeti

A few years ago, when Kenya was still placid and untroubled, I flew to Nairobi, staying overnight at the Norfolk Hotel, a vibrant relic of times colonial. The objective was the Serengeti. The first stop on the way would be Lake Manyara, and the hotel of that name.

I climbed into a small bus outside the Norfolk Hotel after a sizzling English breakfast, and was driven off through the perimeters of Nairobi towards the Kenya-Tanzania border. We reached it. There was a hut and the shabby paraphernalia of immigration and customs checks, and a queue, and shouting posses of Africans selling fruit and ice-creams and other wares. I did the formalities and we drove on, but not far. The bus stopped. It had a punctured tyre. There was a wild to-ing and fro-ing and, in time, it was mended. I reached the Lake Manyara Hotel in late afternoon, having sauntered through a dreary little town called Arusha many miles back.

246

A night passed in fair comfort and, again, a breakfast taken, but of simplicity. A bus conveyed us, a small platoon, to the Lake and there I saw live wild animals and birds for the first time in my life. I was in the midst of luscious forest and swampy glades: jacaranda, tamarind, acacia and mahogany trees abounded; waters speckled by duck of diverse plumage and size and gender and cackle; waders, herons, geese, storks and eagles. The air swam with plovers, larks, barbets. In the meadows, here were bushbuck, zebra, waterbuck, hippo, elephant, giraffe, lion in shadow. All a constellation of wildlife such as I had, as I have said, never observed before, and the more stupefying for that.

I embarked thenceforth in a car with a driver. He was to be chauffeur into the Serengeti and back to Arusha. We set off for the Ngorongoro Crater. I do not recall the name of the hotel I stayed in, perched on a high rim of the crater – a *caldera* (which means a collapsed volcano). It does not matter. The crater is a titanic and wondrous expression of vastness. To look at it from on high is like reading from the Book of Revelation: 'And I beheld, when he had opened the sixth seal – a great earthquake, and the sun became black, and the moon became as blood. And the stars of heaven fell unto the earth – and the heaven departed as a scroll when it is rolled together, and every mountain and island were moved out of their place.' These words are not out of place when looking at this mighty hole in Earth. The crater was swarming with creatures in awesome number but, at a glance however intense and searching from the rim, I saw none. I did next morning, having descended early. Then, I 'shook hands' for the first time with lion and lioness, one couple in the act of mating. In whatever posture the lion is, he is a magnificent thing and MGM, the film distributor, pays him a deserved compliment on the logo.

Within this stupendous hole was a shallow lake, populated by flamingo in their thousands. It was a sight that almost propelled my eyes from their sockets. The flamingo is statuesque and the look-alike of a feminine mannequin clothed in pink with white flashes in lapel and skirt. There is movement, and a chorus of sound: a feathered choir indeed; this silvered lake a carpet of pink changing in afternoon light to mauve, and at dusk to indigo and blue, then utter silence.

247

In the promenade through the crater, I saw other creatures, not least hippopotamus disporting in the water, which they convert to fountains and spirals and whirlpools; circling vultures and fish-eagles and so many other species, winged and not winged.

In the Ngorongoro, I perceived the indignities that man can inflict upon animal, simply by looking and photographing and gaping.

The return was through the Serengeti and the eloquent, spellbinding silences, mirages and vastness of it all. I tarried at Gibbs Farm, still then a model of Englishness in the depths of Africa. I purchased a sensitively-contoured sculpture in hardwood of a family – mother, father, child and baby – which stands on my mahogany desk at home, and is an incessant reminder of this flying visit to Lake Manyara and the *caldera* of Ngorongoro.

JAMES PRENTICE

Switching Children

Many years ago I arranged with my wife that we would have a long weekend away without the children. They would be parked with my mother-in-law and we would be freed to enjoy ourselves at a secret destination.

In fact we flew to Amsterdam where there was a Rembrandt exhibition at the Rijksmuseum.

We spent Friday night and Saturday very happily and on Sunday morning, coming back from the Rijksmuseum after seeing the exhibition, I observed a young couple coming towards us on the same side of the street. I said to my wife, 'Isn't it extraordinary how much that little Dutch girl looks like my niece?'; and almost immediately afterwards I said, 'Good gracious, the man next to her looks like my nephew.'

The amazing thing is that it was indeed my niece and nephew who had been holidaying on the spur of the moment in Belgium and who had driven across to Amsterdam for the day.

Of course this meant that I had to entertain them (not that I had any great objection). We had lunch and dinner together and they drove us to the airport on their way back to Belgium.

On my return to England I telephoned my sister to say that we had gone away to miss my children and had ended up entertaining hers.

MAURICE FOOKS

Borobudur

It was some while before five o'clock, and as is usual for this time in the tropics it was still night, as dark and as soft as velvet. The air was cool, faintly scented with cloves and woodsmoke from early cooking fires. I cycled down the long hill, free-wheeling, shivering a little. A *muezzin* was already wailing his first morning prayer, his minaret invisible. A cockerel crowed in a distant *kampong*, and when I passed an old woman who was lighting an oil lantern she smiled across at me, her teeth glinting unevenly in the guttering lamplight.

A few minutes later and I was at the foot of the hill, and outside the largest Buddhist monument in the world, the eighth-century Javanese temple known as Borobudur. I found my way through the jungle darkness, past the gates and fences, across the dew-damp lawns, around the clusters of sleeping dogs. And just as I was beginning the climb up the temple-pyramid of dark stone terraces, so, with the speed characteristic of these latitudes, a pale grey wash began to limn the edge of the eastern sky. A crisp breeze sprung up, there was the tinkle of a bamboo chime. The dogs behind me began to stir, and I could hear them uttering small yelps of greeting to one another.

Down near the gate was the vague outline of a hut, and from its doorway a small figure emerged. A match flared, and I could see the glow of a newly-lit *kretek* cigarette. Its owner began to climb up towards me, and in the steadily gathering light I could see him adjusting his sarong as he picked his way silently over the stones. The East was waking up: another cool summer's dawn was coming to Java.

The man arrived, slightly breathless. 'You are from Amanjiwo?' he whispered. I nodded. 'Good,' he replied. 'Then I will unlock for you.' He smiled, reached under his sarong for a tiny brass key, undid the bolt and opened the little lych-gate that barred my way. 'Go up, my friend. You are lucky. It will be a good dawn today, I think. And he salaamed me, and left as silently as he had come.

I climbed steadily. A fine conjunction, I thought: a Muslim leading a Christian into a Buddhist monument – into the biggest stupa ever made, and one which yet stood in the middle of the world's most populous Mohammedan nation. The conjunctions of Java are invariably to do with religion: for although there is little that is doctrinaire or fundamentalist or intolerant about the country, it is a place that has been steeped in godly beliefs of one kind or other for thousands of years. The effects of all that worship and devotion linger, like the faint and unmistakable scent of cloves from all those cigarettes, ever present in the Javanese air.

At last, the top – a plateau of grey andesite paving-blocks, with just the rounded bell shapes of six dozen small latticed stupas, from inside which Buddha-figures gazed impassively out over the jungles. It was utterly peaceful, totally quiet. I sat myself on a ledge of volcanic stone, making sure I was facing towards the ever-brightening east. Before long I was quite settled, rapt in a thousand-yard stare, and waiting for the magical moment of what I had heard and read for years was the finest sunrise in the world.

It is seldom that the simple fact of staying in a hotel offers a truly spiritual experience. However seductively their marketers might wish to persuade us otherwise – that the costlier inns are now themselves temples, to hedonism or self-realization or whatever – it is quite idle to suppose that they are much other than commercial entities, designed mainly to separate you from large quantities of cash.

Yet Adriaan Zecha's newest Amanresort in Java, which is called Amanjiwo and which is just a short cycle-ride (happily, all downhill) away from this most lovely of Eastern temples is, to one very limited extent, an exception. During its construction a remarkable deal was cut – a deal that truly does offer the guest the opportunity for a moment of real spirituality. For it transpires that those who stay at Amanjiwo, and those alone, are allowed in through the still-closed gates of Borobudur each morning while it is dark, long before anyone else – and are able thus go and see for themselves the dawning of the day as it should, at least once in a lifetime, be seen.

And all that I had ever heard and read about this moment turns out to be quite true: dawn seen from one of the top terraces of the Borobudur temple is something that, once witnessed, is so blissful as to have a value far, far beyond price. Any deal that permits it, whatever the motivation for cutting it, is by my reckoning an almost saintly act.

To the east of Borobudur, and dominating the flat and fertile Kedu Plain, stand two volcanoes, sturdy ten-thousand-footers called Merbabu and Merapi, one still active and puffing pale smoke from its summit. It is in the low curving col between them that the sun always first appears. If the weather is fair – and it was on my first morning – it starts with a slow, teasing glow, when the whole world turns from grey to salmon and pale gold. then through a long fabulous array of purples, reds and oranges into daybreak itself.

There are many ways in which the actual moment of dawn here is unique and singularly lovely. The simple fact of being on top of a twelve hundred year old monument is one, of course; the fronds of mist lying in the folds of the plateau another; but the most memorable occurrence invariably comes ten minutes or so before the sunrise proper, when there is the appearance of what seems to be a sort of mirage. Two golden sunbeams, wide diverging bands of bright yellow that spear directly up into the skies, seem to announce what is shortly going to happen, a kind of luminous fanfare.

As the beams appear, the few Javanese who are up on the temple-plateau, fall silent too. A reverential calm envelops the temple. And there is no sound, not even a cockerel-crow, from the mist-shrouded *kampongs* below.

Quite suddenly, a thin curved line of unbearable brightness blazes on the lip of the col, a scimitar-blade caught in a flash of lamplight. Swiftly it thickens, first to a broad curve of brass, then to a semicircle of gold. There is a sudden rush of heat – and in the same instant a flood of yellow light bathes the entire temple, and all the eastern Buddhas have their faces lit up as they stare calmly into the bright disc of the sun. The stupas behind change colour, in the same instant, as though washed by golden paint; the old stones that seemed so cold and lifeless before dawn suddenly become warm – sternly impassive and dignified still, but now quite clearly alive.

The watchers gaze, awestruck, until the sun starts to climb up the sky, and it becomes too hot to linger. Down below the gates clang open and the first of the tour buses grind in, and you hear the sounds of ticket-punches and excited Javanese and Sumatran chatter, as the biggest stupa in creation is thrown open for business, once again.

Amanjiwo – the name means peaceful soul – is the fifth in the Aman family to be built so far in Indonesia, the first designed to offer access to a specific site, rather than simply to luxuriate prettily in some marvellous tropical ambiance.

Architecturally the hotel is quite fascinating. It has been designed to mimic, to harmonize with the temple that can be glimpsed from its upper pavilions: so there are domes that look like stupas, columns that look as though they might be worked into the temple galleries, and two parallel semi-circles of suites that each look serenely temple-like, as though each might house at least a *bodhisattva*, if not perhaps a fully-enlightened Buddha.

It is strangely beautiful, the pastel stones and empty spaces almost Nordic in their sparseness. The room interiors and the pools and the gazebos and the two restaurants will be quite familiar to those who travel often and have come to recognize the Aman signatures. The rooms have been styled to meet local tastes, and are as exquisitely spare and elegant as always. The staff, all brought from the local villages, and dressed in simple robes of batik, have a sweet innocence about them: their mere presence, as they pad about, silent and catlike, only adds to the hotel's drenching sense of peace.

But it is the view from within the property that is the most remarkable aspect of the place, the least easy to forget, the most haunting.

It is first seen within moments of arrival. The car grinds up the foothills to where Amanjiwo stands, a couple of hundred feet above the jungles of the plain. It turns left,. crosses a narrow bridge, and heads down a steep slope towards a central rotunda that is modelled to have the look of a monumental stupa. A gaggle of young men and women are on hand here to open the doors. One European manager is there to provide an anchor of familiarity: next, as you climb the few steps up onto the rotunda's great stone floor, so a battalion of small Javan children in costumes of gold and scarlet thread toss rose petals, and cry welcome, to remind you, if it was ever in doubt, that you have been transported into the realm of the exotic and the faraway.

And then there comes the view. The architect has cunningly provided a frame for it, a stone-walled defile that splits the property in two, and which is aimed, arrow-like, directly at the temple below. It takes a moment to realize: the jungle which unrolls like a deep green carpet, coils of woodsmoke hanging over the villages, looks seamless, untouched, unsullied. And then a helpful someone points it out, dead centre – a dark pyramid of stone rising above the foliage, as it has for a more than twelve centuries.

Borobudur is placed cleverly at the centre of every panorama that a guest at the hotel will see. And so – you lie in your bed, and gaze through the french windows and over the pool or out under the gazebo – and there is the temple, a perfectly delineated spectre of godliness, directly in the crosshairs. You swim, come up blinking into the sunlight – and, there it is, as central to what you see as the sacred Mt Meru – on which some say, Borobudur was modelled – is central to the entire Buddhist idea. And it is indeed the very centrality of the temple, its constant presence, hovering, lurking, reminding, that makes Amanjiwo so unusual, so spiritually uplifting a place to be.

The extraordinary setting of the hotel makes it very different from both its other Aman-siblings in Indonesia (which are deliberately sited remotely, and offer their guests peace and privacy alone) and its direct rivals, none of which (except for a locally-run shanty or two) are at all close to Borobudur. Amanjiwo, by contrast, lies just a matter of a few hundred yards from the temple. It is just a few cycleable (or, of course, driveable) miles from a pair of subsidiary temples, Mendut and Pawon. And it has been placed just below the exquisitely misty Menorah Hills, lined with rice terraces, and at the southern edge of a green plain of such rampant fertility and bucolic good cheer, that few guests will want to linger in their suites or by the pool.

The central message of Amanjiwo, and it is a unique message in the current Aman universe, is that one goes there to explore rather than to bask.

One goes to marinate in Java's cultural essences rather than bake in her sunshine. One goes to use this exquisite little place as a base for informing oneself, particularly, about the island's extraordinary ecclesiastical history.

Java, like Sumatra to her west and Bali to her east, stands four-square on the sea-route between India and China. With India long a travelling and trading nation, and China not, places that lay between the two would tend to benefit from the osmotic effects primarily of Indian influence – cultural, linguistic and religious. So Hinduism flourished on the big islands, then retreated (though it remains to this day dominant in Bali); Buddhism, also born in India, came next, flourished in both Sumatra and Java, then retreated (and is now quite extinct); and then Islam, promulgated by the Moghuls when their courts ran India, flourished all across what is modem Indonesia, remaining supreme among the beliefs in the nation today. That the British came and ruled briefly, as did the Portuguese and Dutch and French and Japanese, did nothing to displace the primacy of Islam: it remains pre-eminent, except amusingly tempered by the curious animisms of old Javanese lore.

Borobudur was built during those few hundred years – from the seventh to the tenth centuries – when the newly-proclaimed religion of Buddhism was claiming Javanese attention. During this time of intense intellectual activity the ruling families of the island erected scores of temples of memorial buildings, most of which have long since vanished. But one family in particular, the Sailendras, Lords of the Mountains, evidently thought Buddhism substantial enough a faith to require an unimaginably substantial memorial: so they had 60,000 workers haul a million blocks of stone from the hillsides, place them to cap a small natural rise on the plains, and cut and carve them with a daring and brio that have been equalled by few other temples anywhere else in the world. And these were not primitive Javanese aping the styles of the influential Indians nearby: these Sailendra kings were men of a high and distinct culture: Borobudur is a uniquely Javanese work, a reliquary well worthy of the island in which it for so long lay hidden.

It was in 1814 when Sir Stamford Raffles – one of the most benign, sympathetic and intellectually curious of all British colonial rulers – was

Lieutenant-Governor of Java, that a visitor came to him at his mansion in Semarang to tell of a giant ruined temple that lay in the island's interior jungles, not far from the great *kraton* at Yogyakarta, Java's cultural capital.

Later that year Raffles sent a Dutch engineer named Cornelius to explore: his party duly found, buried by volcanic ash and undergrowth and nearly a thousand years of neglect, the magical ruin of a colossal terraced pyramid. It was square-shaped at the base, but circular, shaped as a magic tantric *mandala* at the top. The eons had left their mark: the temple was waterlogged, half-ruined by subsidence and creepers, with many of its treasures missing, probably long since stolen (or given away, as to a King of Siam). But once it had been cleared and wholly revealed, by hundreds of men working for years, it proved to be an utter marvel, and it stands now (especially after an eleven-year and $25 million UNESCO-supported restoration begun in 1973) as one of the East's, and one of the planet's undisputedly greatest monuments.

Borobudur's rediscovery was important in and of itself, of course; but the sheer magnificence of what Cornelius found and Raffles demanded be restored, also purged the European mind of any lingering prejudices about what was thought to be the primitive state of Asian culture: it led to the dispatch of numbers of other expeditions, including that of Henri Mouhat to Cambodia fifty years later, which was rewarded by the unearthing of a ruin now known everywhere: Angkor Wat. And like the long-known ancient temple complex at Pagan, in Burma, Borobudur and Angkor both derive their architectural origins from India. With Mahabalipuram and Vijayanagara and the Taj Mahal, who would ever dare suggest that the East *could not build?*

There is a particular similarity between the Khmer Wat and Borobudur, in that both have the essential shape, at least in cross section, of a mountain – specifically the sacred Mt Meru, the peak in western Tibet that is at the core of Buddhist myth. But Borobudur – the word is believed to come from *Vihara Budda Uhr*, the *Buddhist Monastery on the Hill* – is a great deal more than this: it also presents a saga, carved in more than a million blocks of volcanic stone arranged in terraces, and that was to be told to those all of those faithful who ventured through the jungles on pilgrimage.

There are nine terraces in all: the sacred Buddhist number. The three circular plateau terraces, from where one now traditionally watches the Java dawn, are built on the top of six others, each square in plan – and it is on long and half-enclosed galleries built into the outer parts of these six that the great Buddhist story is told.

A pilgrim of a thousand years ago, or a traveller today, climbs one of the four narrow staircases and, on reaching the first of the galleries, simply turns left. On the inner and outer walls now on either side of him is the entire story of the Buddhist cosmic vision, told in thousands of carvings that are incised onto 1,460 panels that stretch along a mile of continuous walkway. A visitor circumambulates the first complete terrace (clockwise, as should be done in all Buddhist monuments), then reaches the staircase, climbs to the next gallery and turns left and starts walking again – then ascends again, more walking, up again, again and then again.

And in doing so, even the unschooled beginner notices just what the Buddhist architects of 750 AD planned should be noticed (though it actually took a Russian scholar named Oldenburg to make the first 'translation'). What he discovered was that in the lower terraces the tablets, exquisitely carved, are dominated by images that involve trade and passion and desire and the earthly needs of man. There are ships, elephants, galleons, camels, warriors, dancing girls. Then, as one rises, gallery by gallery, so the story becomes less noticeably earthly, the number of human figures diminishes, the imagery is more concerned with holiness and asceticism and enlightenment, and with the journey towards the Nirvana that only the Buddha himself properly achieved.

While down on the lower levels there are carvings that represent anger and war and suffering, all the misery diminishes steadily as one ascends; upwards through the temple the carved faces achieve ever greater serenity of expressions, until before long, close to the summit, there are scores of *bodhisattvas*, the human figures who are as learned and enlightened as mere mankind could ever be, and who now dominate the imagery.

Finally one reaches the topmost terraces, where there are no galleries at all, no tablets, no story. Just seventy-two Buddhas, each sitting calm and serene inside his stupa of stone latticework, each gazing out over the countryside, contemplative and content. Otherwise, nothing: the upper terraces are devoid of decoration, and are dominated, in essence, by the nothingness that is at the heart of Buddhist enlightenment. The topmost stupa, unlike the others that surround it, is quite empty: it has nothing at its core at all, a perfect symbol of what a truly spiritual person seeks to achieve – everything and nothing, inner peace and intimate self-knowledge.

My guide, who came from a nearby *kampong* and spoke near-perfect English, stood aside as I wandered slowly upwards later that day. He explained where he thought I needed to know, but otherwise held his tongue, perhaps hoping that I would prefer to come to understand the general imagery of the temple, rather than hear from him the fine and overwhelming detail.

But when, at last, I stood at the summit in the heat, close to the place where earlier I had shivered in the dawn, he led me to the south side of the terraces. I thought he was going to show me Amanjiwo, which I could see, sprawled like a ramshackle new temple at the base of the range of hills. But no: instead he pointed at the hills themselves, which, so much smaller than the volcanoes behind me, were rather an insignificance – lined with rice terraces, but otherwise of little obvious merit.

'Look carefully at the summit ridge,' he said. 'Let your imagination wander.'

And so I did, and, just as with the temple-tablets, I realized the depth of meaning in this vision too. For the Menorah Hills, in silhouette, have the undoubted appearance of a man, lying on his back, head to the north, sleeping with an expression of perfect peace on his face. I turned to my guide, who was smiling with pleasure at my new self-discovery.

'He is called Gunadharma,' the man said. 'He was the divine architect of this temple. And now he sleeps. Your hotel is in the shadow of where he is sleeping – between him, and what he made.'

'So let us go. It is uphill. If you bicycle you will be tired when you get back. So maybe you will sleep as well. Between the temple, and the man who made it. A thousand years ago.' And he smiled once again, lit another *kretek*, and in the steamy clove-filled air, we slowly cycled home.

SIMON WINCHESTER

Fellow Travellers

Wilfred Thesiger first visited Afghanistan in 1952. One weekend Bob Dreessen from the American Embassy and I took him some ninety miles south-west of Kabul to visit Ghazni, once the capital of a great military empire. Outside the mud-walled fortress we found the tomb of Sultan Mahmud and two crumbling 'Towers of Victory' built to commemorate the twelve victorious expeditions which he led into the fertile plains of India in the early eleventh century.

That night we stayed at a village teahouse in the Logar valley. Wilfred had recently spent five years exploring southern Arabia, twice crossing the Empty Quarter with camels. Seated beside the hissing samovar, we listened spellbound to his adventures. A man of immense self discipline, he was in tune with the rhythms of nomad life. We could picture him and his Bedu companions crouched round their evening fire waiting to eat, patiently and sometimes for hours, until the last of their number had caught up.

Later that year, Bob told me that an American pilot had just flown over the Hindu Kush. At the top of the Panjshir valley, with his altimeter at 20,000 feet, he had drawn level with a massive snow-capped peak. We decided to reconnoitre this little-known mountain. It was Mir Samir.

Gul Agha, the Tajik lorry driver (*see page 37*), drove us into Panjshir. With us came Ghulam Nabi, another genial Tajik who had started his working life as a *marmitier* in the French ambassador's kitchen and who was now my much-admired cook. Where the motor road ended at Jangalak, Gul Agha introduced us to one of his kinsmen, a sturdy looking yeoman dressed in a long shirt, trousers and a locally made waistcoat with eight pockets, four inside and four out. This was Abdul Ghiyas, who agreed to provide two horses and take us on to Parian, the highest part of Panjshir and up to the summer pastures on the flank of Mir Samir.

By sharing rides on the horses, we travelled forty miles the first day. On the next, we were high up in the meadows with snow cock calling from the rocks around us; and, on the third, we learned just how formidable was Mir

Samir. Rock faces rose sheer from its glaciers. By midday, when frost and ice began to melt around the upper cone, there was a continuous fall of stone and rock. We vowed to return one day.

Our way back was via the Andarab valley, which lies north of the Panjshir. This took us over the Khawak pass which, at 11,640 feet, marks one of the great watersheds of Asia. To the south and east, water flows to the Indus; to the north and west, to the Oxus. A gentle, round-shouldered pass, the Khawak was for many centuries the route over the Hindu Kush preferred by both caravans and conquerors. Among the latter were Alexander and Tamerlane. We ambled down to a welcoming teahouse in the valley bottom. Ghulam Nabi sent a boy to fish and that evening served us delicious grilled trout.

We went back over the Hindu Kush via the higher and little used Parandev pass. After toiling upwards all day, by evening we still had a thousand feet to climb up a vicious funnel pointing to the sky. We camped on a narrow plateau where Bob and I gathered dry artemisia roots for the fire, Abdul Ghiyas found some miniature wild onions and Ghulam Nabi, with the air of a practised conjuror, provided an *omelette aux fine herbes*. After our meal, he spread the embers of the fire, covered them with a layer of earth and lay down to sleep on the warmth.

Next day, we were off at dawn. The sun's rays threw shafts of golden light on neighbouring heights. But we were on a north slope where the cold seemed to freeze our breath. The track was a steep zigzag over frozen snow and rock. The horses had to keep stopping, nostrils quivering and flanks heaving. We were in much the same state.

Three years later, in 1956, I was to return to the Hindu Kush with Eric Newby. Secker & Warburg had advanced him £800 to write a travel book and I had some leave before joining the Embassy in Tehran. Our plan was ambitious: to climb Mir Samir and also visit Nuristan, the wild and little-known region which lay to the east of the mountain. The stalwart Abdul Ghiyas came with us together with two other Panjshiris. But my hopes that Ghulam Nabi might be our cook were dashed.

Adam Arnold Brown, a fine mountaineer and then a headmaster in India, could not join us. Had he been able to, we would surely have been the first to reach the summit of Mir Samir. As it was, a party of German climbers carried off this honour in 1960.

Our journey was chronicled by Eric in his famous *A Short Walk in the Hindu Kush*. First published in 1958, it established his reputation as a travel writer and by now has become a classic, with sales of over half a million. As a travelling companion, Eric had that great quality: enthusiasm. As a writer, he had a sharp eye for detail and he showed a stroke of genius in ending the final chapter, describing our meeting with Wilfred Thesiger in Parian, with the line, 'Gosh, you must be a couple of pansies'. Although Eric indulged in humour at my expense, I regard this as something acceptable in any good friendship. In 1998, we planned to return to the Hindu Kush to make a television film but the BBC eventually decided it would be too difficult logistically and too dangerous personally in a country still torn by tragic ethnic civil war.

Let Wilfred have the last word. 'One evening I encountered two exhausted Englishmen: desiccated, wind-chapped, lame, with bandaged hands, they looked in thoroughly bad shape. Eric Newby and Hugh Carless were returning from their valiant attempt to climb the 20,000 foot Mir Samir, that loomed at the head of the valley.'

HUGH CARLESS

Finnish Misconceptions

For us in Western Europe, Finland is a country beset with misconceptions – like the belief, which died only with the end of the Cold War, that Finland was a form of Soviet colony. There was a distinct awkwardness some years ago, when the Chief of Staff of the Armed Forces, on an official visit to London, was asked casually by a member of the British government (who obviously hadn't read his briefing), 'By the way, General, how many Soviet divisions are there stationed in your country?' The answer was 'none', but the general was naturally pained at having had the question put, and the exchange was reported with some indignation in the Finnish press.

Perhaps the commonest misconception, though, is that the Finns are shrouded in almost perpetual darkness and gloom. In southern Finland, where Helsinki lies, this is not so even in winter. Helsinki airport at four o'clock on a February afternoon, when I arrived there for the first time, looked almost picturesque – as picturesque at least as any airport can look – with crisp reflections of the evening sun off the snow. With little practical idea of what to expect, I was equipped with a large fur hat (a farewell present from the Finair representative in Bangkok) and when the *chef de protocol* came to greet me, wearing a smart trilby and treated me in the lounge to the mandatory smoked reindeer open sandwich, I felt rather too hot and more than a little foolish.

It is not the darkness of the Finnish winter but its length that is the really depressing seasonal factor. The worst months are November, when Helsinki streets are dismally wet and slushy and the winter seems to stretch away interminably to the horizon and beyond; and April, when everyone knows that it is spring everywhere else in Europe but still winter there. 'In November we start to drink,' said one of the first Finns that I met, and the Finnish reputation for hard drinking must owe much to the long winter. Not, as far as I could see, that the Finns drink in total much more that the rest of us, but when they do drink there are – literally – no half measures. I have to admit, though, that only once did I see a Finn known to me personally drink himself legless.

The occasion was an interesting one: an expedition in spring on skis and snowmobiles (motorcycles on skis) to a border police post near the frontier with Norway. (By the end of April, the day in Lapland is longer than in Britain, the sun shines and conditions for cross-country ski-ing are ideal.) On the outward trip, my Finnish friend elected to be towed on skis behind a snowmobile – no mean feat, and accomplished by him in some style. I chose more modestly to sit on a trailer. On our arrival, the border police offered us a sauna, and then lunched us lavishly, at least as far as the drink was concerned. This, incidentally, was the one occasion during four years in Finland when I saw in action that legendary feat – rolling in the snow after a sauna. But the roller was, in fact, an Italian visitor, egged on by the Finns to show how tough he could be!

When the time came to set off on our return, my friend had observed the world through the bottom of a vodka glass more than once too often and was obviously in no shape to repeat his ski-ing prowess of the morning. But despite urgent pleas from the rest of the party he insisted on trying, only to fall every few yards. In the end his skis were confiscated, and he was loaded ignominiously – but still singing – onto a trailer and I found myself promoted to driving a snowmobile.

Later that evening, another member of the party, clearly feeling that some explanation of our friend's behaviour was needed, took me aside and said, 'You know, he never normally drinks like that when there are foreigners around.'

JUSTIN STAPLES

Creatures that go Bump in the Night

Compared with today's airliners, World War II Liberator bombers lumbered and their engines throbbed through your body. They were not built for comfort and, flying at ten thousand feet, they were also cold – even over the Sahara. The war had put a stop to tourism and this, courtesy of the RAF, was my first trip overseas. We flew south across France, over the Med in a thunderstorm and then along the coast of North Africa to Cairo. Huddled in the bomb bay, the cold got to us despite the greatcoats we wore. The small, nicotine-coloured windows gave little opportunity to see the scenery.

I had joined the RAF as the war was drawing to an end and on that flight, from the chilly, damp and grey January dawn of an airfield somewhere in England in 1946, we were en route to the heat of India. There I was to spend much of the next two years at Mauripur, a desert airfield west of Karachi, as part of South-East Asia Command, one of a team controlling the movement of aircraft as they flew troops and supplies back and forth across the sub-continent.

Off-duty days were often spent at Hawkes Bay, some miles west of the airfield. After rattling and bumping across the dusty scrub, sand and rock of the Sind in an open truck, we stayed in a cabin – built, we were told, from glider packing cases – and there enjoyed the pleasures of an almost deserted beach and the sea.

With a silver crescent moon and a million tiny diamonds sparkling in a black sky, we waited one night until we could see a dull glint of light moving slowly at the water's edge a quarter of a mile away. It was the wet shell of a giant turtle in the moonlight. As we made our way towards it we found tracks like the tyre marks of a small car leading straight up the beach. Then, with startling suddenness, from the dune above and almost upon us loomed the huge dark shape of another turtle. We shone our torch on a leathery, bulbous head swinging slowly and menacingly from side to side.

The creatures had come out of the sea to lay their eggs in the dunes. Using their hefty, scaly flippers like arms, they dug holes in the sand leaving the eggs to incubate. They dug deep, too, in the hope that they would be safe from the scavenging packs of stray dogs. Having deposited their eggs the turtles would then heave their lumbering bulk down the beach again back to the sea.

By day we would swim in the sea or paddle out in two-man canvas canoes. Braced by bamboo these were broad-beamed and flat-bottomed with a canvas-covered roll of kapok on both sides to give added buoyancy and stability. Nevertheless they could be turned end over end by a heavy surf. If that caught the canoe, it was driven surging onto the beach upside down, scraping the canoeist's back and neck on the rough sand as it went.

A night fishing expedition was planned. The idea, explained a colleague, was to take a canoe well out to sea about midnight and use a torch to attract the fish, which we would then harpoon with a spear he had made.

We must have been a mile from the shore with the sea swelling gently in the darkness when the canoe gave a violent lurch and rose out of the water. The canvas pressed hard against our thighs as an enormous, firm body swam gliding beneath us – and then another. We guessed we were in the middle of a school of dolphins, but decided not to wait to find out!

The cabin was then a faint speck of yellow light in the blackness – but for us it glowed like a beacon of hope. The dolphins may only have been playing but the fishing expedition was abandoned in seconds. As we headed for that distant light I doubt that two double-bladed paddles could have flashed faster than ours did that night.

PETER HUNT

Supper with Walter Mitty

In the mid 1970s I spent almost three years in Los Angeles as general manager of Angel Records, the US arm of EMI's classical record business. My office was in the Capitol Tower on Vine Street, one of only three noted buildings in Hollywood itself, the other two being the Brown Derby restaurant also on Vine Street and Graumann's Chinese Theatre on Hollywood Boulevard.

Often in the evenings I would go to the Music Center, the performing arts complex newly built by private subscription in downtown Los Angeles with the successful intention of improving and reviving that old business district. The largest of the theatres was the Dorothy Chandler Pavilion which was among other things the home of the Los Angeles Philharmonic Orchestra. In it was the Founders Room, a handsome clubroom for the principal subscribers, and I was lucky enough to carry a Founders card, passed on to me by my predecessors. It had a magnificent set of nineteenth-century Viennese chandeliers originally imported by MGM to lend authenticity to *The Great Waltz*, the 1938 biopic of Johann Strauss II. Mrs Chandler had purchased the set from the MGM warehouse. I often admired them as I sipped a thoughtful cocktail before a concert and enjoyed the civilized pleasures of Los Angeles unknown to casual visitors from the east coast or from Europe.

It is a city difficult for the visitor to understand or to like, quite the opposite of the immediately fascinating San Francisco. Some well-known criticisms are true, such as 'six suburbs in search of a city'; others are unkind: 'Tinseltown', for example. Apart from the blazingly sunny climate – it rained only three times during my three years – it has few obvious attractions other than Disneyland and the Universal Studios tour. However, I soon discovered that by far the greatest attraction is that some very charming and distinguished people live there. Since early in the century, the movie industry had attracted an extraordinary range of artists and musicians as well as the actors, writers and directors. The horrors of the 1930s and 1940s in Europe had driven many more to settle in the Californian sunshine.

Neville Marriner came to direct the Los Angeles Chamber Orchestra for a few months each year. He and his wife Molly introduced me to a circle of patrons of the LACO, many of whom are still my friends over twenty years later.

Several leading figures in the movie business were keen supporters of the Philharmonic Orchestra. Amongst them were Danny Kaye and his wife Sylvia Fine, herself renowned as the writer and composer of many of his best-known songs, who befriended me and entertained me generously. In the Kaye's house I got to know other movie celebrities, from Kirk Douglas and Gregory Peck to Robert Wagner and Natalie Wood, and many others.

In the Music Center one evening before a concert I sat alone in the Founders Lounge contemplating the evening ahead.

Just one work was to be performed, and that was Mahler's Ninth Symphony – one of the most severe and heart-rending pieces ever composed. All of Mahler's symphonies have in them a funeral march: in the Ninth, the whole symphony is a contemplation of death written when the composer knew that his heart disease would soon take him away from the life he loved. The conductor was the revered Carlo Maria Giulini making his very first appearance with the LA Philharmonic. Both as a musician and as a man, Giulini was then and is now renowned for his intense seriousness and his devotion to the inner meaning of every musical work he conducted. In earlier years, as a member of the Philharmonia Chorus, I had many time sung in concerts conducted by him, and I considered his performances of Verdi's *Requiem* amongst the most profound of my musical experiences, worthy to rank with Klemperer's titanic performances of Beethoven's *Missa Solemnis*.

Giulini had recorded for EMI for many years, but I had not seen him for some time as he had been seriously ill the previous year and out of action for months. And that evening I was to take him to dinner after the concert.

Given the circumstances, I had booked a table not far from the Music Center.

His interpretation of Mahler's Ninth was even more poignant than I had anticipated. The audience was deeply moved. I went round behind to congratulate – one might almost say to commiserate with – him and was shocked by his anguished appearance. Always admired for his slim elegance, he had now lost weight: his face white and haggard, his chest almost caved in. He was heartened by the tremendous reception he had received, but clearly exhausted.

We were just about to leave for dinner when Danny Kaye appeared. Although his best-known films had been made twenty years before, Danny had aged not at all. He still looked exactly the same as he had in *The Secret Life of Walter Mitty* or *Wonderman* and reinforced the impression by wearing in public the same clothes – on this evening, the familiar white trenchcoat. He asked me to introduce him to Giulini and enquired what were our plans. When I said we had in mind a quiet supper at the Ambassadors Hotel nearby, he suggested we came back to his house in Beverly Hills, where he would himself cook us some supper.

I looked at the haggard, exhausted Giulini, expecting him to decline regretfully, but saw in his eye a gleam of interest. 'I am very tired,' he said. 'Is it far?' When I said it was about twenty miles, he looked disappointed, but brightened up when I said it would not take long and that I would drive him there and back. Off we went to Beverly Hills.

Danny was a keen cook, particularly of Chinese dishes, for which he had installed in the kitchen a row of huge stainless steel woks. I had been his guest at a Chinese dinner on various occasions. Usually there would be eight sitting down to dinner whilst Danny stood by his woks producing a stream of delicate dishes.

However, on this occasion he rapidly prepared green salads and excellent omelettes and then sat down to quiz Giulini earnestly about the technique of conducting.

Danny's hobby was to immerse himself in the technicalities of highly skilled professions: as with Chinese cookery, so also with piloting jet planes and assisting his friend Michael De Bakey at operations of open-heart surgery. I think he may have been allowed to tie the sutures. These hobbies were clearly reminiscent of the dream sequences in the film of *The Secret Life of Walter Mitty*, and may indeed have inspired them.

In recent years, Danny had taken up conducting symphony orchestras for charity fund-raising concerts. As a mimic of genius, he was able to produce some delightfully comic turns, but he strove constantly to improve his baton technique so that purely musical items could sound almost as good as with a professional conductor. At concerts at the Music Center, he did not sit in the audience, but preferred to observe the conductor from the wings at the side.

'Now Carlo,' he said, ignoring my habit of calling him Maestro, 'on the downbeat, when is the exact moment of entry for the orchestra? I think it is when the point of the baton reaches the bottom of the beat,' gesturing with an imaginary baton. 'Don't you agree?'

Giulini did agree, a little nervously. I realized that even though he was himself world famous as a conductor, he was excited but a trifle overawed by the glamour of being entertained by one of the best-known stars of Hollywood's golden age.

They went on talking until after 2 a.m. when Giulini remembered that he had to repeat his Mahler interpretation the following night. I drove him back to his hotel near the Music Center and thought that he seemed much to have enjoyed his unexpected supper.

A few years later, many people were surprised that the ascetic Giulini accepted the position of Music Director of the Los Angeles Philharmonic, but I was not.

MICHAEL ALLEN

When did the UK actually join Europe?

You can have plenty of argument over the real point when the United Kingdom became a full part of the European Community. Perhaps only I know the full secret of how and when exactly the knot was joined. I am prepared to let everyone in on it at the cost of a glass or two.

After all the rebuffs from the French and a wobbly persistence from British governments of both major parties, the Treaty of Rome was at last signed by the Prime Minister in the person of the Rt. Hon. Edward Heath on 22 January 1972.

I know that is true because I was in the Egmont Palace in Brussels when the deed was done. I remember how late Heath was for the ceremony and we all sat, or in my case stood against the wall, trying to keep cool in the ornate but overheated chamber.

Since my task there was to provide pictures and a story for BBC tv-news, I confess to feeling a bit miffed when it came out that the delay was caused by some woman. She had thrown a bottle of ink all over Ted Heath's nice city suit as he got out of his car outside the Palace. Fortunately one of my colleagues was on hand to get that, but the news filtered only slowly into the chamber where all the usual dignitaries were gathered including the King of the Belgians. King Baudouin was a nice affable chap and I managed to have a word or two with him off the record, but I confess I forgot to ask him about the significance of the ink throwing.

Some people claim our fate was sealed on that occasion.

To my mind though, that was not the actual occasion for the cross-over for the UK from being a free-wheeling member of EFTA to getting into bed with the rest of Europe as a fellow member of the Community.

Was it then attendance at the special summit called by Georges Pompidou for the newly enlarged EU? The Prime Ministers of the UK, Ireland and Denmark duly joined the original six in Paris in the autumn of 1972. It was quite a successful joining together, so pleased were they all that they signed a pledge to achieve full economic and political Union by 1980.

It was a pledge that very quietly was left to drift to oblivion until quite recently.

But no, I wouldn't say that that date was definitive either.

What about 5 January 1973, when our new Commissioners arrived in Brussels to take up their tasks?

It was a day of dreadful weather. Fog clung to the entire northern part of Europe and the Continent was well and truly isolated. This meant that Sir Christopher Soames and George Thomson couldn't get into the airport at Zaventem and had to be diverted to Schiphol which by some miracle was briefly open.

The plan was that they would then come down from the Netherlands by rail.

We all had to wait for them on the down platform at Brussels' Gare du Nord. With everything clinging wet, it was a miserable gathering, a few journalists and the newly appointed *chefs de cabinet* of our new Commissioners. David Hannay was looking just a mite worried. 'Oh God, the old man will be in a frightful mood,' I remember him saying.

But it wasn't as bad as that. The UK's champions seemed resigned to their new role. They gave us a few words to report, none of which I can recall now. And we went our various ways to sit it out in the Berlaymont while the Commission President, Xavier Ortoli, spent the night with his colleagues to share out portfolios. That went well and they held the first Commission meeting in a reasonably good humour, Soames with responsibility for External Affairs and Thomson looking after the new Regional Policy dossier.

But I believe that for the general public the real watershed in our island story can be detected a few days earlier.

As the final minutes of 1972 ticked away, most of the British contingent in Brussels were well into a good knees-up party at the Queen Vic. This was a rather up-market pub on the Rondpoint Schuman which unhappily fell victim to the vicious competition for beer drinkers that the capital of Europe offers. There was a lot of noise and singing of patriotic songs. I remember we celebrated the 1973 New Year and the UK's newer status in Europe twice: once as the local clocks chimed midnight and an hour later when Big Ben did the same.

But even then, I was not quite satisfied that the line had finally been drawn.

My task, simply put, was to give pictures to the BBC and through them to the great British public to prove that all was changed forever.

On New Year's Day, I conceived the idea then of showing British civil servants streaming into the Berlaymont Building to take up the burden of running Europe alongside their European colleagues.

The problem was that it was a public holiday and the doors were locked and barred. There was no streaming except from the heavens.

Fortunately in my earlier months of poking about in Brussels, I had made the acquaintance of the janitors, the canny people who ran the building. They had been most helpful in getting me into forbidden places before, and I found salvation with them again.

One of them was doing duty in his den despite the holiday. He listened for my plea for help and rustled around behind his desk where he kept the flags of all nations.

While we set the camera up outside, he expertly ran the Union Jack up the tallest flagpole in front of the building.

The pictures appeared on the evening news bulletins pretty well everywhere. That's when I reckon people knew there was no going back.

ROBERT ELPHICK

Across the Channel and into the Trees

A-jabber with alien tongues and impenetrable local jargon, inhabited by ravenous anthropophagites great and small, the graveyard of many a parliamentary, political and diplomatic reputation, obeying customs unknown to Englishmen and laws known only to the Gods, its procedural jungle pathways tortuous, dimly lit and beset with traps for the unwary and snakepits for the unwelcome, the dreaded Brussels Euro-jungle is a place where the tenderfoot can disappear without trace in broad daylight, and where even seasoned old-timers with leopard-skin bandannas round their hats go pale beneath their tans if caught out in the bush after sunset. Brussels also has some of the best restaurants and pubs, and brightest public servants, in the world.

I joined the Foreign Office in 1956, serving in the Middle East, South-East Asia and Western Europe, in large, medium and small diplomatic missions of acknowledged efficiency. In London, I sat on the NATO and WEU desk in a *mouvementé* period; and, later on, got shacked up with the policy planning staff with Percy Cradock (latterly foreign affairs adviser at Number 19), Roger Tomkys (now Master of Pembroke College, Cambridge) and Charles Powell (subsequently for many years one of Mrs Thatcher's key Private Secretaries). It was an orderly, appetising and oxygenated existence, involving no obviously incurable diseases, little map reading or hand-to-hand fighting, and really very few unpleasant insects.

But Arcady is never forever; Olympus is not an abiding abode for mortal men. In 1973, on Britain's entry into the European Community, I was seconded from the FO to the European Commission in Brussels, as one of the directors (in Whitehall terms, 'under secretaries') responsible for external relations. Most of the time I was condemned, as Sisyphus might well have been, to trying to propitiate the United States, to appease the old commonwealth, and to cope with agricultural trade problems in the GATT. In addition – and as an act of malice towards the then only professional diplomat in that neck of the Commission's woods – I was assigned supervision of the EC Protocol Service, and of a new unit set up to rationalize policy on external diplomatic representation.

The initial 'culture shock' on arrival in Brussels was pretty massive, even for a professional. Language alone was a problem: to draft documents much of the time, and to speak most of the time, in French, demanded a level of effort greater than that which I had normally had to make during four years in the British Embassy in Paris. The French language demands facial exertions different from those required when one mutters away in English; the throat, cheeks and lips used to rebel after eight or nine hours non-stop; and I regularly suffered from French 'face-ache' in the first week or two back in Brussels after a spot of furlough. A greater difficulty was the shortage of

Brussels staff, compared with the ample availabilities of Whitehall. In consequence, the work load was consistently heavy. Another kind of handicap was imposed by the bureaucratic tradition of the Commission: old timers used to joke that it was an amalgam of the worst practices of each of the civil services of France, Germany, Italy and Benelux – the six founding members of the European Community.

Certainly, staff discipline was more relaxed, obedience to instructions less unquestioning, than in 'the Office'. There seemed little or no career-planning or in-house training. I looked in vain for the kind of teamwork and the coordinating structures familiar to me both within the Foreign Office and between government departments in Whitehall. One had to watch out for banana skins from the ill-intentioned. Hierarchy did not seem to matter too much – the Luxembourger head of my protocol service (grade A4) was junior in rank to his Italian number two (grade A3 *à titre* personnel). There were other novelties and horrors, like giving press conferences and being grilled by the external relations committee of the European Parliament. Worse, I was constantly required to rush off and *do* something, instead of composing elegant and judicious Blue Minutes.

As for the EU overseas offices for which I had assumed responsibility, they were very few, of recent creation and operating on an improvised, even hand-to-mouth basis. Confidentiality and discretion was less than what I had been accustomed to. One privileged delegation was rumoured to possess an ancient cipher machine which no one knew how to use and which was therefore left locked up in a safe. There was no diplomatic bag service, or secure telephone link, to anywhere or anyone. On one occasion, I had to report to the *chef de cabinet* of my Commissioner in Brussels, from a slightly dodgy situation in Latin America, by means of a telex sent from the local post office in Persian (in which we were both naturally fluent). Indeed, the Commission took pride in being a 'house of glass'. Asked by a Foreign Office friend how I was finding things, a few weeks after my first arrival in Brussels, I recall replying that while in London you locked away official papers on leaving the office at night, in Brussels you left your files on your desk, but locked up the telephone, so that office cleaners did not spend their evenings making long international calls to distant relatives. Internal organisation, too, could be – dare I say – inspirational. Thus, I recall the Washington delegation once reporting the same US government policy development twice to Brussels, in two separate telexes, drafted by two different officials who had not consulted each other or their boss. In another overseas office, its head – a senior German from Bonn's generally weak reconstructed post-war civil service – occasionally assigned the same piece of work simultaneously to two separate officials, to see which one made a better job of it – a procedure proudly described by its practitioner as using a 'two-headed eagle'.

The foregoing will rightly appear arrogant and condescending. To start with, I do confess to having missed the planning staff in particular, and the diplomatic service in general; and to have longed for the day when I could 'come in from the cold'. Indeed, during those early years with the Commission, I must have given the impression of a fastidious and slightly narcissistic Guards officer who had suddenly found himself an outcast, on transfer to a line regiment stationed in a remote outpost of some insalubrious equatorial colony.

But these personal feelings were mistaken, and anyway faded with time. I came to realize that I found myself in a set-up which had more in common with a swinging London merchant bank, or the upper layers of a dynamic multinational company, than with a long-established imperial bureaucracy. There were not a few precocious prima donnas; a good working relationship with colleagues had to be earned, rather than expected as of right; knowledge was power – you did not share it too widely (as even cabinet ministers may find, on moving from Whitehall to commerce). Average ability in the Brussels bureaucracy seemed to me to fall slightly below that habitual in top Whitehall departments. But the senior continental officials – at least in DGI, the external relations Directorate General in which I served – were people of marked ability and intelligence, who believed in what they were doing. These, and Euro-colleagues from the agricultural and industrial policy departments, possessed international negotiating skills, developed over long years doing the same sort of job, that were unsurpassed – perhaps even unmatched – anywhere in the world. I admired them and felt I had much to learn: initially, they were probably less convinced that they had much to learn from me. Yet, although it took time for my face to fit, in the end it was possible to rub noses and undergo tribal initiation.

On my first day in the Foreign Office, in September 1956, a clerk in the training department, to whom I expect that I had been more than usually gracious (perhaps even *de haut en bas*), ushered me out of his office with the words, 'No matter how rigorous and searching we make the selection process to Branch A of the Foreign Service, we tend to find that the percentage of idiots in the intake remains constant.' I was to remember this, twenty years later, swinging in a hammock slung between fever trees in Etterbeek. Clearly, one had to join them, if one could not beat them; there was no alternative but to go native. To keep the opposition guessing, I began to switch constantly between Higher School Certificate French, barrack room Flemish, Goon Show German, largely invented Italian, long forgotten Greek (mostly 'water is best' and 'everything is in a state of flux'), and broad Harry Lauder Scots ('there's aye muckle a slappy steen, at ilka body's door'). I duly locked up my telephone; left my papers strewn across my desk; cast banana skins behind me; set aside hierarchy; instructed two juniors to do something which I then did better myself; dined as often as possible at 'Le Cygne', 'Comme Chez Soi' or the 'Villa Lorraine'; and generally daubed my cheeks, and other accessible parts of my anatomy, with the comitological war paints of the relevant EU tribal Indabas.

But there was a price. It became difficult, when briefly out of the trees and back across the Channel, to speak good enough English to get past the porter's desk at the Travellers' Club in native dress; and quite impossible, on eventual return to Blighty after fifteen years of Brassholes, to get any sort of job outside the University of Sussex. But I console myself. I am glad to say that I have happily since recovered full command of my native tongue. One must-a be dankful for ze small *merçis, nicht*?

LESLIE FIELDING

Coffee Everywhere in Arabia

Thirty years ago, shopping in Abu Dhabi was a pretty limited activity and the few shops that I visited were new and located outside the souk. On one occasion, in 1967, I had been to check whether the weekly consignment of fresh vegetables had arrived at the 'supermarket'; it had not. I then went to our Indian friend who imported British daily newspapers to see whether he had added anything of interest to his modest collection of other goods; he had not. But one had to be quick: he once imported one dozen identical standard lamps which were all sold within hours of appearing in his shop.

There was usually little reason to go into the souk itself, but today I made a small detour. I walked behind the Indian shop into the soft white sand, past our tailor – 'Chand brothers, civil and military' according to the label in my trousers – and into the shade of the souk. There a friendly voice called '*tafadhl*' to me from a group of Arabs perched cross-legged on their chairs around a small low coffee table set between two little shops.

It was Tarish (*see page 107*), transformed from the geological sample-washer, clad in dark blue baggy overalls, to the urbane man about town. I had spent many hours sitting on a dune in the oil field with Tarish, but here he was, to me, hardly recognizable in his spotlessly clean white *kandura*. He invited me to meet his uncles and their friends. They gathered every day for a couple of hours in the same place to drink coffee and exchange news. One of them provided the table and chairs from his shop nearby. These were set in a gap between the coral stone buildings to catch the feeble draught in the otherwise hot, humid and still air. Another uncle brought coffee and dates. Their ages were difficult to determine because they dyed their beards black and concealed their hair under flowing head-dresses.

After the usual greetings, cut short for me as a foreigner, I was offered a seat on a rough wooden chair. Tarish, the youngest and deferring to his uncles, picked up in his left hand the brass coffee pot (*dhalla*), blackened by many years of boiling on the charcoal fire. With his right hand he selected from the enamel bowl of murky water several small china cups without handles. He held the cups, stacked inside one another, shook the water out of them and then poured into the top cup a small amount of burning hot, light coffee. It seemed to be no more than enough to cover the bottom of the tiny cup, but it was enough to enable him proudly to let the coffee pot rise and fall as he poured without spilling. I noted the sprig of matting from the trunk of a date palm poked into the spout to hold back the grains of the roughly ground and lightly roasted coffee and cardamom seeds (*hail*). Tarish offered coffee to his uncles, who all declined, saying that they had just drunk. He stood waiting to offer me more, taking my cup in his hand to pour again. After the second time, I returned the cup to him gently shaking it to indicate that I had had enough.

When I finished my coffee, an uncle offered me fresh dates. These were the *khalas*, the last dates of the season; after them and through the winter months there would be only the dried, boiled dates (*tamr*).

Courtesy had been shown and soon the animated conversation resumed, reinforced by gesticulations and a small cloud of dust as a thin bamboo camel stick struck the ground. I understood scarcely a word.

The source of the delicious dates was the large oasis Al 'Ain, meaning the spring, which is situated one hundred miles to the east of Abu Dhabi. Al 'Ain oasis features prominently in the lives of many of the Arabs, as they retreat there in the summer. They go to enjoy the gardens and the fresh running water of the ancient underground man-made channels (*falaj*), as well as to escape the heavy coastal humidity and the torrid heat of the cloudless skies. Before the advent of cars, the journey took up to seven days on camels across the burning sand. The travellers were sustained by brackish water from the few wells along the route until they camped the last night on the high dunes overlooking the Al 'Ain plain. These last few miles were relatively easy; even the camels were encouraged by the approaching green of the date palm waving in the wind and the 'thud thud' of the Blackstone diesel engines pumping water for the gardens. Children came running barefoot, ahead of family members, joyfully to greet the safe arrival of the travellers. As they entered the shade of the gardens, the sound like a bell of the pestle and mortar grinding beans welcomed them and promised a few small cups of delicious pale coffee.

After a time I said my farewells to Tarish and his chattering uncles and continued my walk through the souk. One shop had a row of sacks open to display the contents: all dried goods, whether vegetables, fruit or fish alongside spices and herbs, and all contributing to the powerful and enticing smell. Another shop sold cloth, the bolts laid out to interest the few customers. The jewellery shop contained some watches and silver ornaments but, as with all the shops, it told of the great poverty that was Abu Dhabi, a poverty that oil revenues were just starting to disperse. The souk was typical of those of the area. One entered a passageway about ten feet wide with shops on both sides, built of coral stone and mud brick and roofed with palm frond matting. Few shops had glass windows; some had shutters. The goods were laid out on the floor or on low shelves, while others were hung on hooks. The shopkeeper made space among his wares for himself to sit or stand.

I had been working in the desert, far removed from the upheavals in family bliss occasioned by the oil company's decision to move from comfortable, reliable and very civilized Bahrain with its hotels, clubs and schools, asphalted roads, villas with mature gardens, a social life unequalled, and a substantial expatriate population. Why move to Abu Dhabi? The Ruler was determined that his people should all benefit from the revenue derived from the oil so recently found in their territory. A year earlier in 1966 the oil company, which had headquarters in London and Bahrain, agreed to construct houses and offices in Abu Dhabi and to move there from Bahrain. This was an important first step in the modern development of a new city; but at the time of our arrival the only Abu Dhabi hotel, the Beach Hotel, provided shared accommodation and 'take your water glass to your room after dinner, there is no water in the tap'. We were told that the company would provide a club and a school. The villas were new and untried, as was the water and electricity supply. There was not an inch of asphalt road. Social life would be of our own making within the small expatriate population. As the move got underway, I had been called to a distant corner of the desert.

A friend had told me that the sheikhs in Bahrain were selling good cars cheaply: cars they had no further use for. He could buy one for me and put it on the barge with the other cars coming to Abu Dhabi. A message came from Bahrain: 'found ideal car, send 500 dinars immediately'. I sent the money and in due course the barge arrived, the twenty cars on it doubling the saloon car population in Abu Dhabi, and mine was delivered to my house.

Returning from the desert, I was eager to see my new possession. An 'ideal car' for a young petroleum engineer? I had no idea what that was. I did not know that those of us who had come to Abu Dhabi from the desert were entering a small, very jealous European society: a society very reluctantly transplanted from Bahrain, one where every move was watched and every social gaffe regaled with embellishments. We were junior to and, of course, considered to be less sophisticated than our colleagues from Bahrain. They said that we could not understand the sacrifice they made in the move, a sacrifice for our benefit. We were to keep a low profile and know our position.

My 'ideal car' turned out to be a twelve-cylinder Oldsmobile, which was the largest in the range and probably the largest car in Abu Dhabi. I could straddle the potholes in the road while my seniors had to drive into each sandy hole and try to drive out again in their Minis and Austin 1100s. As I sailed by in my air-conditioned comfort, I could raise and lower my seat, the windows and the radio aerial at the touch of a switch, while they struggled with overheated engines to escape the soft sand.

The year is now 1998. The old Abu Dhabi has long ago totally disappeared. There is no doubt in our minds, as we enter one of the many supermarkets, that we will find a splendid array of fresh fruit and vegetables. One hot summer morning recently I visited the shop of our Indian friend, now occupying several floors in a new twenty-storey building. His shop, which could be in any affluent world capital, is similar to so many in Abu Dhabi today, and the building is one of dozens towering towards the sky. I found all that I needed and much more: I could have bought silk flowers, caviar, computers and electric coffee grinders.

I came out onto the street, not a grain of sand here, and passed between two jewellery shops piled high with gold, protected from the burning heat and rising humidity by plate glass and excessively powerful air conditioning. I was relieved to turn the corner into the shade and a slight breeze when I heard the voice of Tarish. *'Tafadhi'* was the call from a group of Arabs perched cross-legged on their chairs around a small low coffee table in the shade – between two thirty-storey buildings.

DAVID HEARD

Dining Out

During a training exercise in India our company pitched camp in a remote region about fifty miles from Bareilly. On the second day a message arrived with an invitation to the British officers from the local *tehsildar* (the head man of a *tehsil*, which is about the size of an English county) to dine with him that evening. He apologized for the fact that his house was inaccessible to motor vehicles, but that he would send other transport. This duly arrived in the shape of two elephants with their drivers. Much to the amusement of the sepoys, the three of us, two on the larger and more sedate animal, and the junior company officer on the smaller and more frisky one, mounted and rode off at a cracking pace across fields and tracks until we reached our host's residence some five miles distant. There in front of the main building was laid out in a large circle a most lavish feast, the whole dining area being surrounded by a thousand flickering lights. After the formal courtesies had been exchanged, we were seated in places of honour among about thirty other guests – all local dignitaries. There followed a seemingly endless succession of delicious courses interspersed with music and dancing by professional entertainers. The evening passed pleasantly by and we became aware of many other arrivals outside the ring of lights – perhaps four or five hundred villagers had come to join the party. The murmur of voices, the companionable bubbling of hookahs, the desultory conversation with our amiable hosts, the music, the dancing, the superbly seasoned food all set beneath the brilliant canopy of stars made us feel very close to the heart of India. It was with genuine regret that we bade farewell, mounted our elephants and returned to reach camp an hour before dawn.

PETER FRANCIS

Getting Away from it All

After a long and enjoyable lunch in the City with a cricketing friend, I was walking back to Fleet Street when I noticed a model cargo boat in the window of the shipping agent Clarksons. Handsome and shining, the *Pozarica*, some 2,500 tons, was irresistible. In the front office a clerk said, 'She's sailing tomorrow evening from Liverpool.'

He agreed that I could join her as a passenger and, before he could announce her ports of call, I requested him not to tell me. 'I wish,' I said, 'to get away from it all. I will board your ship with such sum in travellers' cheques as you may require and pay as I go.' The clerk, entering into the spirit of my great escape, said £100 would be acceptable, told me how to find the *Pozarica* and undertook to inform her master of my unusual request.

When I arrived at the docks a steward conducted me to a cabin. He said: master's compliments and would I join him for breakfast? There were port noises and we headed for the open sea. I slept well and in the morning the scouse steward brought a cup of tea. As we seemed to be alongside again I reminded the steward of his company's undertaking not to tell me where I was or for what foreign parts the *Pozarica* was bound.

Although the steward stopped short of tapping his forehead, his expression indicated doubts about my sanity. He said, 'So you're the daft bugger who doesn't want to know where he's going.' At breakfast the master, mate, engineer and my fellow passenger, a retired hospital matron, maintained the charade. Yes, I was told, there was time to go ashore and explore providing I was back for lunch.

I walked down the gangway, turned towards the dockyard gates and very soon approached a shopping area. Obviously, purchases were out because foreign currency from the purser would have destroyed my determination on adventure. Then, glancing at the shops, I recognized Woolworth and Marks & Spencer. I was in Swansea.

EDWARD BISHOP

In Africa, think Big

It is often instructive and frequently salutary to reflect on the sayings of great men and women. One harbours the vain thought that in years to come travellers in outer space might peruse this very volume in order to find inspiration during their long sojourn to the edge of the universe. Assuming of course that the universe has an 'edge' but that is another matter altogether. The recorded utterances of the great and the good vary considerably. Some have the immediate clarity of pure spring water. Others are equally refreshing once they have been distilled and allowed to mature for a while. Take the following example:

> *'Never take a cold bath in Africa, unless ordered to do so by a doctor.'*

Such was the suggestion in *Hints to Travellers* offered by Dr William Henry Cross in 1906. If the innocent traveller were to accept this 'hint' without question, he could easily find himself going without a bath of any kind for a considerable period of time, hot water being a rare commodity in

> *'that mysterious land! Surrounded by a lot of sand and full of grass and trees'.*

At least that is how Hilaire Belloc described it in 1898. I admit, things may have changed since then but Belloc, in poetic mood, captures something of the Africa travellers know and love. The land where a bath of any description is welcome. As you may have gathered, I am distilling the remarks of Dr Cross.

It is up to the truly great names to speak with clarity and purity.

> *'In Africa, think big.'*

That is water from the spring. Clear, sparkling, refreshing and spoken by none other than the great Cecil Rhodes.

I had occasion to reflect on this profound statement when attempting to travel from Lagos in the west of the continent to Capetown in the south. After exertions that would reduce the labours of Hercules to a mere picnic,

I managed to travel from the centre of Lagos to the airport. At first I imagined I had chosen to travel on a day when the entire Islamic population was bound for Mecca, Christians for the Holy Land and the remainder for any part of the world that would accept them. I was wrong. It was a normal day in Nigeria. Everyone wanted out, as the saying goes. Given the fact that the international terminal was teeming with life and hand-to-hand fighting was breaking out in front of most airline counters, the airline officials appeared remarkably serene.

Obtaining my ticket was a tedious business that involved mediating sundry potential serious disputes, plotting my way through several tons of hand luggage and encountering counter staff who were so relaxed that they claimed they had no record whatsoever of my ever having booked a ticket. The latter fact was hardly surprising as all computers in the building had been out of action throughout the afternoon, enabling the staff to enjoy some serenity in the midst of what appeared to be a minor civil war.

As evening fell the busy world was far from hushed and agitated travellers continued to be plagued by the fever of life, which was rapidly developing into a battle for survival. In short, no work had been done and I remained stranded. Then, in the twinkle of an eye, all, well almost all, was resolved. The computers flickered into action; the staff yawned into sluggish activity and renewed fighting broke out yet again throughout the concourse. My ticket was duly delivered and I prepared for the long and hazardous journey through customs and immigration. I shall pass over that prolonged and frustrating experience. To this day it distresses me and I have no desire to pass on that distress to the reader, especially if he or she be on their lonely way to the edge of space.

I felt a small twinge of anxiety when, in the relative peace of the departure lounge, I examined my ticket. I was booked to travel from Nigeria to Zaire and then onwards to South Africa. In Zaire there would be just two hours to wait for my onward connection. Travellers will know too well that the western and African concepts of time do not always harmonize. When Lord Hemingford remarked that in Africa it is always five minutes to twelve, he may have been expressing what I am trying to convey. On the other hand he may not. No matter, suffice to say time and timetables can be a problem for the western traveller in the continent. Unlike the noble Lord's clock, I was alarmed.

The journey to Zaire passed pleasantly enough. At one point there was a minor commotion at the back of the plane when a thirsty traveller produced a spirit stove and prepared to brew a pot of tea. Fortunately he was restrained by members of the same group who had fought with such determination in the departure lounge, and we landed safely.

> '*Fatal Africa*,' observed the great Henry Morton Stanley,
> *one after another travellers drop away.*'

How right he was, I thought, when in Zaire only two passengers disembarked. A youngish man dressed in blue jeans and a check shirt, and myself. We crossed the tarmac together and were mercifully reunited with our luggage. Compared to Lagos the terminal in Zaire was a haven of tranquillity. In fact it was so peaceful we began to feel somewhat nervous. We stumbled across the dimly lit departure lounge looking for a place to check in for our next flight. Not one booth was illuminated. Our feelings of apprehension increased as not only had the travellers disappeared but seemingly everyone else had gone also. The man in the check shirt (a seasoned traveller and, I was later to discover, a very important man in the business world) suggested that I guard the luggage while he went to try to find some signs of life. I glanced at my watch. Our 'plane was due to leave in half an hour. After five minutes or so he returned.

'Bad news,' he said.

I confessed that I was hardly surprised.

'There's a war on. Our connecting flight arrived early and because of possible trouble departed immediately.'

I could see our speed downhill was increasing rapidly.

'The next flight is in three days. It's useless to try to get into town. Apart from being too dangerous, every hotel is occupied by journalists.' In times of crisis when one feels the need to gain inspiration from the sayings of the great, it is important to be selective. Stanley who, after noting how his companions in Africa disappeared, went on to speak about *'the rabid fury of the native guarding every entry and exit, the unspeakable misery of life within the wild continent, the utter absence of every comfort, the bitterness which each day heaps upon the poor white man's head . . . '*

Clearly at this juncture Stanley was not our man but good old Rhodes was.

'In Africa, think big.'

I have already mentioned that my new-found companion was what might be called casually dressed. I, although only occupying a lowly position as a junior layman in the Church of England, was smartly dressed as I was due to be met in South Africa by an archdeacon and archdeacons, as guardians of church fabric, know a thing or two about sartorial elegance.

'Come,' I said confidently. 'I shall be a most important traveller. A VIP in fact. You, dressed as you are, must take on the role of my bodyguard.'

We picked up our cases and set off to explore the dark terminal. Those who frequent airports will have noted that whenever a new building is designed the architect is given one instruction that must be followed come what may. It is that every arriving and departing passenger must be made to walk as far as possible. We walked along deserted corridors, empty departure halls and through vacant offices. The campaign that day had been hard fought and after half an hour or so we were feeling somewhat tired and dispirited when, to our delight, we met another human being. Unlike the most famous encounter in African history, between the great Livingstone and Stanley, the man we met was certainly not looking for us nor did he seem particularly pleased to see us. In order to gain an immediate advantage, and in keeping with the military spirit of the day, I threw him a command.

'Please take us immediately to the VIP lounge.'

He looked at me and took a longer look at my casual companion

'That's my bodyguard. He must stay by my side at all times.'

The lone figure turned and we followed. Even VIPs are not exempt from the architect's rule and after a hike of fifteen minutes or so we arrived outside a splendid private lounge.

'Where is the book?' I demanded in a polite but firm tone.

The lonely man who seemed to know everything produced a leather-bound volume and we inscribed our names therein.

'If we do that now,' I said *sotto voce* to my bodyguard, 'they won't throw us out in the morning. Once you're in the book, you're in.'

By now my newly-appointed bodyguard was thinking along the same lines as Cecil Rhodes.

'Mr Waite will need some food,' he said. 'We shall also need something to drink.'

The lonely man looked abashed.

'I shall need money,' he muttered.

'No problem,' said the bodyguard. He rummaged in his briefcase and produced a little box. He opened it, revealing at least two dozen miniature Swiss Army penknives. 'Take these,' he said. 'We have no money but plenty of these.'

For the first time that evening, the lonely man smiled, accepted one of the penknives and disappeared to return within thirty minutes with an old-fashioned 10 Downing Street lunch, namely beer and sandwiches.

We spent the next three days in the VIP lounge eating and drinking like real VIPs thanks to our little stock of knives. At 4 a.m. on the third and final morning, our slumbers were disturbed by a posse of military men with instructions to search the room. As our names were 'in the book' we were safe and returned to sleep, only to be awakened some two hours later by a visit from none other than the President of the Republic, who was on his way to the battle zone. I chatted pleasantly enough with him as VIPs do while my bodyguard lurked in the corner of the room with half a dozen machine-gun-toting bruisers. Finally, after a refreshing early morning beer or so, the President departed, and later that morning we left also.

As I flew across that great continent en route to the south, there was time to further ponder the wisdom of Rhodes and in particular his expansive thinking. At least, I thought, think as big as you can, given the limitations of the situation, and if you can't think big enough, perhaps a miniature Swiss Army knife might help you to survive for a day or so even if you don't win every round of the battle. And you never will . . . in Africa.

TERRY WAITE

A Note on the Architecture of the Travellers Club

Our building fronts Pall Mall, demurely lodged between the stately Athenaeum and the grandiose Reform, as if Mozart were sitting between Bach and Beethoven. Sir John Betjeman thought the Travellers (1832) and the Reform (1841) the loveliest of Sir Charles Barry's buildings, while the *Survey of London* calls it the first of his masterpieces. The design was derived from Raphael's Palazzo Pandolfino in Florence and, as a turning point in English architecture, it was a major influence on many later Victorian buildings.

The prettiest aspect of the house is its Florentine back, glimpsed through the trees of the gardens. Its handsomest rooms are the Library, overlooking those gardens, and the dining room, called the Coffee Room. This last takes up the full 69 feet of the Club's frontage and is a fine sight with its three towering chandeliers alight, its walls now restored to colours close to the original.

The most elegant of rooms, the Library, is sectioned into three parts by sets of columns that are now, as described in 1839, 'of a wainscot or pale oak colour'. Below the ceiling of the middle section runs a cast of the frieze from the Temple of Apollo at Bassae, unearthed in 1811 by C R Cockerell, a founder member of the Club. Apollo rides with Artemis in a chariot drawn by roe deer, Greeks battle with Amazons, Lapiths with centaurs. Below them is an intricately carved oak chimney piece that had been available for sale when the Club was at the design stage. Barry thought it appropriate and snapped it up for £20. For he did not confine himself to the architecture of the building but designed much of its furniture and its handsome brass gasoliers, long since electrified. He was not, however, responsible for a curiosity in the entrance hall, where an open fire glows redly through the winter months. Immediately above it there is a handsome window overlooking the central courtyard while a cunning architectural trick hides the chimney.

John Summerson observed of the Travellers that it is the pioneer of the post-Waterloo clubs, a smaller, but in another sense, perhaps greater building than the Athenaeum. Its greatness lies, indeed, in its scale and proportions. It was designed to welcome the traveller home, to invite and not to overawe.

GRAHAM BINNS

The Authors

We asked each contributor to write his own biography for us. The Editors.

ALLEN, MICHAEL (*b.* 1932) Read Russian at Cambridge and English at Oxford. Joined EMI 1956; spent over 30 years in international management of classical records. General Manager, Angel Records USA (Los Angeles 1974–1976); otherwise based in London, travelling frequently in Europe, USA and Far East. Retired 1989 as Commercial Director of EMI Classics. Particular interest: early music movement and classic American musicals. *See pages 24, 124, 162, 205 and 264*

ARMITAGE, ST JOHN CBE (*b.* 1924) Specialist in Middle East affairs. Served with Arab armies in Transjordan, Saudi Arabia and Oman, searched for locusts in Kenya and the Aden Protectorates and oil in Libya and, as a member of HM Diplomatic Service, spent 16 years in Iraq, Lebanon, Saudi Arabia and the United Arab Emirates. *See page 208.*

BAILEY, ANTHONY JOHN, MIPR, MIPRA (*b.*1970) Public relations executive and freelance journalist. Managing Director, Eligo International 1997–present. Media adviser to numerous national and international statesmen and Royalty 1990–present. Manager of Management Communications, IBM, EMEA (Paris 1995–6). Senior Account Director, Burson-Marsteller (London, Lima, Cairo 1991–5). Particular interests: Eastern and Central European history and politics. *See page 166.*

BARRY O'BRIEN, RICHARD (*b.*1930) Journalist: 37 years as reporter on *Daily Telegraph, Sunday Telegraph* and *Daily Mail* covering home & foreign news ranging from Profumo affair in 1963, to Middle East wars and African famine in 1970s–1980s. Travelled widely in Middle East and Africa reporting

289

from Israel, Lebanon, Jordan, Egypt, Turkey, Cyprus, Iraq, Sudan, Ethiopia, South Africa and other countries. *See page 225.*

BINNS, GRAHAM (*b.* 1925) Served WW2 in both Royal Navy and Indian Army. Fulbright Scholar USA. 5 years in Arts Council followed by 30 years in broadcasting and communications. Managed radio and tv stations overseas. Deputy Chairman, Capital Radio 1974–82; Director, Duke of York's Theatre 1980–84. Hellenophile with contrasting interest in Wild West Indies. *See pages 29 and 287.*

BISHOP, EDWARD (*b.*1924) Following service Royal Navy & SEAC Newspaper, journalist *Singapore Free Press, Daily Telegraph, Daily Mail, Financial Times.* Author of *The Battle of Britain, The Wooden Wonder, Emma Lady Hamilton, Blood and Fire, Wellington Bomber, The Hurricane, The Debt We Owe.* Currently *Daily Telegraph* aviation and SOE obituarist. *See 115, 190 and 280.*

BRAMALL, FIELD MARSHAL THE LORD, KG, GCB, OBE, MC (*b.* 1923) Professional soldier. Enlisted 1942; commissioned 1943. War service in N.W. Europe, June 1944–May 1945. Served in British Commonwealth Occupation Force in Japan 1947; in UK,Middle East and Berlin 1948–62; on staff of Earl Mountbatten 1962–64; C.O. 2nd Battalion Royal Greenjackets during confrontation with Indonesia 1965–67; commanded 5 Airborne Brigade 1967–69; 1st Armoured Division 1970–72; British Forces Hong Kong 1973–76. C-in-C UK Land Forces 1976–78. Chief of General Staff 1979–82 (during Falklands). Chief of Defence Staff 1982–85. HM Lord Lieutenant of Greater London 1986–98. President of MCC 1988–89. Chairman of Trustees Imperial War Museum 1989–98. Current Chairman Travellers Club. Joint author of *The Chiefs: an anecdotal history of the Chiefs of Staff.* Interests: international affairs on defence, cricket, painting and travel. *See page 35.*

BRASHER, CHRISTOPHER WILLIAM, CBE Started working life as an engineering apprentice earning £2.10s a week. Progressed via two expeditions to the Arctic, junior oil company executive, Sports Editor of *The Observer,*

BBC–TV reporter, Head of General Features, BBC–TV. Managing Director Fleetfoot Ltd, Chief Executive London Marathon 1980–95, Chairman Reebok UK 1990–92, Berghaus 1993–98, Brasher Boot Co 1993 – semi-retirement in 1999. Author (with Sir John Hunt) of *The Red Snows*; and of various books on the Olympics etc. Interests: horse racing, mountains, orienteering, social running, fly fishing. *See page 26.*

BROOK-SHEPHERD, GORDON, CBE (*b.* 1918) Double First History, Cambridge 1938. Lieut-Colonel Intelligence Corps WW2 (mentioned in despatches). Foreign Correspondent, Diplomatic Correspondent and Associate Editor, *Daily* and *Sunday Telegraph* 1948–1986, travelling world-wide. Chairman, SOS Children's Villages UK 1989–present. Author of 19 works on modern European history specializing in Central Europe. Interests: shooting, fly fishing, tennis, travel, music and good food. *See page 142.*

BROWNRIGG, HENRY (*b.* 1943) Educated Winchester and New College Oxford. Secretary, Oxford Union. Worked for international mining group Charter Consolidated, latterly as Divisional Manager. Sloan Fellow of London Business School. Collects & deals in Asiatic & Islamic art. Author of *Betel Cutters in the Samuel Eilenberg Collection* (1992). Major interest: Asian culture & politics. *See page 129.*

CARLESS, HUGH CMG (*b.* 1925,India) Studied Persian at SOAS 1940–43. After 4 years in army and 3 years at Cambridge, joined Foreign Service 1950. Served in Foreign Office, Afghanistan, Iran, Europe and Latin America, lastly as Ambassador to Venezuela. Executive Vice-President, Hinduja Foundation 1986–97. Married to painter, Rosa Maria Frontini. *See pages 37, 122 and 258.*

CARSWELL, PROFESSOR JOHN (*b.*1931) Artist, writer and historian. Archaeological draughtsman at Jericho 1951. Taught fine art at American University of Beirut 1956–76. Museum Director at University of Chicago 1978–87. Director of Islamic Department, Sotheby's 1987–96. Archaeological research in Middle East, Maldives, Indian sub-continent, Central Asia and Gobi Desert. Author of *Coptic Tattoo Designs* (1958), *New Julfa* (1968), *Kütahya*

Tiles (1972), *Blue-and-White* (1984), *Arab Seafaring* (new edn. 1996), *Iznik Pottery* (1998). One-man exhibitions in London 1966, New York 1968, and retrospective in Stockholm 1998. Interests: travel and research. *See page 11.*

COTTESLOE, JOHN FREEMANTLE – THE RT HON LORD COTTESLOE, KSTJ JP DL (*b.* 1927) Served RN 1944–1966 – last seagoing appointment C.O. HMS *Palliser*, Fishery Protection frigate during 'Cod War'. Retired to manage family estate and business. High Sheriff of Buckinghamshire 1969–70. Deputy Lieutenant 1978. HM Lord Lieutenant 1984–1997. Hon Dr University of Buckingham 1993. Deputy President Royal Show (to HRH the Princess Royal) 1996. Chairman Radcliffe Trustees. Succeeded to peerage 1994; sits on Cross Benches. *See page 163.*

DALE, SIR WILLIAM, KCMG (*b.*1906) Barrister, Government legal adviser, Whitehall with extensions to Palestine (1934), Sarawak (with Rajah Brooke), Libya, Beirut (1968–73 General Counsel UNWRA). Director of Legislative Studies, Institute of Advanced Legal Studies, London. Author of *Translations of Bontempelli*; *Law of the Parish Church* (7th edn 1998); *Legislative Drafting: a New Approach* (1977); *The Modern Commonwealth* (1983); *Time Past Time Present* (autobiography 1994). Amateur musician. *See pages 14, 68 and 239.*

ELLETSON, HAROLD DANIEL HOPE. Business consultant and former Member of Parliament. Author of *The General against the Kremlin* [a biography of General Lebed] (1998). Lives in Lancashire. *See page 50.*

ELPHICK, ROBERT Spent most of his life in journalism, ending his career as spokesman for European Commission in Brussels & London. Reuters Correspondent in Moscow 1958–62; in Algiers 1963–4. Joined BBC as Assistant Diplomatic Correspondent 1964, covering Eastern & Central Europe from Vienna. Transferred to Bonn as BBC–TV's first Europe Correspondent 1972. Other lengthy assignments in India, Vietnam, Amman & Beirut. Joined the EC in 1977. *See pages 216 and 268.*

ELY, ROBERT (*b.* 1930) After National Service in the Suffolks and Modern Languages at Trinity Hall, joined B.A.T. 1953. Worked in Europe, East and West Africa, Trinidad and Chile. Retired as Head of Public Affairs worldwide 1990. Now works voluntarily for several charities. Interests: languages, travel and meeting people. *See pages 111 and 187.*

FIELDING, SIR LESLIE KCMG FRSA FRGS HON.LLD (*b.*1932) Joined Foreign Service 1956. Served Tehran (Oriental Secretary), Singapore, Phnom Penh (chargé d'affaires 1964–66), Paris; and on West European Desk and Policy Planning Staff, London. Transferred to European Commission, Brussels 1973 as Director; EC Ambassador, Tokyo 1978–82; Director General for External Relations, Brussels 1982–87. Vice-Chancellor, University of Sussex 1987–92. Industrial consultant 1992–97. Interests: teleology in the natural sciences and in comparative religion. *See pages 105, 179 and 270.*

FOOKS, MAURICE (*b.*1915) Qualified as solicitor 1937; now consultant. War service with RAF including spell in India and Ceylon. Interests: chess, languages, travel, anything not involving physical exercise. *See pages 178 and 248.*

FORSTER, ANTHONY S (*b.* 1920) After 6 years in Army, almost entirely abroad in Middle East, Italy and Germany, joined book publishers Methuen 1947, concerned mostly with academic books. Managing director 1973, retired 1978 to south-west France to translate books and lead a country life. *See pages 22, 135 and 223.*

FRANCIS, PETER (*b.*1921, Mauritius) Commissioned into 9th Jat Regiment, Indian Army, 1941. Arakan, Imphal and Burma campaigns with XIV Army 1942–45. Shell International Petroleum, Thailand, Singapore, Ceylon, East and West Africa 1946–1976. Independent Schools Careers Organisation, Western Regional Director 1977–1996. In retirement reading for Arts degree, Open University. *See pages 55 and 279.*

THE AUTHORS

GUINNESS, THE HON SEBASTIAN (*b*.1964) A film maker now living in New York. Discovered the source of the Mekong river 1994 with Anglo-French expedition. Travels widely in the Far East documenting disappearing customs and cultures. Interests: politics, literature and languages. *See page 65.*

HAY, DR EWEN DAVID AGNEW (*b*.1931) After resident hospital jobs at St Thomas's Hospital London, served in Royal Navy for short service commission largely spent as Medical Officer of Antarctic guardship. For over 30 years thereafter, a Chelsea general medical practicioner. Retired to sheep farm in north-west Hampshire where he grew up as a boy. *See page 102.*

HEARD, DAVID OBE (*b*. 1939) Studied geology and physics at Keele. Joined Iraq Petroleum group and went to Abu Dhabi with Abu Dhabi Petroleum Co 1963. Involved in discovery giant oil fields and start of oil exports. Since 1980 represents interests of same group in Abu Dhabi. Travelled to China, USA, South Africa, many European and Arab countries. Married Dr Fraure Heard-Bey, well-known UAE historian. Interests: walking, reading, Arab and United Arab Emirate affairs. *See pages 107 and 275.*

HERRMANN, FRANK, FSA (*b*. 1927) Book publisher 1947–1976 (Faber, Methuen, Ward Lock etc). Director Overseas Operations Sotheby's (1978–81). Antiquarian book auctioneer (founder-director Bloomsbury Book Auctions). Author of *the English as Collectors* (1972 & 1999); *Sotheby's: Portrait of an Auction House* (1981); & *Giant Alexander* series (children's books 1964–1972). Regency porcelain enthusiast. Conceived this volume. *See pages 74, 126 and 198.*

HUNT, PETER MBE FIPR (*b*. 1927) External Affairs Adviser, Coca-Cola GB. Joined company 1958. Served with RAF in India; was an evening newspaper reporter and PR consultant. Director, Public Relations, Coca-Cola Europe, then Director, Government & Industry Relations, Northern Europe. President, Institute of Public Relations 1978 and of British Soft Drinks Association 1988–90. Member Tree Council. *See page 262.*

THE AUTHORS

HURD, DOUGLAS – THE RT HON LORD HURD OF WESTWELL CH CBE
PC. HM Diplomatic Service 1942–66. Secretary of State for Northern Ireland
1984–5. Home Secretary 1985–9. Foreign and Commonwealth Secretary 1989–
1995. Author of several novels and more serious pieces. *See page 213.*

KIDD, GERALD LE BLOUNT OBE MBE MD (*b.*1910) Started own practice,
London. Led Law Society delegation Germany 1936. Met Hitler. Warned
government of Nazi war preparations. Pilot, Civil Air Guard. RAF ranker
1940. Wing Commander Biggin Operations 1942. Parliamentary candidate.
Liberal executive. Administrator 20 years leprosy hospital, Essex. Senior
partner Lincoln's Inn Fields. Author of two volumes of poetry. Interested in
all sports. *See page 101.*

LEIGH FERMOR, PATRICK MICHAEL DSO OBE(MIL.) DLITT (KENT &
WARWICK) CLITT. Travelled in Europe & Balkans 1933–35. Enlisted Irish
Guards 1939; 'I' Corps 1940; SOE 1941. Campaigns of Albania, Greece,
Crete, Middle East & Western Europe. Author of a number of books: one
novel, translations from French & Greek, occasional verse. Now lives in
southern Greece. Interests: literature, history, travel, painting, religions etc.
See page 172.

MACKENZIE-YOUNG, PETER LDS RCS (*b.*1915) Qualified as a dental
surgeon. Appointed House Surgeon, London Hospital 1940–41 during
London Blitz. Served in Royal Navy as dental surgeon, demobilised in 1946
as Surgeon Lt Commander. Opened dental practice in London 1946.
Appointed Registrar and then onto teaching staff of dental schools at London
Hospital and Royal Dental Hospital. Retired from private practice 1989.
Interests: music, family and cooking. *See pages 6, 83 and 137.*

MORGAN, SIR JOHN KCMG. H M Foreign Service. Served in Moscow
(twice) Peking and Rio de Janeiro. Ambassador to Korea, Poland and Mexico.
Now retired. *See pages 54, 114 and 212.*

PIKE, SIR MICHAEL KCVO CMG (*b*.1931) Edited *Cherwell* at Brasenose, Oxford after National Service in Middle East. Joined Foreign Service 1956. Served in Korea, Singapore, Poland, USA and Israel. Royal College of Defence Studies 1982. Ambassador Hanoi 1982–84; Minister NATO 1985–87; High Commissioner Singapore 1987–1990. Collector of oriental porcelain & occasional marathon man. *See page 40.*

PRENTICE, JAMES LLB (*b*.1927) Educated Bradfield College and Liverpool University. Joined Lloyds 1951, then Willis, Faber & Dumas Ltd. Founded overseas broking department; especially active in France, Belgium, Nordic countries, Turkey, Greece and Japan. Ardent library builder, enthusiast with pen and paintbrush and assists with music recitals at Lacock Abbey, Wiltshire. *See page 246.*

PURDUE, ARTHUR WILLIAM (BILL) (*b*.1941) After 3 years as Instructor-Lieutenant Royal Navy, joined Newcastle upon Tyne Polytechnic as Lecturer in History 1967–76; Lecturer, then Senior Lecturer in History, Open University 1976–present; consultant to University of East Asia, Hong Kong 1982; Northumberland County Councillor 1987–present. Author with J M Golby of *Civilisation of the Crowd* (1984) and *the Making of the Modern Christmas* (1986); and author of *The Second World War* and *Merchants and Gentry in North East England 1650–1830* (both 1999). Member of Northern Counties Club, Newcastle upon Tyne [and only contributor to this volume from a member of a reciprocal club, of which there are 125 worldwide. *The Editors*.]. *See page 192.*

RHODES, SIR PEREGRINE ALEXANDER KCMG. Army 1944–49 (Captain). First at Oxford (Lit. Hum.). Diplomatic Service 1950–85, High Commissioner Cyprus, Ambassador Greece, Chief of Assessment Staff Cabinet Office. Director General British Property Federation 1986–94. Chairman Travellers Club 1994–98. Interests: photography, reading. *See page 156.*

THE AUTHORS

STAPLES, JUSTIN, CMG (*b.* 1929) After two years' National Service training as an RAF navigator, entered Foreign Office 1954. Apart from three assignments in London (first on Thai language studies) spent diplomatic career alternating between S.E. Asia and Western Europe. Final postings as Ambassador to Thailand (1981–1986) and Finland (1986–1989). *See pages 86 and 260*

STARK, SIR ANDREW KCMG CVO DL (*b.* 1916) Served war in Army, Green Howards; later Major on Eisenhower's staff throughout Overlord. Joined Diplomatic Service 1948. Service in London included being Private Secretary to Eden and Macmillan. Posts abroad were Vienna, Belgrade, Rome, Bonn, New York (as British Under-Secretary-General in UN) and Ambassador in Copenhagen. On retirement joined boards of Maersk, Scandinavian Bank and Carlsberg. Interests: literature and international affairs. *See page 196.*

TALLBOYS, RICHARD CMG OBE FCA LLB (*b.*1931) 8 years at sea 1947–55; 7 years in accounting profession. Australian Government Trade Commissioner 1962–68 (Africa, Singapore, Indonesia). HM Diplomatic Service 1968–88: overseas appointments to Brasilia, Phnom Penh, Seoul, Houston (Consul General) and Hanoi (Ambassador). Chief Executive, World Coal Institute 1988–93. Since 1993 occasional consultant and lecturer on Asia. Co-author of *Fifty Years of Business in Indonesia* (1996). *See pages 88 and 219.*

THESIGER, SIR WILFRED KBE DSO (*b.* 1910, Addis Ababa) Educated at Eton and Oxford. As early as 1934 showed his aptitude as an intrepid traveller, bringing to successful conclusion a hazardous exploration of the Aussa Sultanate in Abyssinia. In 1935 joined the Sudan Political Service, and soon found an opportunity off-duty for serious Saharan travel. During the war served with distinction under Wingate in liberation of Abyssinia; and with SOE in Syria, and SAS in Libya. Later spent 5 years with the nomadic Bedu in southern Arabia, and several more among the marsh dwellers of Iraq: these experience he described in two classic books which, with his fine photographs, made his reputation – *Arabian Sands* (1959) and *The Marsh Arabs* (1964). He continued for years to travel adventurously in Africa and

297

Asia, and to publish a further series of remarkable books: *Desert, Marsh and Mountain* (1979); *Visions of a Nomad* (1987); *The Life of My Choice* (1987); *My Kenya Days* (1994); *The Danakil Diary* (1996); and *Among the Mountains* (1998). He now lives permanently in England, and is occasionally sighted at the Travellers Club, which he joined in 1932. *See page 43.*

Composed for W.T. by G.H.W.

TOMKINSON, MICHAEL FIL FRGS (*b*.1940) Proprietor, Michael Tomkinson Publishing 1970-present. Read Modern Languages at Oxford before returning to Foreign Office 1963. Resigned in 1968, but not before eluding June War by joining Middle East Command's expedition to Socotra as linguist. Based in Tunisia 1970–1990, Nairobi 1990–1994 and in Cotswolds since, writing and editing translations of *inter alia* his *Kenya, Norway, The Gambia* and *Tunisia*. *See page 60.*

TOWNER, JOHN (*b*.1939) Entered Colonial Service (Hong Kong Government) 1961 and FCO 1972. Chinese studies provided basis for later diversification into things Japanese. Since 1994 has concentrated on private interests and business involving Europe, Middle East and East Asia. *See page 242.*

WAITE, TERRY CBE (*b*.1939) Wide international experience in education and development. Former adviser to the Archbishop of Canterbury. Fellow Commoner Trinity Hall, Cambridge. *See pages 3 and 281.*

WEBB, CHARLES FRGS (*b*.1962) After studying Chinese at University in Leeds and Shanghai, joined Reuters and was posted to East Africa. From 1989–1996, at Control Risks Group, based in London and SE Asia. Main professional focus, political risk management. Now director Ciex Ltd, London. Keen sailor, mountaineer, diver, photographer. *See page 79.*

WEBB, GEORGE HANNAM CMG OBE (*b*. 1929, Kenya) Educated England. Colonial Service Kenya 1954–63. Diplomatic Service 1963–85, in Thailand, Ghana, Iran and USA. Staff of City University, London 1985–93, Senior

Fellow. Chairman of Travellers Club 1987–1991. Author of *The Bigger Bang – a financial revolution* (1987); *Kipling's Japan* (with Sir Hugh Cortazzi, 1988). Interests: literary (editor since 1980 of quarterly *Kipling Journal*). *See pages 9 and 184.*

WILLEY, PETER ROBERT EVERARD, TD FRAS. After war service entered teaching profession. Senior Housemaster Wellington College. Founded GAP 1976. Since 1982 Tutor and Lecturer (Fine Arts and Literature) Bristol University. Since 1959 has directed over 20 historical/archaeological expeditions to Middle East, particularly Iran and Syria, Central Asia and India researching history of the Nizari Ismaili state (the Assassins). Author of *Castle of the Assassins* (1965) and sequel to be published 1999. Interests: travel, literature, opera & music, photography. *See page 244.*

WINCHESTER, SIMON (*b.* 1944) Until 1994 a foreign correspondent for *The Guardian* and *The Sunday Times*, based in Ireland, America, India and China, covering most of the non-European world. Currently a freelance writer, living in New York City. *See pages 91, 145 and 249.*

WORDIE, PETER CBE (*b.*1932) After National Service in the Argyll and Sutherland Highlanders, embarked on a career in shipping. Founder and Chairman of Western Ferries 1968 and Stirling Shipping 1972, both based in Glasgow. Author of *The Royal Game* (1980). Main interest: books on postal polar history. *See pages 49 and 166.*

WRIGHT, SIR DENIS GCMG. HM Ambassador to Iran 1963–71 and Ethiopia 1959–63; also served in Romania, Turkey, Yugoslavia and USA. Hon Fellow of St Edmund Hall and St Antony's College, Oxford. Author (with James Morris & Roger Wood) of *Persia* (1969); and author of *The English amongst the Persians* (1977); *The Persians amongst the English* (1986). *See page 97.*